Learn C++
for Game Development

Bruce Sutherland

Apress·

Learn C++ for Game Development

ISBN-13 (pbk): 978-1-4302-6457-6

ISBN-13 (electronic): 978-1-4302-6458-3

Publisher: Heinz Weinheimer
Lead Editor: Steve Anglin
Development Editor: Matthew Moodie
Technical Reviewer: Michael Thomas
Editorial Board: Steve Anglin, Mark Beckner, Ewan Buckingham, Gary Cornell, Louise Corrigan,
James T. DeWolf, Jonathan Gennick, Jonathan Hassell, Robert Hutchinson, Michelle Lowman,
James Markham, Matthew Moodie, Jeff Olson, Jeffrey Pepper, Douglas Pundick, Ben Renow-Clarke,
Dominic Shakeshaft, Gwenan Spearing, Matt Wade, Steve Weiss
Coordinating Editor: Anamika Panchoo, Kevin Shea
Copy Editor: Teresa Horton
Compositor: SPi Global
Indexer: SPi Global
Artist: SPi Global
Cover Designer: Anna Ishchenko

Distributed to the book trade worldwide by Springer Science+Business Media New York, 233 Spring Street, 6th Floor, New York, NY 10013. Phone 1-800-SPRINGER, fax (201) 348-4505, e-mail orders-ny@springer-sbm.com, or visit www.springeronline.com. Apress Media, LLC is a California LLC and the sole member (owner) is Springer Science + Business Media Finance Inc (SSBM Finance Inc). SSBM Finance Inc is a Delaware corporation.

For information on translations, please e-mail rights@apress.com, or visit www.apress.com.

Apress and friends of ED books may be purchased in bulk for academic, corporate, or promotional use. eBook versions and licenses are also available for most titles. For more information, reference our Special Bulk Sales–eBook Licensing web page at www.apress.com/bulk-sales.

Any source code or other supplementary materials referenced by the author in this text is available to readers at www.apress.com. For detailed information about how to locate your book's source code, go to www.apress.com/source-code/.

Contents at a Glance

Contents

About the Author

Bruce Sutherland is a video game developer working at Firemonkey Studios in Melbourne, Australia. He is currently working on iOS and Android titles written in C++ for both platforms. Bruce has worked on Real Racing 3, the Dead Space series, and The Elder Scrolls: Oblivion among others in his nine-year video game development career.

About the Technical Reviewer

Michael Thomas has worked in software development for more than 20 years as an individual contributor, team lead, program manager, and Vice President of Engineering. Michael has more than 10 years of experience working with mobile devices. His current focus is in the medical sector, using mobile devices to accelerate information transfer between patients and health care providers.

Acknowledgments

I would like to thank my wife for the support and encouragement she provides while trying to write books and ship video games at the same time. Both of these are time-consuming and demanding pursuits and Claire's support is greatly appreciated.

I'd also like to thank the team at Apress for the endless support, encouragement, and advice they provided while I was writing this book. Converting programmer speak into plain English is a task they carry out effortlessly.

Introduction

The C++ programming language remains the de facto language for many game development studios around the world. This is true because C++ provides a convenient, low-level programming language that allows developers to straddle the line between high-level software engineering and low-level coding to the metal. This makes it the language of choice for many high-performance and real-time computer programming projects.

C++ is a language in active development. Many of the examples in this book use features that were ratified and released in the C++11 standard. Some of the features used are not yet supported by one of the major compiler vendors. This active and progressive language development is a major reason for C++ remaining a widely used and relevant language. The fact that it's the only way to write portable, in-house code across all of the types of computers and processors you find today makes learning C++ a handy skill to have. Devices that support C++ range from mobile phones, game consoles, ATMs, smart watches, to even glasses! C++ programmers will never be short of work. I hope you find this book an invaluable resource in your journey to learning the C++ programming language.

Chapter 1

Beginning C++

The C++ programming language was designed by Bjarne Stroustrup at Bell Labs, beginning in 1979. The goal of the language was to provide useful features from other languages of the time, such as Simula, with faster runtime performance. C was chosen as the basis for this new language due to its execution speed, portability, and wide adoption.

The first major extension Stroustrup added to C was class support. Classes allowed a new programming paradigm to be used with C: object-oriented programming (OOP). Stroustrup's new language quickly became known as *C with Classes*, eventually changed to *C++* in 1983.

C++ has been in continual development since its inception. New features were added regularly throughout the 1980s and 1990s and many of these have become essential tools for game developers. Examples of these features that are covered in this book are *virtual functions*, *templates,* and the *Standard Template Library*.

An ISO standard for C++ was first published in 1998. Standardizing a language gives compiler writers a common set of features to implement if they wish to achieve C++ compatibility. Standardization also benefits programmers writing code in C++ as it allows them to use a common set of features that they can expect to behave in the same way when using multiple compilers or multiple operating systems and computer architectures. There have been four C++ standards released to date. The original standard is known as C++98. C++98 was added to with C++03, and new experimental features were added to the language with C++TR1 (C++ Technical Review 1). The current C++ standard is C++11.

This book focuses on the most up-to-date version of the standard. However, this presents us with some challenges, as not all compilers have been updated to support all of the latest features of C++'. It can be taken for granted that when I refer to C++ in this book I mean C++11; any topics that require explicit reference to older C++ standards will be clear. The Microsoft' C++ compiler included with its Visual Studio integrated development environment (IDE), for example, does not include support for constant expressions or type aliasing. (Don't worry if you don't understand these terms; they are new C++11 features and are covered in the section relating to templates.) Notes are added to the text in sections where relevant features are not supported by one of the major compilers.

Compilers

C++ is a compiled language; this means that the code is read by a program that converts the text source files created by a programmer into instructions that can be executed by a processor. Different settings in compilers, or different compilers, can be used to turn source files into instructions suitable for completely different processor architectures, such as x86 and Armv7.

The major compilers currently in use are the following:

- Microsoft Visual C++ Compiler (MSVC)
- GNU Compiler Collection (GCC)
- Apple LLVM
- Clang

These are the compilers that this book is most concerned with, as they are the most likely to be encountered by game developers. MSVC is the compiler included with the Microsoft Visual Studio IDE and used when writing programs for Windows and Microsoft game consoles such as the Xbox One. GCC is common on Linux platforms and is the default compiler used when building native Android applications. Apple LLVM is the C++ compiler used when building OS X and iOS applications. Clang is a relatively new program that acts as the front end for the LLVM compiler (also used in the Apple ecosystem) and is included as an optional compiler by the current Android Native Development Kit (NDK).

Some of the samples included in this book might not compile on your compiler of choice if that compiler is incompatible with all of the latest features of C++11. Switching compilers if possible or updating your software to the latest versions are possible options to work with these features.

Programming Paradigms

Programming paradigms are closely related to high-level programming styles. C++ does not enforce a particular paradigm and provides flexible features to enable programmers to program in the following paradigms.

Procedural Programming

Procedural programming involves writing ordered statements in blocks known as functions (also known as procedures). Functions are used to encapsulate code that can be reused and to improve code readability. C is also a procedural language and C++ contains the entire C language as a subset, allowing C++ programs to be written in a fully procedural manner. Part 1 of this book covers the aspects of C++ necessary to write procedural programs.

Object-Oriented Programming

OOP is supported through the addition of classes to C++. OOP involves designing a program as a set of discrete objects. These objects hide their implementation and data from the calling code (encapsulation), which allows specific implementation details to be changed at a later time without affecting other sections of the program. Inheritance and polymorphism are other important aspects of the C++ OOP paradigm. OOP programming is the focus of Part 2 in this book.

Generic Programming

Generic programming is most likely the least understood paradigm in C++ despite its widespread use via the Standard Template Library. Templates allow programmers to write classes that can operate on different types via specializations. Template metaprogramming is a powerful technique that confers the ability to write programs within the code that generate values and code at compile time. Templates and Metaprogramming are covered in Part 4 of this book.

C++ Game Programming

C++ has been a major language of choice for game developers since its inception. All major gaming platforms have supported and currently support C++ compilation. This includes Windows, Linux, OS X, iOS, Xbox One, PlayStation 4, Wii U, and Android.

Part 5 of this book covers advanced C++ topics that programmers will find useful as hardware becomes more powerful. These include design patterns, streams, memory management, concurrency (multithreaded programming), and a look at how we can write code that supports multiple game development platforms.

Our First C++ Program

Let's take a look at a simple C++ program before we get started with the details of C++. Listing 1-1 shows a simple C++ program written in Microsoft Visual Studio Express 2012 for Windows Desktop.

Listing 1-1. Our First C++ Program

```cpp
// Chapter1.cpp : Defines the entry point for the console application.
//

#include "stdafx.h"
#include <iostream>
#include <string>

using namespace std;

int _tmain(int argc, _TCHAR* argv[])
{
        cout << "What is your name?" << endl;

        string name {};
        cin >> name;

        cout << "You said your name is: " << name << endl;

        return 0;
}
```

The first two lines of this source code are comments. A double forward slash indicates that all text following the // on the same line should be ignored by the compiler. Block comments are also supported and are opened with /* and closed with */. You will see several uses of both forms of comment throughout this book.

There are then several lines beginning with #include. This tells the compiler to include other files into our program. We cover the difference between source and header files in Chapter 6.

The next line tells the compiler that we want to use the standard namespace. Namespaces are also covered in Chapter 6.

The program then begins with the _tmain function. This is the first function called by the program when writing Windows applications that target the console. Different operating systems have different entry points and you'll see these throughout this book as different examples are written to target different operating systems and compilers. You should be able to easily alter the samples to use the entry point for your system of choice.

The cout operator writes the text following the << operator to the console window. The cin operator stops the program and waits for the user to enter text. We store the text entered into the name variable and then use it to echo back the input the user entered.

The last line returns the value 0 from the function to let the operating system know that we finished without error.

As you can see, this simple program asks for the user's name and then repeats that name back to the user. Congratulations: You've written your first C++ program.

Summary

This chapter has given you a very brief introduction to the C++ programming language. We've looked at the basic history of the language, the current main C++ compilers, its major paradigms, and a simple C++ program.

The next chapters look at how we can create some simple games using the C features of C++, beginning with a look at the fundamental built-in types and operators in C++.

The examples in Chapters 2 and 3 are simple programs that will help you to understand how C++ types and operators behave. The examples beginning in Chapter 4 see us begin to create a text adventure game that we will develop to completion throughout the remainder of the book. Text adventure games were very popular on early computers and they are an excellent way to learn C++ for game development without requiring you to learn the intricacies of a platform-specific windowing system or graphics application programming interface (API).

Procedural Programming

The roots of the C++ programing language come from the C programming language. C provides the basis for the C++ procedural programming paradigm.

Procedural programming involves using variables and functions to create reusable procedures that constitute a full program. This part of the book introduces you to the features provided in C++ that would allow you to write fully procedural programs.

This part of the book begins by looking at C++'s built-in types, operators, arrays, pointers and references, and functions before finally looking at flow control statements and methods of structuring your programs.

Part 1

Procedural Programming

Chapter 2

Writing a Guessing Game with C++ Types

You will begin the process of learning C++ by learning about the different built-in types that the language supports. C++ has built-in support for integers, floating point numbers, booleans, and enumerators. This chapter covers all of these types. We also look at the different types of operators that can be used to manipulate and compare these types of values. It is useful to understand how C++ handles variables before we begin to create programs in the language. To start, we take a look at the difference between dynamically and statically typed languages, which includes how we declare and define variables in C++.

Dynamic Versus Static Typed Languages

Variables in programming languages can be handled in two different ways. Dynamically typed languages do not require the programmer to state explicitly which type should be used to store the value. Dynamically typed languages can switch the type of a variable on the fly depending on how it is being used.

Statically typed languages require the programmer to tell the compiler explicitly which type to use to represent the data the variable will store. C++ is a statically typed language and creating variables in C++ is a two-step process.

Declaring Variables

When we are introducing a new variable into a program, we are said to be declaring the variable. This essentially means that we are telling the compiler that we would like to have a variable of a specific type and with a specific name. C++ compilers require that all variables be declared before they can be used in our programs. An example of a variable declaration would be:

```
int numberOfObjects;
```

This declaration tells the compiler that we would like to have an integer with the name numberOfObjects; it does not tell the compiler what the variable contains or what it should be used for.

Defining Variables

We can define our variable once we have declared it. Defining a variable involves telling the compiler what its initial value should be. This is an example of a variable definition:

```
numberOfObjects = 0;
```

It's fairly common that we will define and declare some variables at the same time. Combining the declaration and definition would resemble this line:

```
int numberOfObjects = 0;
```

We'll be looking at the places where it is appropriate to declare names to the compiler compared to defining them as we move through this book. The rules for declaring and defining different variables and types depend on the context in which they are being used.

Integers

The first set of types that we will be looking at in C++ is the integer types. The previous sections have already shown how to declare and define an integer variable. To recap:

```
int numberOfObjects = 0;
```

This line of code declares and defines an integer variable. What this means to the compiler is that we want to create a variable that is capable of storing whole numbers. Examples of integers are –1000, 0, 24, and 1345219. Integers can contain both positive and negative numbers.

The type int is just one of several different types that can store integers. The others are char, short, and long. Table 2-1 shows the different ranges of values that can be stored in these types when using MSVC.

Table 2-1. The MSVC Integral Types, with Minimum and Maximum Values

Type Name	Number of Bytes	Minimum Value	Maximum Value
char	1	–128	127
short	2	–32,768	32,767
int	4	–2,147,483,648	2,147,483,647
long	4	–2,147,483,648	2,147,483,647
long long	8	–9,223,372,036,854,775,808	9,223,372,036,854,775,807

As you can see there are five main types of integers when using C++. It's important to select a variable that can accommodate all of the possible values you might wish to store. Failing to use a type with enough possible values results in wrapping. That means that if you had a char variable that currently stored 127 and you tried to add a one, the value in the variable would *wrap* and your variable would then contain –128.

Unsigned Integers

C++ also supports unsigned versions of the integer types shown in Table 2-1. Table 2-2 shows the ranges that these unsigned variable types can store.

Table 2-2. MSVC's Unsigned Integral Type Ranges

Type Name	Number of Bytes	Minimum Value	Maximum Value
unsigned char	1	0	255
unsigned short	2	0	65,535
unsigned int	4	0	4,294,967,295
unsigned long	4	0	4,294,967,295
unsigned long long	8	0	18,446,744,073,709,551,615

Using unsigned types extends the range of available positive integers at the expense of losing all negative integers. These types should be used in all cases where negative numbers will not be needed.

Two's Complement

Before we move on to look at some other types of variables, it is important to understand how the integer values we have covered are represented by the computer. You've seen that unsigned numbers of varying numbers of bytes can store numbers ranging from 0 through to their maximum size. In the case of a single-byte char that maximum number is 255.

This happens because a single byte is made up of 8 individual bits. Each bit represents the next power of two from the last. Table 2-3 shows how you can think of the bits in a byte.

Table 2-3. The Bits Making Up a Single Byte: The Top Row Shows the Bit Number and the Bottom Row Shows the Value This Byte Represents When Using Unsigned Variables

8	7	6	5	4	3	2	1
128	64	32	16	8	4	2	1

Table 2-3 shows the bit values for an unsigned char. When we have an unsigned char variable that stores the value 255, all of the bits are *turned on*. This would be represented by 11111111 in binary. If we add a 1 to this number the values will *wrap* and we will end up back at 00000000 as the 8 bits cannot store a higher value. This is something that you will need to be aware of when using unsigned integer variables.

When you want to represent negative numbers using signed variables, the processor will use *Two's Complement*. Two's Complement works by using the highest bit to represent whether the number is positive or negative. The highest positive number that can be stored in a char variable is 127 and is represented in binary by 01111111. Adding 1 to this number gives us 10000000, which is −128 and once again shows you how wrapping occurs in practice.

Switching between a positive and negative number is a simple process. You have to switch all of the bits and add one. The number 1 is represented in binary by 00000001. To flip 1 to -1 we first flip all of the bits to 11111110 (which is -2) , then add 1 to give us 11111111.

This is a brief introduction to how a processor represents the integer values your programs will store in memory. We will cover some more binary representations of numbers in Chapter 3 when we look at binary operators.

Floating Point Numbers

Floating point numbers in C++ are used to represent numbers with a decimal point. Examples of these are −10.5, 0.3337, and 89.8376.

Like the signed integer types, floats can be used to store positive and negative numbers. Unlike integers, though, there are no unsigned versions of floating point numbers. Defining a floating point is done in the following way:

```
float decimalNumber = 1.0f;
```

When defining floating point variables in code, the value must be followed by an f. The reason for this is that a number with a decimal point but no f is a double.

The current floating point standards require that floats be represented with 32 bits (or 4 bytes). Thirty-two-bit floating point numbers might not have a large enough range for what we would like to achieve under given circumstances, so C++ also supplies the double type. The float type can be thought of as a single precision floating point number and the double type is then a double precision floating point number. A double can be defined as follows:

```
double doubleNumber = 1.0;
```

Single precision floats are usually sufficient for all but a few scenarios in game development and are generally faster and more efficient for the types of tasks we carry out.

Boolean Values

Booleans are simple values that can only contain true or false. Booleans are usually, but not always, implemented as a single byte char. A value of 0 is usually used to represent false and any nonzero value is true. We rarely use numbers to represent booleans, as C++ contains the true and false keywords. A couple of boolean variable declarations would be:

```
bool isTrue = true;
bool isFalse = false;
```

We've already seen in the previous section that functions can return boolean values to help create statements that make sense to a human reader:

```
bool numberIsNaN = isnan(nan);
```

Booleans will also become useful once we start looking at flow control statements in Chapter 5.

Enums

C++ allows us to create an enumerated list of values. This is useful if we wish to convey sets of things that have readable names. An example of an enum in C++ is:

```
enum class Color
{
        Red,
        Green,
        Blue
};
```

This has effectively contained a new type in C++, Color. We can create new variables of type Color like this:

```
Color currentColor = Color::Red;
```

Using enums is a useful way to create code that is highly readable. Compare the preceding line to this:

```
unsigned int currentColor = 0;
```

This code essentially does exactly the same as the preceding line, but it is much more difficult to understand. We have no way of knowing that 0 was the color red and it was also possible to assign the number 10 to currentColor, which wouldn't be a valid color.

Enums also allow us to assign a value to each element. In the Color enum we currently have Red assigned the value 0, Green 1 and Blue 2. In the enum definition we could have used the following:

```
enum class Color
{
        Red,
        Green = 10,
        Blue
};
```

In the preceding enum, Red is still 0, and Green is 10; however, Blue is 11, as it directly follows Green. There are few occasions where we need to specify the values of enums as they are most useful for creating more readable code; but it is useful to understand that this is possible because you will come across code written by others that will use this feature.

It's also important to note that the enum class is a C++11 construct. Prior to C++11 the enum would have been created using the following:

```
enum Color
{
        Red,
        Green,
        Blue
};
```

C++11 style enums are known as strongly typed enums. The compiler will not allow you to accidentally use integers in place of the enum values. It also wouldn't have been possible to use the value Red in two different enums.

```
enum Color
{
        Red,
        Green,
        Blue,
};

enum TrafficLights
{
        Red,
        Amber,
        Green
};
```

This is not allowed with older enums, as the code to define a variable would look like:

```
Color currentColor = Red;
TrafficLights = currentLight = Red;
```

As you can see, we have no way of knowing which Red is to be used. This is even worse with the Green value, as it would have a different integer representation: 1 in Color and 2 in TrafficLights. This could cause bugs in our code as it would be valid to use the TrafficLights version of Green when we really meant to use the Color version. The compiler would assume that we meant Blue as both Color::Blue and TrafficLights::Green are representations of 2. Using an enum class, however, means the code must look like this:

```
Color currentColor = Color::Red;
TrafficLights = currentLight = TrafficLights::Red;
```

As you can see, the strongly typed version of enums is much better and provides us with more explicit code. Always use an enum class where possible in new code.

Enums are the last type introduced in this chapter. We can now spend the rest of the chapter looking at the different types of operators that C++ supplies to work with our types.

Switching from One Type to Another

Sometimes while writing our programs we will have a value stored as one type, such as an int, but we would like to use the value from our variable along with a value stored in another variable. Fortunately C++ can automatically convert from some types to others. The following lines of code provide some examples:

```
char charNumber = 1;
int intNumber = charNumber;
float floatNumber = intNumber;
```

C++ can implicitly convert numbers from one type to another. Going from smaller types to larger types and from integer types to floats and floats to doubles as well as from integer types to bools are all legal and carried out automatically by the compiler.

static_cast

Whereas moving from a smaller type to a larger type is safe, moving from a larger type to a smaller type can cause a loss of data. For example:

```
int largeNumber = 1000;
char smallNumber = largeNumber;
```

In this case, the large number would likely be truncated from 1,000 to 127, as that is the largest number that a signed char variable can hold. This type of data loss is known as a narrowing conversion. C++ compilers give warnings about this type of conversion and many game development studios like to keep their code error-free or enable compiler settings that cause all warnings to become errors. Fortunately C++ provides us with a method to tell the compiler that we were converting this value on purpose. This method is known as a static cast. An example of the usage of static_cast would be:

```
char smallNumber = static_cast<char>(largeNumber);
```

This code tells the compiler that we are purposefully converting our type to a char and it will not output any warnings for the conversion.

It's also good practice to use static_cast when carrying out conversions to larger types (actually called widening conversions) to make it clear and obvious to other programmers that we have used the conversion on purpose and that it is not actually a mistake.

static_cast is evaluated by the compiler at compile time and will cause a compilation error if we are trying to convert between incompatible types.

A Simple Guessing Game

We'll use what you have learned about declaring and defining variables and integers to create a simple guessing game. In the beginning the game will be basic; however, we will add to the game throughout the remainder of this chapter to make the output more like a game.

For now we will ask the player to input a number and output that number and a random number selected by the program. Listing 2-1 shows the program written to compile using C++ 4.7.3.

Listing 2-1. A Simple C++ Guessing Game

```cpp
#include <ctime>
#include <cstdlib>
#include <iostream>
#include <string>

using namespace std;

int main()
{
        // Generate unique random numbers using the current time
        srand(time(NULL));
        // Get a random number between 0 and 99
        unsigned int numberToGuess = rand() % 100;

        cout << "Guess a number between 0 and 99" << endl;

        unsigned int playersNumber {};
        cin >> playersNumber;

        cout << "You guessed: "
                << playersNumber
                << " The actual number was: "
                << numberToGuess
                << endl;

        return 0;
}
```

Our guessing game source code begins by including the C++ header files necessary for the features we use and declares that we will be using the std namespace.

```
#include <ctime>
#include <cstdlib>
#include <iostream>
#include <string>

using namespace std;
```

The entry point for our program when using GCC is:

```
int main()
```

Listing 1-1 showed that the entry point when using MSVC was:

```
int _tmain(int argc, _TCHAR* argv[])
```

The first four lines of the main function are used to obtain a random number. The srand function carries out an operation known as seeding. This uses the current time returned from the time function to generate a sequence of random numbers.

```
// Generate unique random numbers using the current time
srand(time(NULL));
```

We declare and define a variable, numberToGuess, to store the value that we would like our player to guess. The rand function returns the number and we use the modulus operator (%) to ensure that the number remains less than 100. We cover the modulus operator in more detail in Chapter 3.

```
// Get a random number between 0 and 99
unsigned int numberToGuess = rand() % 100;
```

The remaining code is similar to Listing 1-1. We use cout to write text for the player to read and use cin to allow the player to enter a guessed number. We finish by returning 0.

```
cout << "Guess a number between 0 and 99" << endl;

unsigned int playersNumber {};
cin >> playersNumber;

cout << "You guessed: "
        << playersNumber
        << " The actual number was: "
        << numberToGuess
        << endl;

return 0;
```

Summary

This chapter has given you a brief introduction to the built-in data types provided by C++ as well as also taking a look at enums and the usage of `static_cast` to convert between these built-in types.

We then used this knowledge to create a very simple program to guess a number chosen by the computer. At the moment, we do not have the ability to test whether the player guessed correctly; that will come later in Part 1 when we look at flow control statements in Chapter 6. Chapter 3 covers the operators that are available in C++. Operators are the means with which C++ allows us to create logical programs that calculate and compute outcomes from our statements.

Chapter 3

Creating Calculators with Operators

C++ provides operators that allow you to express all sorts of mathematical formulae in computer programs. You have access to operators that allow us to carry out algebra, compare values, and even manipulate the individual bit pattern of a variable's value directly. This chapter is going to cover these C++ operators and end by having you create a simple command line calculator.

The Assignment Operator

The first operator we are going to look at is the assignment operator. We have already been using the assignment operator in the previous chapters as it is the operator that allows us to assign a value to a variable. This operator uses the = symbol:

```
int number1 = 1;
```

As you can see we have assigned the value of 1 to an integer variable named number1. We can also assign variable values to other variables:

```
int number2 = number1;
```

Here the program will read the value stored in number1 and assign that value to the variable number2. As we saw in the previous chapter, the assignment operator can also automatically convert from one variable type to another.

```
char charNumber = 1;
int intNumber = charNumber;
```

The assignment is one of the most widely used operators in C++; thankfully, it's also easy to use and fairly obvious in nature.

The assignment operator can also be used in some pieces of code that aren't necessarily very readable. Take the following line, for instance:

```
number1 = number2 = number3 = 1;
```

C++ compilers will evaluate these statements from right to left. 1 is assigned to number3, which would be assigned to number2, which would be assigned to number1, and all three variables will end up storing 1. I wouldn't recommend writing code like this.

Arithmetic Operators

C++ also allows us to carry out basic arithmetic operations and we have five of these available:

- Addition operator
- Subtraction operator
- Multiplication operator
- Division operator
- Modulo operator

The Addition Operator

The addition operator behaves exactly as you would expect: It allows us to add two numbers together. The addition operator can add a value from the right to a value on the left and the result can be used in a statement, like this:

```
int sum = number1 + number2;
```

Here we have added number2 to number1 and stored the result in a third variable named sum.

It is also possible to use the same values in all of the places in our addition statement, for example:

```
int number = 1;
number = number + number;
```

Here we end up with 2 being stored in the variable number after this code has executed.

The Subtraction Operator

The subtraction operator works exactly like the addition operator, although unsurprisingly it subtracts one number from another and creates a result:

```
int number1 = 2;
int number2 = 1;
int result = number1 - number2;
```

This code would cause the value 1 to be stored in the variable result.

The Multiplication and Division Operators

These operators are also fairly self-explanatory; the multiplication operator multiplies numbers together and the division operator divides the number on the left by the number on the right:

```
int number1 = 4;
int number2 = 2;
int multiplied = number1 * number2;
int divided = number1 / number2;
```

The result of the multiplication would be 8 and the result of the division would be 2.

The division operator, like the subtraction operator, has a result that depends on the order of the variables.

```
int divided1 = number1 / number2;
int divided2 = number2 / number1;
```

After executing these lines of code, divided1 would store 2 as earlier but divided2 would store 0 as 4 cannot divide into 2. You can think of the results of the division as being rounded down to the nearest whole integer. The following example shows a similar result.

```
int number1 = 5;
int number2 = 2;
int divided1 = number1 / number2;
int divided2 = number2 / number1;
```

In the preceding code, divided1 will contain 2 after execution. The actual math would be 5/2 = 2.5 or 2 remainder 1, but as integers can only store whole numbers we lose the extra 0.5 or remainder. 2/5 = 0 remainder 5, and again we lose the remainder; therefore divided2 will store 0.

```
float divided2 = static_cast<float>(number2) / static_cast<float>(number1);
```

Casting both numerator and denominator to float values (or dividing two float variables) would have yielded a result of 0.5f. This is why it is important to use the correct type of variable for the job at hand.

The Modulo Operator

Our guessing game in Listing 2-1 has already shown a usage of the modulo operator. This can be thought of as a remainder operator, as it will return the remainder of dividing one number by another.

```
int numerator = 12;
int denominator = 10;
int remainder = numerator % denominator;
```

The variable remainder shown here will store the value 2 as 12 divided by 10 equals 1 remainder 2.

A Simple Arithmetic Calculator

We will now write a simple program that can show the results of the arithmetic operators. Listing 3-1 shows the code that will take two numbers and add them together. This sample code was created using Xcode and the main function is suitable for creating command-line programs for OS X.

Listing 3-1. Adding Two Numbers

```
#include <iostream>
using namespace std;

int main(int argc, const char * argv[])
{
        cout << "Enter your first number: " << endl;
        float number1 = 0.0f;
        cin >> number1;

        cout << "Enter your second number: " << endl;
        float number2 = 0.0f;
        cin >> number2;

        float result = number1 + number2;
        cout << "The result of adding your two numbers is: " << result << endl;
        return 0;
}
```

We once again use cin and cout to communicate with users and ask them to enter two numbers. We then store the result of an addition in the variable result and print the output to the console. An example of the output from this program is shown here:

```
Enter your first number:
40
Enter your second number:
10
The result of adding your two numbers is: 50
```

Listing 3-2 shows a subtraction version of this program.

Listing 3-2. Subtracting Two Numbers

```
#include <iostream>
using namespace std;

int main(int argc, const char * argv[])
{
        cout << "Enter your first number: " << endl;
        float number1 = 0.0f;
        cin >> number1;

        cout << "Enter your second number: " << endl;
        float number2 = 0.0f;
        cin >> number2;
```

```
        float result = number1 - number2;
        cout << "The result of subtracting your two numbers is: " << result << endl;
        return 0;
}
```

Listing 3-3 shows a multiplication version of this program.

Listing 3-3. Multiplying Two Numbers

```
#include <iostream>
using namespace std;

int main(int argc, const char * argv[])
{
        cout << "Enter your first number: " << endl;
        float number1 = 0.0f;
        cin >> number1;

        cout << "Enter your second number: " << endl;
        float number2 = 0.0f;
        cin >> number2;

        float result = number1 * number2;
        cout << "The result of multiplying your two numbers is: " << result << endl;
        return 0;
}
```

Listing 3-4 shows a division version of this program.

Listing 3-4. Dividing Two Numbers

```
#include <iostream>
using namespace std;

int main(int argc, const char * argv[])
{
        cout << "Enter your first number: " << endl;
        float number1 = 0.0f;
        cin >> number1;

        cout << "Enter your second number: " << endl;
        float number2 = 0.0f;
        cin >> number2;

        float result = number1 / number2;
        cout << "The result of dividing your second number into your first is: "
            << result << endl;
        return 0;
}
```

Last but not least, Listing 3-5 shows a modulo version of this program.

Listing 3-5. Finding the Remainder Between Two Numbers

```
#include <iostream>
using namespace std;

int main(int argc, const char * argv[])
{
        cout << "Enter your first number: " << endl;
        int number1 = 0;
        cin >> number1;

        cout << "Enter your second number: " << endl;
        int number2 = 0;
        cin >> number2;

        int result = number1 % number2;
        cout << "The remainder from dividing your second number into your first is: "
                << result << endl;
        return 0;
}
```

We have to change the variables in Listing 3-5 to `int` from `float` as the modulo operator can only operate on integer values.

Now that we have covered the arithmetic operators, we will take a look at relational operators.

Relational Operators

C++ allows us to compare variable values using relational operators. These operators allow us to work out if two variables are equal, not equal, one is greater than the other, or one is less than the other. There are also operators to work out if variables are less than or equal, and greater than or equal.

Each of these operators provides a true or false result that can be stored in a bool. C++ provides the following relational operators:

- Equality operator
- Greater-than operators
- Less-than operators

Equality Operators

The equals operator is ==. We can use this in the following way:

```
bool isEqual = number1 == number2;
```

`isEqual` will contain `true` if `number1` and `number2` store the same value; otherwise it will contain `false`.

C++ also contains an inequality operator that can be thought of as a not equals operation. It can be used as follows.

```
bool isNotEqual = number1 != number2;
```

As we can see, the inequality operator uses an exclamation mark before the equals symbol. This operator provides true when the two values are not the same and false if they are the same.

Greater-Than Operators

C++ also allows us to work out if a value stored in a variable is greater than another. We can do this as follows:

```
bool isGreater = number1 > number2;
```

We can also tell if a number is greater than or equal to another:

```
bool isGreaterThanOrEqual = number1 >= number2;
```

Less-Than Operators

We can work out if a value is less than another using the less-than operator:

```
bool isLessThan = number1 < number2;
```

As with greater-than, there is a less-than or equal to operator:

```
bool isLessThanOrEqual = number1 <= number2;
```

We will create some small programs to show off the relational operators just as we did with the arithmetic operators.

Simple Comparison Calculators

Listing 3-6 shows the source code for a simple program that tests the equality of two values.

Listing 3-6. Using the Equality Operator

```
#include "stdafx.h"
#include <iostream>

using namespace std;

int _tmain(int argc, _TCHAR* argv[])
{
        cout << "Enter your first number: " << endl;
        int number1 = 0;
        cin >> number1;
```

```
        cout << "Enter your second number: " << endl;
        int number2 = 0;
        cin >> number2;

        bool result = number1 == number2;
        cout << "It is "
                << result
                << " that your first number is equal your second."
                << endl;

        return 0;
}
```

This sample application was created using Microsoft Visual Studio. The program will end very quickly after the second value has been entered, so a good trick is to set a breakpoint on the return line using the F9 key and to use debug mode to run the program using the F5 key.

The boolean value in this sample will be printed out as a 1 when the operation results in a true value and 0 when the result is false.

Listing 3-7 shows a simple program using the inequality operator.

Listing 3-7. The Inequality Operator

```
#include "stdafx.h"
#include <iostream>

using namespace std;

int _tmain(int argc, _TCHAR* argv[])
{
        cout << "Enter your first number: " << endl;
        int number1 = 0;
        cin >> number1;

        cout << "Enter your second number: " << endl;
        int number2 = 0;
        cin >> number2;

        bool result = number1 != number2;
        cout << "It is "
                << result
                << " that your first number is not equal your second."
                << endl;

        return 0;
}
```

Listing 3-8 contains the source code for an example of the greater-than operator.

Listing 3-8. The Greater-Than Operator

```
#include "stdafx.h"
#include <iostream>

using namespace std;

int _tmain(int argc, _TCHAR* argv[])
{
        cout << "Enter your first number: " << endl;
        int number1 = 0;
        cin >> number1;

        cout << "Enter your second number: " << endl;
        int number2 = 0;
        cin >> number2;

        bool result = number1 > number2;
        cout << "It is "
                << result
                << " that your first number is greater than your second."
                << endl;

        return 0;
}
```

Listing 3-9 shows a use of the greater-than or equal to operator.

Listing 3-9. The Greater-Than or Equal To Operator

```
#include "stdafx.h"
#include <iostream>

using namespace std;

int _tmain(int argc, _TCHAR* argv[])
{
        cout << "Enter your first number: " << endl;
        int number1 = 0;
        cin >> number1;

        cout << "Enter your second number: " << endl;
        int number2 = 0;
        cin >> number2;

        bool result = number1 >= number2;
        cout << "It is "
                << result
                << " that your first number is greater than"
                << " or equal to your second."
                << endl;

        return 0;
}
```

Listing 3-10 shows an example of the less-than operator.

Listing 3-10. The Less Than Operator

```
#include "stdafx.h"
#include <iostream>

using namespace std;

int _tmain(int argc, _TCHAR* argv[])
{
        cout << "Enter your first number: " << endl;
        int number1 = 0;
        cin >> number1;

        cout << "Enter your second number: " << endl;
        int number2 = 0;
        cin >> number2;

        bool result = number1 < number2;
        cout << "It is "
                << result
                << " that your first number is less than your second."
                << endl;

        return 0;
}
```

Finally, Listing 3-11 shows a use of the less-than or equal to operator.

Listing 3-11. The Less-Than or Equal To Operator

```
#include "stdafx.h"
#include <iostream>

using namespace std;

int _tmain(int argc, _TCHAR* argv[])
{
        cout << "Enter your first number: " << endl;
        int number1 = 0;
        cin >> number1;

        cout << "Enter your second number: " << endl;
        int number2 = 0;
        cin >> number2;

        bool result = number1 <= number2;
        cout << "It is "
                << result
                << " that your first number is less than "
```

```
            << " or equal to your second."
            << endl;

        return 0;
}
```

So far we have looked at arithmetic operators for carrying out basic mathematical operations and relational operators for comparing the values stored in variables. The next set of operators supplied by C++ is the bitwise operators, which allow us to modify the individual bits that make up our values.

Bitwise Operators

All of the values we have seen so far have been backed by bits stored in computer memory. In a binary computer system, a single bit can either contain a one or a zero. We represent higher numbers than these by using different patterns of bits. This section covers the operators that allow us to manipulate bits.

As a programmer you will generally deal with data sizes in terms of numbers of bytes rather than numbers of bits. A byte is a collection of 8 bits. We have already seen that the char data type consists of a single byte and that an int consists of 4 bytes. This means that a char consists of 8 bits and an int is 32 bits.

We can think of the 8 bits of a byte as being represented in the same manner as in Table 3-1.

Table 3-1. The Unsigned char Bit Sequence for 137

128	64	32	16	8	4	2	1
1	0	0	0	1	0	0	1

The bit sequence in Table 3-1 represents the unsigned char value of 137. We have a bit telling us that the value consists of a 1, an 8, and a 128. These are added together to give us 137.

The bitwise operators allow us to set and unset individual bits, test if bits are set, and even merge bit patterns together. A set bit means that its value is 1 and an unset bit has the value 0. The rest of this section looks at the bitwise operators available in C++ as well as the hexadecimal representation of numbers.

Hexadecimal Number Representation

When we normally write numbers, such as 11, we are using the decimal number representation. Decimal numbers have a base 10 format. We say it is base 10, as we have 10 unique digits, 0 through 9. Once we add one to 9 in a column, we reset the column to 0 and add a one to the column to the left, so 9 becomes 10, 19 becomes 20, and 1999 becomes 2000.

> **Note**   It's probably not a coincidence that we have 10 fingers, or digits, on our hands and that our modern counting systems are all based on the base 10 number system. The binary numbers we have been looking at so far are actually numbers in the base 2 representation of numbers!

Table 3-1 shows how we can represent numbers in the binary format. 1 is 1, 2 in binary is 10, and 137 in binary is 10001001. Once we get to 32-bit values we have to keep track of 32 individual bits, and things are even worse now that we are seeing processors that can operate on 64-bit values. To make life easier for all, the hexadecimal number format can be used to represent large bitfields. Despite the "hex" part leading us toward believing that we are dealing with sets of six, hexadecimal values actually work in sets of 16, or base 16. The hexadecimal representation uses the digits 0, 1, 2, 3, 4, 5, 6, 7, 8, 9, A, B, C, D, E, and F where A, B, C, D, E, and F represent 10, 11, 12, 13, 14, and 15, respectively.

Table 3-1 can be used to work out that the binary value 1111 is actually the number 15. We can represent the 8-bit value of 15 in C++ using the following line of code:

```
unsigned char hex15 = 0x0F;
```

If we wish to print a value out onto the console in hex format we tell cout in the following manner:

```
cout << std::hex << number << std::dec << number;
```

For the rest of this section we use simple 8-bit binary representations of numbers to show how the bitwise operators change values in our code. This small section on hexadecimal numbers is useful, as we would use this format for binary values in source code for shipping game titles.

C++ provides us with the following bitwise operators:

- AND operator
- OR operator
- Exclusive OR operator
- Left Shift operator
- Right Shift operator

The Binary & (AND) Operator

The & operator is known as the AND operator. Listing 3-12 shows how the & operator is used.

Listing 3-12. The Bitwise & Operator

```
#include "stdafx.h"
#include <iostream>

using namespace std;
```

```
int _tmain(int argc, _TCHAR* argv[])
{
        unsigned int first = 0x0F;
        unsigned int second = 0x18;
        unsigned int anded = first & second;

        cout << hex << showbase;
        cout << first << endl;
        cout << second << endl;
        cout << anded << endl;

        return 0;
}
```

> **Note**   We are using unsigned int and not unsigned char in these examples as cout prints character
> symbols when using char types but converts to human-readable numbers when using int types.

We are using the & operator on the variables first and second in Listing 3-12 and storing the result in anded. The first use of cout tells the output stream that we would like to show numbers in the hex format. The showbase specifier tells the output stream that we would also like to show the 0x part of the number. The output from this program would look like the following:

```
0xf
0x18
0x8
```

0x0f and 0x18 were our input numbers and 0x08 is the output generated. Table 3-2 shows how we derive this result.

Table 3-2. The Result of Using Bitwise & on 0x0F and 0x18

	128	64	32	16	8	4	2	1
first	0	0	0	0	1	1	1	1
second	0	0	0	1	1	0	0	0
anded	0	0	0	0	1	0	0	0

Table 3-2 shows how we can derive 0x08 as the result of an & between 0x0F and 0x18. We begin with the right-most column and work our way to the left.

In the 1s column we have a 1 in first and a 0 in second; therefore the result bit is 0.

In the 2s column we have a 1 in first and a 0 in second; therefore the result bit is 0.

In the 4s column we have a 1 in first and a 0 in second; therefore the result bit is 0.

In the 8s column we have a 1 in first and a 1 in second; therefore the result bit is 1.

In the 16s column we have a 0 in first and a 1 in second; therefore the result bit is 0.

All other columns have 0s in both values.

As you can see, to be able to have a 1 in a bit column in our result value the corresponding bit column also had to be 1 in the first *and* second values. If either of the values was a 0 then the result bit at the same column is also a 0.

The Binary | (OR) Operator

The Bitwise |, or OR, operator is used to determine if either of the bits in a given column is set to 1 in either of the two supplied values. Table 3-3 shows the result of using | with the same 0x0F and 0x18 values as the previous example.

Table 3-3. The Result of Using Bitwise | on 0x0F and 0x18

	128	64	32	16	8	4	2	1
first	0	0	0	0	1	1	1	1
second	0	0	0	1	1	0	0	0
ord	0	0	0	1	1	1	1	1

The result of the | on the two values is 0x1F. We derived this using the following method from left to right.

In the 1s column we have a 1 in first; therefore the result bit is 1.

In the 2s column we have a 1 in first; therefore the result bit is 1.

In the 4s column we have a 1 in first; therefore the result bit is 1.

In the 8s column we have a 1 in first; therefore the result bit is 1.

In the 16s column we have a 1 in second; therefore the result bit is 1.

All other columns have 0s in both values.

Using the | operator is as simple as using the & operator; however, the resulting bit for each column is set to 1 if either of the bits from the two input values were 1.

The Binary ^ (Exclusive OR) Operator

Our last bitwise operator is the ^ (or Exclusive OR/XOR) operator. This operator differs from the | operator by requiring that one of the two input values bits is set, but not both. Table 3-4 shows this in practice.

Table 3-4. The Result of Using Bitwise ^ on 0x0F and 0x18

	128	64	32	16	8	4	2	1
first	0	0	0	0	1	1	1	1
second	0	0	0	1	1	0	0	0
xord	0	0	0	1	0	1	1	1

The result from 0x0F ^ 0x18 is 0x17. As you can see, every column that contains a 1 and a 0 resulted in a 1 being placed into the result. The columns that contain two 1s or two 2s all result in 0s being stored.

The Left Shift (<<) Operator

You can use the left shift operator to move bits to the left by a specified number of bits. The following code shows how we can use the shift operator.

```
unsigned int shifted = 1 << 1;
```

If you print the value stored in shifted you will see that it contains the number 2. This is because the bit to the left of the first bit represents 2. The following patterns show what has happened.

128	64	32	16	8	4	2	1
0	0	0	0	0	0	0	1
0	0	0	0	0	0	1	0

If we had shifted the number of bits by 2 then shifted would have contained 4. When we use the left shift operator, all of the bits at the right of the pattern are set to 0. This ensures that we do not introduce new values into our variable.

A more complicated way of thinking about the shift operator is to imagine that we are multiplying the left value by 2 raised to the power of the number of shifted bits. In our example, we had $1*(2^1)=2$. If we had shifted by 4 bits we would have $1*2^4=16$.

The last thing you should consider when using left shift is what happens to values on the end. Consider the following line of code.

```
unsigned int shifted = 0x80000000 << 1;
```

This code shows that we will shift the end bit off of the end. In this case shifted will store 0 after execution. As all bits to the right of the shift are set to 0, any bits that are shifted out of the variable will be lost.

The Right Shift (>>) Operator

The right shift operator carries out the opposite operation to the left shift operator.

```
unsigned int shifted = 0x2 >> 1;
```

`shifted` contains 1 after executing this line of code. Again, if you shift values off the end then they are lost.

There is a significant difference between the left and right shift operators. When left shifting, all of the new values are set to 0. When right shifting the new bits depend on whether your value is a `signed` or `unsigned` type. Unsigned types have the values at the left of the bit pattern set to 0. Signed types have these set to the value contained in the sign bit. This means that positive values will have these bits set to 0 and negative values will have these bits set to 1. If you're having trouble remembering why this would be, you should go back over the description of twos complement numbers in the previous chapter.

Bitwise operators can be fairly complex to get your head around, but they can be a very powerful tool for a programmer. The next set of operators that we will be looking at is the logical operators.

Logical Operators

We are going to cover logical operators here without covering any source examples. Logical operators are at their most useful when combined with flow control statements, which we will look at in Chapter 6. There are two logical operators: Logical AND (&&) and Logical OR (||). These behave differently to the Bitwise & and | operators, so it is critical that you ensure that you are choosing the appropriate operator for the task at hand.

Logical operators operate on two boolean values and return a boolean result.

The && Operator

The && operator simply tells us whether two booleans are both true. For example:

```
bool isTrue = true && true;
bool isFalse = false && true;
bool isFalse = true && false;
bool isFalse = false && false;
bool isTrue = true && true && true;
```

There isn't any more to the && operator than this.

The || Operator

The || operator is as simple as the && operator. Some results when using || are as follows:

```
bool isTrue = true || true;
bool isTrue = false || true;
bool isTrue = true || false;
bool isFalse = false || false;
bool isTrue = true || false || false;
```

As you can see, the result is only false when all parameters in the || chain are false where they were all true, to provide a true result using &&.

Another class of operators we can use in C++ are the unary operators. So far all of the operators we have looked at have required two input values to create an output value. Unary operators can work on a single variable.

Unary Operators

C++ provides a set of operators that can be used with a single variable as opposed to the operators that take two operands as we have seen so far. There are arithmetic, logical, and binary unary operators, which we look at in this section. First we take a look at the arithmetic unary operators.

Arithmetic Unary Operators

The arithmetic unary operators are the plus and negative operators, and the increment and decrement operators.

Unary Negative Operator

The unary negative operator is used to negate a given value just as we do in general arithmetic. -x means negate x. If x happened to be 4 then the value would become –4, if it was –3 the value would become 3. It can be used in C++ code as follows:

```
int negatedValue = -4;
int positiveValue = -negatedValue;
```

positiveValue would contain 4 after executing these lines of code.

Unary Plus Operator

The unary plus operator simply returns the same value as it reads and therefore finds little use in practical programming.

```
int valueA = 1;
int valueB = +valueA;
```

In the preceding code, valueB would also contain the number 1.

The Increment and Decrement Operators

The increment operator allows us to increase a value by one and the decrement operator allows us to decrease a value by one. If we place the operator before the variable name, it is said to be a preincrement or predecrement operator. If we place it after it is said to be a postincrement or postdecrement operator. Listing 3-13 shows a small MSVC program that outputs various values using these operators.

Listing 3-13. The Increment and Decrement Operators

```
#include "stdafx.h"
#include <iostream>

using namespace std;

int _tmain(int argc, _TCHAR* argv[])
{
        int value = 0;
        cout << value << endl;
        cout << value++ << endl;
        cout << ++value << endl;
        cout << value-- << endl;
        cout << --value << endl;
        return 0;
}
```

The output from this program is the following:

```
0
0
2
2
0
```

We achieve this in the following way. 0 is output in the first cout line as the variable value was initialized to 0. The second cout also prints 0 as the postincrement operator returns the value of the variable, then increases it; therefore, we print out 0 then add 1. The third cout uses a preincrement operator; therefore, 1 is added to the variable, giving 2, which is then returned to cout for printing. Our fourth cout uses a post decrement operator that causes the value 2 to be returned from the variable before it is decremented to 1. The last cout decrements the variable to 0 before returning it to the cout command for printing.

These operators will be useful when we look at arrays in Chapter 4.

The Logical Not Unary Operator

Logical Not allows us to flip the value of a boolean value. Using !, true becomes false and false becomes true. We could determine if two values were not equal in the following way:

```
bool notEqual = !(valueA == valueB);
```

This is a simple example of how to use the ! operator.

The One's Complement Operator

The operator, ~, can be used to flip all of the bits in a variable. Listing 3-14 shows a program to print the output from the ~ operator.

Listing 3-14. The ~ Operator

```
#include "stdafx.h"
#include <iostream>

using namespace std;

int _tmain(int argc, _TCHAR* argv[])
{
        int test = 0x0000000F;
        cout << hex << ~test;
        return 0;
}
```

This program will write out 0xFFFFFFF0, which is the value 0x0000000F with all of the bits flipped from 0 to 1 and 1 to 0.

Summary

In this chapter we have covered all of the basic operators that we will be using to construct procedural programs. These operators allow us to carry out arithmetic on variables, compare the relationships between values in variables, and even carry out complicated operations on individual bits inside variable values.

Every program we write uses combinations of these operators to carry out complicated and complex tasks. The examples so far in this book have been basic programs that help us to understand the effects of these operators on the types provided by the C++ programming language. The examples beginning in Chapter 4 will actually start us on our journey into creating a text adventure game using C++.

Summary

Chapter 4

Beginning C++ Game Development with Arrays

We will begin to create our first C++ game in this chapter. So far this book has looked at the various types supplied by the C++ programming language as well as the operators that can be used to alter and compare these types. The next major area of the C++ programming language that you should understand to begin constructing complex programs is data storage. The individual types in C++, such as int and char, can hold single values, but often we will want to be able to remember multiple values all relating to similar things. We could achieve this by creating a unique variable for every object with a value that we wish to remember; however, C++ provides us with arrays to store multiple values together. This chapter takes a look at how arrays are used in C++ and also explores how we can use arrays to begin our text adventure game.

The C++ Array

We looked at the various types supplied by C++ in Chapter 2, but each of the examples involved looking at only a single variable at a time. When writing programs, we would rather work with multiple pieces of data, as this is the type of task that computers are exceptionally good at. The following line of code shows how we can define an array that contains five integers.

```
int intArray[5] = { 0, 1, 2, 3, 4 };
```

This code creates an array of five integers each containing the values 0 through 4. The individual variables contained within an array are often referred to as the *elements* of the array. Listing 4-1 shows how we can use this array in a simple program.

Listing 4-1. C++ int Array

```cpp
#include <iostream>

using namespace std;

int _tmain(int argc, _TCHAR* argv[])
{
        int intArray[5] = { 0, 1, 2, 3, 4 };
        cout << intArray[0] << endl;
        cout << intArray[1] << endl;
        cout << intArray[2] << endl;
        cout << intArray[3] << endl;
        cout << intArray[4] << endl;
        return 0;
}
```

The array operator [ ] is used to specify an *index* into an array. The index is a value that specifies the offset of the variable that we would like to access. A common misunderstanding in computer programming is the fallacy that programmers "count" from zero. This is not strictly the case; programmers *offset* from zero and indexing into arrays is a perfect example of this.

The index 0 specifies that we would like the first element from the array and the index 1 specifies that we would like the second element. Listing 4-1 supplied indexes to the array using hard-coded literal values. You can also index into an array using a variable. Listing 4-2 gives an example of this.

Listing 4-2. A Variable Array Index

```cpp
#include <iostream>

using namespace std;

int _tmain(int argc, _TCHAR* argv[])
{
        int intArray[5] = { 5, 6, 7, 8, 9 };

        unsigned int index = 0;
        cout << "Index: " << index << endl;
        cout << "Value: " << intArray[index++] << endl;

        cout << "Index: " << index << endl;
        cout << "Value: " << intArray[index++] << endl;

        cout << "Index: " << index << endl;
        cout << "Value: " << intArray[index++] << endl;

        cout << "Index: " << index << endl;
        cout << "Value: " << intArray[index++] << endl;

        cout << "Index: " << index << endl;
        cout << "Value: " << intArray[index++] << endl;
        return 0;
}
```

We use an unsigned int as the array index, as we will never require a negative index into our array. Our index is initialized to 0 to access the first element and we use the post increment operator to increase the index by one after we print each value from the array.

> **Note**   You must make sure to initialize the array index to 0 in Listing 4-2 to ensure that we access the first element of the array. If you had failed to initialize the index in production code, the variable could contain a random value and access memory outside of the array. This always leads to bugs that are hard to locate and fix. The same principle of always initializing should apply to all of your variables to avoid this problem.

Listing 4-2 has also changed the values in the array to prevent the same values from being printed out for both the index and value lines. This helps show the relationship between the index and the values contained within the array.

Arrays can be constructed using any type in C++. Listings 4-1 and 4-2 show arrays using the int type but we could just as easily have used float, short, or bool (for example). char arrays have special meaning in C++ under certain circumstances as they can be used to represent C style strings.

Before we can look at the functions that C++ provides to manipulate C strings, you need to understand how pointers work and their relationship with arrays and memory.

Pointers

Pointers are a fundamental aspect of the C++ language that allows it to deliver fast runtime performance as a low-level programming language. Where variables allow us to manipulate the values stored at specific locations in memory, pointers let us manipulate variables that store addresses to other variables.

The concept of pointers can be a difficult one to explain, so let's jump straight into some examples. Listing 4-3 shows how we can use a pointer to find the value stored at a given memory address.

Listing 4-3. Using Pointers in C++

```
#include <iostream>

using namespace std;

int _tmain(int argc, _TCHAR* argv[])
{
        int     variable = 5;
        int*    variablePointer = &variable;

        cout << "Value of variable: " << variable << endl;

        cout << "Address of variable: " << &variable << endl;
```

```
    cout << "Value of variablePointer: " << variablePointer << endl;

    cout << "Value of variablePointer + 1: "
          << variablePointer + 1 << endl;

    cout << "Value of memory at dereferenced variablePointer: "
          << *variablePointer << endl;

    cout << "Value of memory at dereferenced variablePointer + 1: "
          << *variablePointer + 1 << endl;

    return 0;
}
```

This code creates an int variable and assigns it the value of 5. We then create a pointer to the variable.

```
int     variable = 5;
int*    variablePointer = &variable;
```

The * operator after the type name tells the compiler that we are creating a pointer. A pointer is a variable with a value that is a memory address rather than an actual value. We assign the address of variable to variablePointer by using the address-of operator &.

Figure 4-1 shows the output generated by the code in Listing 4-3.

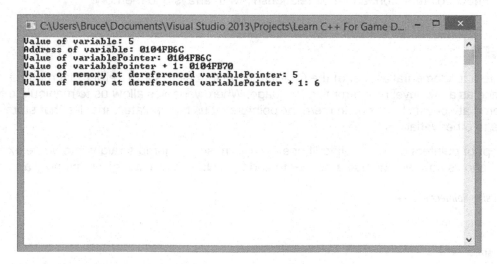

Figure 4-1. The output from Listing 4-3

The first line shows the value of variable using cout as usual.

```
cout << "Value of variable: " << variable << endl;
```

The second line prints out the hexadecimal address of the variable using the address-of operator.

```
cout << "Address of variable: " << &variable << endl;
```

The third line prints out the value of variablePointer. As variablePointer stores the address of the variable, the value output is the same.

```
cout << "Value of variablePointer: " << variablePointer << endl;
```

Pointer Arithmetic

Listing 4-3 and Figure 4-1 show the results of pointer arithmetic.

```
cout << "Value of variablePointer + 1: " << variablePointer + 1 << endl;
```

This line shows that we can add to addresses stored by pointers; we can also subtract, multiply, and divide pointers. Addition and subtraction usually make the most sense. The program has printed 0104FB6C as the address of variable. As the difference between the two addresses is 4 bytes, variablePointer + 1 is 0104FB70. This is not a coincidence. The size of an integer in my program is also 4 bytes. The compiler has added the size of 1 int to the address when we have used the addition operator with the int*. The compiler will always add on the size of the data type pointed to by the pointer multiplied by the number we are adding to the pointer variable. If our pointer had been a short it would have added 2 bytes, not 4. If we had added 5 to the int pointer, the compiler would have added 20 to the stored address.

Dereferencing Pointers

Once we have a pointer, we occasionally would like to know the value of the variable pointed to by the pointer. You can see this in action in the last two cout statements in Listing 4-3.

```
cout << "Value of memory at dereferenced variablePointer: "
     << *variablePointer << endl;

cout << "Value of memory at dereferenced variablePointer + 1: "
     << *variablePointer + 1 << endl;
```

The pointer dereference operator is *. When this operator is used with a pointer variable, the compiler will fetch the value of the variable pointed to by the pointer. In this case we dereference the pointer and retrieve the value 5. The next line shows that the * operator is evaluated before the arithmetic operator. In this case the 1 is added to the value pointed to by variablePointer and not the address that is stored there; therefore the output from this line is 6.

Pointers and Arrays

The timing of the description of pointers goes hand in hand with the description of arrays as the array index operator is carrying out pointer arithmetic for us behind the scenes. Compare Listing 4-4 with Listing 4-2.

Listing 4-4. Using a Pointer with an Array

```
int _tmain(int argc, _TCHAR* argv[])
{
        int intArray[5] = { 0, 1, 2, 3, 4 };

        cout << "Value: " << *intArray << endl;
        cout << "Value: " << *(intArray + 1) << endl;
        cout << "Value: " << *(intArray + 2) << endl;
        cout << "Value: " << *(intArray + 3) << endl;
        cout << "Value: " << *(intArray + 4) << endl;
        return 0;
}
```

Listing 4-4 creates a program that outputs the values stored in the array. However, it accesses the values in the array by manipulating a pointer as opposed to using the index operator. Once again we have used parentheses in our program to dictate the order in which our operators are evaluated.

As you can see, the array is created as usual; however, this time it is clear that the variable `intArray` is actually a pointer to an `int`. We can manipulate the array variable using pointer arithmetic to achieve the same result as using the index operator. The first value is accessed by dereferencing the pointer, and each subsequent value is accessed by dereferencing the pointer after it has been offset using pointer arithmetic.

Now that you know how to access arrays using either the index operator or pointers, we are ready to tackle C style strings.

C Style Strings in Arrays

Listing 1-1 showed the use of a C++ style string using the `string` class. We look at this class in detail in Chapter 13 once we have covered classes in more detail. Until then we can use arrays to represent C style strings.

> **Note**   It is recommended that STL strings are used in new programs. STL strings automatically resize to store strings of varying length and generally hide all of the complicated memory management processing that can be involved when working with C style strings. This chapter covers C style strings, as you are likely to come across these very often when dealing with older game code and legacy game engines or libraries.

Listing 4-5 shows how we can access a C style string via pointer.

Listing 4-5. A C Style String

```
#include <iostream>

using namespace std;

int _tmain(int argc, _TCHAR* argv[])
```

```
{
        char* cStyleString = "CStyleString";

        cout << cStyleString << endl;

        return 0;
}
```

The value "CStyleString" in quotes is known as a *string literal*. The compiler creates a table of all of the string literals in our program and stores them together in memory. We can access these string literals by assigning them to a char*. When we use cout with a char* that stores the address of a string literal it will print out the entire string and then stop.

C++ achieves this by adding an extra character to the end of C style strings, the null terminator. We can see this in action using the code in Listing 4-6.

Listing 4-6. The NULL Terminator

```
#include <iostream>

using namespace std;

int _tmain(int argc, _TCHAR* argv[])
{
        char* cStyleString = "CStyleString";
        cout << (cStyleString[12] == '\0') << endl;

        return 0;
}
```

This program will print out a 1 as the 13th character of our string matches the null terminator character, \0. As you can see, we can store the address of the string into a char*, and we can then access individual characters using either pointer arithmetic or array indexing.

Note   Characters by default in C++ programs (and in this book) all use the American Standard Code for Information Interchange (ASCII) encoding. ASCII characters can be represented using single quotes such as 'a'. The null terminator is a special character and as such must be preceded by a \, '\0' using '0' would represent the number zero and not the null terminator character. The actual decimal value of 'a' is 87, '0' is 48, and '\0' is 0. You can find a full list of ASCII values at www.asciitable.com/

Working with C Style Strings

C++ provides *functions* to work with C style strings. We cover how functions operate and write our own in Chapter 5; for now we list the different functions that C++ provides to work with strings.

strlen

strlen tells us how many characters are in a given string excluding the null terminator; this is shown in Listing 4-7.

Listing 4-7. strlen

```
#include <iostream>

using namespace std;

int _tmain(int argc, _TCHAR* argv[])
{
        char* cStyleString = "CStyleString";
        cout << strlen(cStyleString) << endl;

        return 0;
}
```

This program outputs 12.

strcmp

strcmp compares two strings and returns 0 if they match. Listing 4-8 contains an example.

Listing 4-8. strcmp

```
#include <iostream>

using namespace std;

int _tmain(int argc, _TCHAR* argv[])
{
        char* cStyleString1 = "CStyleString";
        char* cStyleString2 = "CStyleString";
        cout << strcmp(cStyleString1, cStyleString1) << endl;

        return 0;
}
```

This program outputs 0.

strcpy

strcpy copies a string from one array into another. Listing 4-8 provides an example.

Listing 4-8. strcpy

```
#include <iostream>

using namespace std;

int _tmain(int argc, _TCHAR* argv[])
{
        char* cStyleString1 = "CStyleString";
        char cStyleString2[13];
        strcpy(cStyleString2, cStyleString1);

        cout << cStyleString2 << endl;

        return 0;
}
```

It's important to note that cStyleString2 contains enough space to store the 12 characters of the string literal plus an extra character for the null terminator.

strcat

strcat allows us to join, or concatenate, two strings. Listing 4-9 provides an example.

Listing 4-9. strcat

```
#include <iostream>

using namespace std;

int _tmain(int argc, _TCHAR* argv[])
{
        char cStyleString1[13];
        strcpy(cStyleString1, "CStyle");
        char* cStyleString2 = "String";
        strcat(cStyleString1, cStyleString2);

        cout << cStyleString1 << endl;

        return 0;
}
```

cStyleString1 must have enough space to store the combined string, therefore we create an array with space for 13 characters. We then use strcpy to copy "CStyle" into this array. strcat is used to copy "String" into the end of cStyleString1 from cStyleString2.

> **Note**   There are more functions supplied by C++ for working with C style strings; however, it is better to use
> the string class supplied by the Standard Template Library (STL) in modern C++ programs. We cover
> STL strings in Chapter 13. You can find a reference for C style string functions at
> www.cplusplus.com/reference/cstring/

Text Adventure Game

As you work through this book we will build a text adventure game on the console. In this chapter
we have looked at arrays, pointers, and C style strings. In the last two chapters we have looked at
types, operators, and interacting with the user using cin and cout.

We will begin by making our game a personal experience by asking the players for their name.
This will be used to make the game seem as though it knows the players while they play through the
game. Listing 4-10 shows the code that asks the players for their name.

Listing 4-10. Asking for the Player's Name

```
#include <iostream>

using namespace std;

int _tmain(int argc, _TCHAR* argv[])
{
        cout << "Welcome to Text Adventure!" << endl << endl;
        cout << "What is your name?" << endl << endl;

        char playerName[1024];
        cin >> playerName;

        cout << endl << "Hello " << playerName << endl;

        return 0;
}
```

This code stores the player's name into a char array that contains 1,024 letters. The game would run
into trouble if the player was to enter more characters than this, so we will use a string instead, as
shown in Listing 4-11.

Listing 4-11. Using an STL String for the Player Name

```
#include <iostream>
#include <string>

using namespace std;

int _tmain(int argc, _TCHAR* argv[])
{
        cout << "Welcome to Text Adventure!" << endl << endl;
        cout << "What is your name?" << endl << endl;
```

```
        string playerName;
        cin >> playerName;

        cout << endl << "Hello " << playerName << endl;

        return 0;
}
```

Now the players can enter a name as long or as short as they like without issue. We will cover why the string class is safer than a character array in Chapter 13.

Note   We could use character arrays for player input until we cover strings. However, I do not like to encourage the development of bad habits. If a player was to enter too many characters for our array to hold we would suffer a buffer overrun and introduce bugs into our code that will cause the program to crash. STL string does not suffer from this problem for reasons that are covered in Chapter 13.

Summary

This chapter has covered C++ arrays that allow us to store groups of data of the same type in *contiguous* memory. Contiguous means that the elements of the array follow each other directly in memory without having to jump to another location.

This can be seen in action when we index arrays or carry out pointer arithmetic. Modern processors are designed with caches to operate at peak efficiency when dealing with contiguous memory addresses and arrays, therefore, are vitally important to the performance of modern video games.

We cover more exotic data layouts later in this book when we introduce the STL, but it is important to understand arrays to be able to write fast and efficient code under many circumstances.

C style strings are also an important concept to understand. Many current games are still written using this style of string, although the STL provides a better string class implementation. This is usually because it can still be faster to operate on arrays directly rather than work with classes. However, accessing arrays directly comes with some concerns about program stability, especially when dealing with user input. Overrunning the end of a buffer and overwriting memory used by other variables is a common cause of hard-to-find bugs and potential security vulnerabilities in many games.

This chapter also introduced the concept of a function. Chapter 5 covers functions in more detail and you will learn how to write some of your own.

5

Chapter

Functions, the Building Blocks of C++

Modern games consist of hundreds of thousands of lines of code and can be worked on by teams consisting of hundreds of people. C++ provides the ability to separate code into blocks called functions to allow us to build more modular programs.

A function allows us to write a routine that can be reused throughout our program. The benefits of this are significant. You saw this in the last chapter when we looked at some of the C++ functions for working with strings. We did not have to write our own code to determine if two strings were the same; instead, we could simply *pass* them both into a function and the *return* value told us the result of the function.

This chapter covers how we write functions, including how to pass values to a function, how to pass pointers to functions, and a special type of pointer, the reference.

Writing Our First Function

A C++ compiler requires that functions are declared and defined before they can be used, just as with variables. It's also possible to define and declare a function at the same time. Listing 5-1 shows the code for a simple program that calls a single function.

Listing 5-1. Our First Function

```
#include <iostream>

using namespace std;

void PrintHello()
{
        cout << "Hello!" << endl;
}
```

```
int _tmain(int argc, _TCHAR* argv[])
{
        PrintHello();

        return 0;
}
```

Listing 5-1 contains a function named PrintHello. Functions in C++ always follow the same format and PrintHello is as simple as a function can be. It does not return any values to the code that calls the function and we also cannot pass any parameters to the function. To tell the C++ compiler that we do not want the function to return a value, we specify void as its *return type*. We can call a function by placing its name in our code followed by parentheses, as we have done with PrintHello.

Passing Parameters to Functions

Functions tend to be more useful when we can pass values to them. We do this by specifying parameters in the function *signature*. Listing 5-2 shows a function that contains parameters in its signature.

Listing 5-2. Passing Values to Functions Through Parameters

```
#include <iostream>

using namespace std;

void PrintSum(int valueA, int valueB)
{
        cout << valueA + valueB << endl;
}

int _tmain(int argc, _TCHAR* argv[])
{
        PrintSum(3, 6);

        return 0;
}
```

The function PrintSum takes two parameters. Both parameters are of the type int and are named valueA and valueB. When we call PrintSum in _tmain we pass it the values 3 and 6. Inside the function the variable valueA contains the value 3 and valueB contains 6. The output from the program is 9. Another way to achieve this result would be to return the sum from the function.

Return Values

Functions can return values to the calling code to be stored within variables or passed as parameters to other functions. Listing 5-3 shows how to return a value from the function.

Listing 5-3. Returning Values from Functions

```
#include <iostream>

using namespace std;

int ReturnSum(int valueA, int valueB)
{
        return valueA + valueB;
}

int _tmain(int argc, _TCHAR* argv[])
{
        int sum = ReturnSum(3, 6);
        cout << sum << endl;

        return 0;
}
```

The function ReturnSum has a new return type in its signature: It now reads int rather than void. Inside the function you now see that we use the return keyword to return the value from the + operator. We store the returned value from ReturnSum into the variable sum, which is then used with cout to print the result 9 to the console.

Any of the built-in types can be used as parameter or return types. The functions we have looked at in Listings 5-1, 5-2, and 5-3 all pass and return their function by value. This means that the compiler will make a copy of the values when they are being passed to or from the function. Sometimes we would like to be able to alter the values that come into our function so that the calling code can access the new values, and we can do this by passing in pointers.

Passing by Pointer

Listing 5-4 alters our previous example to pass the result of our sum back to the calling code using a pointer.

Listing 5-4. Passing by Pointer

```
#include <iostream>

using namespace std;

void ReturnSum(int inValueA, int inValueB, int* outValue)
{
        *outValue = inValueA + inValueB;
}
```

```
int _tmain(int argc, _TCHAR* argv[])
{
        int sum = 0;
        ReturnSum(3, 6, &sum);
        cout << sum << endl;

        return 0;
}
```

Listing 5-4 initializes the variable sum to contain the value 0. ReturnSum now does not return a value; instead it takes a pointer to an int as its third parameter. When we call ReturnSum we pass the address of sum using &sum. Inside ReturnSum we alter the value stored at the pointer using the following line:

```
*outValue = inValueA + inValueB;
```

The pointer dereference operator is used to tell the compiler that we want to change the value stored at the pointer and not the pointer itself. In Listing 5-4 this achieves the result of altering the value of sum from 0 to 9.

Note   Pointers can be set to not contain a value. This is achieved by assigning nullptr to them. We'll cover nullptr in Chapter 6 when we look at flow control statements.

As well as being able to pass values by pointer, we can also pass them by reference.

Passing by Reference

When we pass by pointer we must explicitly dereference the pointer to be able to retrieve its value. There's also a possibility that the pointer might not point to a valid memory address but instead be assigned a nullptr. If we dereference a nullptr our program will crash. If we use a reference then we do not have to deference to obtain the value, we do not have to worry about nullptrs and we do not have to use the address of operator when passing the initial variable to the function. You can see this in Listing 5-5.

Listing 5-5. Passing by Reference

```
#include <iostream>

using namespace std;

void ReturnSum(int inValueA, int inValueB, int& outValue)
{
        outValue = inValueA + inValueB;
}
```

```
int _tmain(int argc, _TCHAR* argv[])
{
        int sum = 0;
        ReturnSum(3, 6, sum);
        cout << sum << endl;

        return 0;
}
```

We now use the reference operator on the type for outValue; this looks like int&. We're beginning to see the same operators being used for different purposes in different contexts. When defining a variable, the & operator after the typename tells the compiler to make the variable a reference. When placed before a variable name, when assigning to a variable, or when passing to a function it becomes the address-of operator.

Sooner or later in our programs we will want to pass large amounts of data into a function. One option could be to add many parameters to the function signature, but this makes the code difficult to maintain, as every time we change the function signature we will also have to change every call. Luckily structures provide an alternative.

Structures

So far all of the variables we have been using have been single variables. Individual variables are useful, but sometimes they can only take us so far. We will alter the sum example once again to show how we can use a structure with a function. Listing 5-6 shows an example of passing a structure to a function.

Listing 5-6. Passing a Structure to a Function

```
#include <iostream>

using namespace std;

struct SumParameters
{
        int     valueA;
        int     valueB;
        int     result;
};

void ReturnSum(SumParameters& params)
{
        params.result = params.valueA + params.valueB;
}

int _tmain(int argc, _TCHAR* argv[])
{
        SumParameters sum;
        sum.valueA = 3;
        sum.valueB = 6;
```

```
        sum.result = 0;
        ReturnSum(sum);
        cout << sum.result << endl;

        return 0;
}
```

Listing 5-6 begins by defining our structure. We do this using the struct keyword. Immediately after the keyword is the name we would like to use for our structure. This name behaves as though we have created a new type. We can see this in the first line of _tmain where we declare the variable sum.

Once we have a variable that is of a structure type, we can use the . operator to access its *member* variables. We assign the values 3, 6, and 0 to the members of sum and then pass it by reference to the function ReturnSum. The compiler would have made a copy of all three members if we had passed the structure by value and therefore we would not have been able to read the proper result of the sum from the result member.

You can use the information you have learned about functions in this chapter to modify the game we have been writing.

Adding Functions to Text Adventure

We began our Text Adventure game in Chapter 4. At that time you didn't know that we could store data in structures or that we could use functions to make more readable programs. In this chapter we will create a structure for the player and create a function that will be responsible for welcoming the player. We do both of these in Listing 5-7.

Listing 5-7. Adding the Player struct and WelcomePlayer Function to Text Adventure

```
#include <iostream>
#include <string>

using namespace std;

struct Player
{
        string m_name;
};

void WelcomePlayer(Player& player)
{
        cout << "Welcome to Text Adventure!" << endl << endl;
        cout << "What is your name?" << endl << endl;

        cin >> player.m_name;

        cout << endl << "Hello " << player.m_name << endl;
}
```

```
int _tmain(int argc, _TCHAR* argv[])
{
        Player player;
        WelcomePlayer(player);

        return 0;
}
```

Our program is now much more readable than before. The Player structure will be responsible for storing all of the data related to our player object; for now we only need to keep track of the player's name. We pass the player variable by reference to the WelcomePlayer function. This allows us to add all of the code necessary to welcome our players to a single function and this function can assign the player's name from cin directly into the Player reference.

Our _tmain function now has code that is almost plain English. This is the goal of our code for the most part. Code that is human readable is very valuable when writing game programs. A lot of the code written, especially code to be reused between projects, must be maintained by teams of programmers. Having code that can be understood just by reading through it reduces the time it takes to understand and make alterations to the code.

Summary

This chapter has covered the C-style functions and structures you can use while writing programs in C++. Functions are the basic building blocks that allow us to write procedural programs. We have learned how to use parameters and return values to help us write readable programs. We've also looked at how pointers and references can be used to pass data into and out of functions. Finally, we looked at how we can group variables into structures. Grouping data in this way allows us to create our own types within the language. These types also aid us in writing programs that other programmers can easily understand. You saw this put to good effect in our Text Adventure game when we created a Player structure to group together data relating to our player.

Our programs are beginning to take a real form but they are still limited to carrying out basic arithmetic. In the next chapter we will look at control flow statements that will allow our programs to make decisions or repeat tasks over a large set of data.

Chapter **6**

Making Decisions with Flow Control

The programs that we have been writing until now have been very linear. That is, they begin with the first line in `main` and carry on executing each line at a time until the program finishes with the return statement on the last line of `main`. Sometimes we might decide to carry out different code paths based on values we have stored in variables or repeat a section of code until some condition is satisfied.

C++ provides us with statements that allow us to carry out these decisions and repetitions. This chapter introduces the `if`, `switch`, `for`, and `while` statements. These statements collectively are known as the flow control statements. We'll end the chapter by using flow control statements to add some decision making to our Text Adventure game.

The if Statement

The first flow control statement that we will look at is the `if` statement. This statement allows us to execute inside its curly braced block *if* the boolean we pass to it is true. Listing 6-1 shows a simple if statement.

Listing 6-1. The if Statement

```
#include <iostream>

using namespace std;

int main(int argc, const char * argv[])
```

```
{
        if (true)
        {
                cout << "Print This!";
        }
        return 0;
}
```

This if statement will always enter into the block associated with it. This block begins with the opening curly brace immediately following the statement and ends with the corresponding closing curly brace. If we were to change the value in the expression from true to false the block would not be entered and we would not see the output printed on the console.

> **Note**   The examples in this chapter have been created using Xcode. Be sure to check that the main statement is correct for the integrated development environment (IDE) and platform you are using.

The else and else if Statements

The if statement allows us to make decisions in our code but usually we also want to be able to execute code on other conditions or as a default. We can use the else and else if statements to add more execution blocks to our if statements. Listing 6-2 shows how to use the else statement.

Listing 6-2. The else Statement

```
#include <iostream>

using namespace std;

int main(int argc, const char * argv[])
{
        if (false)
        {
                cout << "Print This When True!";
        }
        else
        {
                cout << "Print This When False!";
        }
        return 0;
}
```

Our if statement now evaluates to false. If this were to happen in Listing 6-1, we would see no output from our program; however, the else statement in Listing 6-2 ensures that we will still see output. Listing 6-3 adds an extra if into the code.

Listing 6-3. The else if Statement

```
#include <iostream>

using namespace std;

int main(int argc, const char * argv[])
{
        if (false)
        {
                cout << "Print This When True!";
        }
        else if (true)
        {
                cout << "Print This When Else If Is True!";
        }
        else
        {
                cout << "Print This If All False!";
        }

        return 0;
}
```

Here you can see that the extra else if statement will cause the code to execute its block and miss the else block. Listing 6-4 shows that we can have multiple else if blocks.

Listing 6-4. Multiple else if Blocks

```
#include <iostream>

using namespace std;

int main(int argc, const char * argv[])
{
        if (false)
        {
                cout << "Print This When True!";
        }
        else if (false)
        {
                cout << "Print This When First Else If Is True!";
        }
        else if (true)
        {
                cout << "Print This When Second Else If Is True!";
        }
```

```
        else
        {
                cout << "Print This If All False!";
        }

        return 0;
}
```

We can, in fact, have as many else if statements as we like. The else statement is also optional: It is completely valid to have cases where no else statement is necessary.

Now we'll take a look at the for loop, which allows us to execute the same code block multiple times.

The for Loop

The for loop allows us to iterate as many times as necessary. Listing 6-5 shows a simple for loop in action.

Listing 6-5. A for Loop

```
#include <iostream>

using namespace std;

int main(int argc, const char * argv[])
{
        for (unsigned int i=0; i<10; ++i)
        {
            cout << "Loop Iteration: " << i << endl;
        }

        return 0;
}
```

The for loop statement consists of three parts:

- An initializer, which sets the initial value of the loop index variable (i.e., unsigned int i=0).

- A test, in which the loop will continue to execute until the test statement evaluates to false (i.e., i<10).

- A continuation statement, which is executed at the end of each successful loop before starting the next one (i.e., ++i).

The for loop in our example results in the output being printed to the console 10 times with the values 0 through 9 appended to the end.

A more powerful example of this is to combine the for loop with an array, as shown in Listing 6-6.

Listing 6-6. A for Loop Over an Array

```cpp
#include <iostream>

using namespace std;

int main(int argc, const char * argv[])
{
    unsigned int array[10];

    for (unsigned int i=0; i<10; ++i)
    {
        array[i] = i * 2;
        cout << "Loop Iteration: " << array[i] << endl;
    }

    return 0;
}
```

This example shows how we can use the for loop index variable to index into an array. Here we initialize each element of the array via iteration and print the results to the console. We can use this technique to execute code on each element of an array, which is especially useful when writing games.

Sometimes we do not know beforehand how many iterations of a given loop we would like to execute. Thankfully C++ provides us with another loop statement that can handle this case, the while loop.

The while Loop

A while loop just executes until its accompanying statement evaluates to false. Listing 6-7 shows a simple example.

Listing 6-7. A while Loop

```cpp
#include <iostream>
using namespace std;

int main(int argc, const char * argv[])
{
    unsigned int array[10];
    unsigned int count = 0;
    while (count < 10)
    {
        array[count] = count * 2;
        cout << "Loop Iteration: " << array[count++] << endl;
    }

    return 0;
}
```

Another type of while loop is the do . . . while loop. Listing 6-8 shows an example of this type.

Listing 6-8. A do . . . while Loop

```
#include <iostream>

using namespace std;

int main(int argc, const char * argv[])
{
        unsigned int array[10];
        unsigned int count = 0;

        do
        {
            array[count] = count * 2;
            cout << "Loop Iteration: " << array[count++] << endl;
        } while (count < 10);

        return 0;
}
```

The main difference between these two types of loop is that the do . . . while version will always execute at least once. The test occurs at the end of the first iteration of the do . . . while whereas the test occurs at the beginning of a standard while loop.

If count in Listing 6-7 had been initialized to 10, the loop would never have run, whereas in Listing 6-8 it would have run once (and caused an array overrun).

There are also times when we are programming when we want to execute specific code for a given value contained in a variable. C++ provides the switch statement for these moments.

The switch Statement

A switch statement can be used in place of an if . . . else if block when we have a set of literal values that we wish to differentiate between. Listing 6-9 shows an example using an enum.

Listing 6-9. The switch Statement

```
#include <iostream>

using namespace std;

int main(int argc, const char * argv[])
{
        enum class Colors
        {
            Red,
            Green,
            Blue
        };
```

```
        Colors color = Colors::Red;
        switch (color)
        {
            case Colors::Red:
                {
                    cout << "The color is Red!";
                }
                break;

            case Colors::Green:
                {
                    cout << "The color is Green";
                }
                break;

            default:
                {
                    cout << "Unknown color!";
                }
                break;
        }

        return 0;
}
```

You can see from this example that the switch statement can be used to create blocks of code (cases) that will execute for values that we are aware of at compile time. enums are perfect candidates for this type of statement. Listing 6-9 did not include a case block for the Blue value. This omission allowed us to look at the default case. The default case is supplied to provide a default behavior to the switch so that we can properly handle situations that need either a default behavior or to catch an error.

Listing 6-9 also sees the introduction of the break keyword. This new keyword allows us to break out of a statement block. If we had missed this in our switch, the program would have created the following output (assuming we add endl to each line):

```
The color is Red!
The color is Green!
Unknown color!
```

Missing the break in each block would cause the code to flow from one block to the next. Sometimes this is the behavior we desire, but more often than not it is a bug.

Note   This is our first mention of code bugs! Games are large projects and bugs can be caused by many complicated interactions in code. This example of missing a single word is just one example of how bugs can enter our code.

The break statement can be used to exit any of the loops we have covered in this chapter. If we had a for loop and had a condition where we would like to stop execution, then we would be able to use break, and the same goes for both versions of the while loop. C++ also provides the continue keyword to control loops.

The break and continue Keywords

Listing 6-10 shows an example loop that contains both the continue and break statements.

Listing 6-10. Using continue and break

```cpp
#include <iostream>

using namespace std;

int main(int argc, const char * argv[])
{
    unsigned int array[10];
    unsigned int count = 0;

    do
    {
        if ((count % 2) == 0)
        {
            ++count;
            continue;
        }

        array[count] = count;
        cout << "Loop Iteration: " << array[count++] << endl;

        if (count == 10)
        {
            break;
        }
    } while (true);

    return 0;
}
```

The output from our program is the following:

```
Loop Iteration: 1
Loop Iteration: 3
Loop Iteration: 5
Loop Iteration: 7
Loop Iteration: 9
```

The first if statement that contains a mod operator and a relational equals operator tells the loop to skip all of the even numbers when executing. Our output shows this by printing the current iteration count.

The second if statement tells the loop to break once the count reaches 10. The last flow control statement that we will look at in this chapter is the goto.

The goto Statement

The goto statement is frowned on by modern C++ developers, so I include it in this chapter merely for the sake of completeness, so that you are aware of its existence and can work with it in legacy code.

> **Note**   goto really is a rare sight in code today. In eight years I have only ever seen it used in a single game! This Wikipedia entry explains some of the concerns that exist with the goto statement: http://en.wikipedia.org/wiki/Goto#Criticism_and_decline

Listing 6-11 modifies Listing 6-10. This time we use a goto to end the loop rather than a break.

Listing 6-11. The goto Statement

```cpp
#include <iostream>

using namespace std;

int main(int argc, const char * argv[])
{
        unsigned int array[10];
        unsigned int count = 0;

        do
        {
            if ((count % 2) == 0)
            {
                ++count;
                continue;
            }

            array[count] = count;
            cout << "Loop Iteration: " << array[count++] << endl;

            if (count == 10)
            {
                goto finished;
            }
        } while (true);
```

```
    finished:
        return 0;
}
```

A goto consists of two parts:

- A label
- The goto statement

A label is inserted into the code, which creates a named point to which we can jump. In this example our label is finished. We can then use this label to have the goto command jump directly to that point.

I have seen this used to move between the game loop, the frontend loop and a pause loop in game code before. It's also been known for goto to be used to jump to error handling code. This might seem to be a good idea, but there are always better options such as using break, a state machine for game state, or return values or exceptions for handling errors.

In this chapter we have covered the essential flow control statements provided by C++. It's now time to put these to good use in our Text Adventure game.

Adding a Game Loop to Text Adventure

For our Text Adventure to be a compelling game, we must add a loop that allows the player to interact. We looked at the for loop and the while loop in this chapter. A for loop provides us with a set number of iterations, so a while loop would be better suited to our needs for a game loop.

Listing 6-12 shows how we can use an enum, functions, references, relational operators, and a while loop to write code that begins to resemble an interactive program.

Listing 6-12. The Text Adventure Game Loop

```
#include <iostream>
#include <string>

using namespace std;
```

The Player struct and WelcomePlayer functions have not changed since Chapter 5.

```
struct Player
{
        string m_name;
};

void WelcomePlayer(Player& player)
{
        cout << "Welcome to Text Adventure!" << endl << endl;
        cout << "What is your name?" << endl << endl;
```

```
        cin >> player.m_name;

        cout << endl << "Hello " << player.m_name << endl;
}
```

We create a new function, GivePlayerOptions, to display the different choices players currently have available to them.

```
void GivePlayerOptions()
{
        cout <<
            "What would you like to do? (Enter a corresponding number)"
            << endl << endl;
        cout << "1: Quit" << endl << endl;
}
```

The GetPlayerInput function reads the player's commands from the console and stores them into a string reference.

```
void GetPlayerInput(string& playerInput)
{
        cin >> playerInput;
}
```

We use an enum, PlayerOptions, to represent the choices the players can enter. For now we only have representations of Quit and None.

```
enum class PlayerOptions
{
        Quit,
        None
};
```

This function takes a reference to a string that represents a choice that could be made by the player. The literal string "1" is used to represent the Quit option at the moment.

We use an if...else statement here to decide whether the player has entered an option that we recognize. Strings can be compared using the compare function and will return 0 if the two strings match. If the player's input matched "1" we set the chosenOption value to PlayerOptions::Quit, and it is initialized to PlayerOptions::None. chosenOption is used as the return value of the function.

```
PlayerOptions EvaluateInput(string& playerInput)
{
        PlayerOptions chosenOption = PlayerOptions::None;

        if (playerInput.compare("1") == 0)
        {
            cout << "You have chosen to Quit!" << endl << endl;
            chosenOption = PlayerOptions::Quit;
        }
```

```
        else
        {
            cout << "I do not recognize that option, try again!"
                << endl << endl;
        }

        return chosenOption;
}
```

The RunGame function returns a bool, the shouldEnd variable. This function is designed to be called from a loop and simply calls the other functions that represent the different stages of our game at the moment. The return value from EvaluateInput is checked to determine if the player has decided to quit the game.

```
bool RunGame()
{
        bool shouldEnd = false;

        GivePlayerOptions();

        string playerInput;
        GetPlayerInput(playerInput);

        shouldEnd = EvaluateInput(playerInput) == PlayerOptions::Quit;

        return !shouldEnd;
}
```

Our program's entry point is still the main function. This function calls WelcomePlayer then executes a while loop that will iterate until the player has selected the quit option.

```
int main(int argc, const char * argv[])
{
        Player player;
        WelcomePlayer(player);

        bool isPlaying = true;
        while (isPlaying)
        {
            isPlaying = RunGame();
        }

        return 0;
}
```

We have now written a program that is beginning to resemble a game. We have put the core game loop into place and from here we will be able to add new functionality to our existing functions.

Summary

This chapter has introduced the flow control statements that are a core part of the C++ programming language. These statements allow us to write game code that creates compelling interactive experiences for our players. We can use `if` and `switch` statements to execute different code paths depending on the values stored in variables at runtime. These values could be calculated from the current state of the game or might be obtained from player input. You have also seen how we can use loops to execute code repetitively. The `for` loop can be used to carry out an iterative block of code over a fixed number of iterations and the `while` loop can be used to continue iterating until some condition is met. You've also seen how we can use the `continue` and `break` keywords to gain finer control over our loop execution.

We then used what we have learned to build a game loop for our Text Adventure game. We read input from the player inside a `while` loop until they enter the option to quit. We used an `if` statement to determine if the option the user entered matches the value we have chosen to represent quit.

The next chapter looks at program structure. It will show you how we can split our code across multiple source files so that we can create projects that are more manageable. So far our program has been relatively short and we have been working on our own. Professional game projects can have tens of thousands of files and tens to hundreds of programmers all working at the same time. You will learn how you can use source and header files, as well as namespaces, to modularize your code.

Chapter 7

Organizing Projects Using Files and Namespaces

In Chapter 6 we ended with a file that contains functions and structures that were related to completely different high-level concepts. Some were there to control the game loop, others to obtain user input and write output, and a structure to represent the player model. Eventually this code would become difficult to manage and work with if we were to continue down this path of adding everything to a single file.

We have already seen that we can split new functions into declarations and definitions as well as being able to use the #include directive to be able to use functionality that is contained within separate files. All of the examples we have used so far have used the using namespace std; directive. In this chapter we look at how we can organize our own programs into separate files and also create namespaces to group together functionality. To wrap up, we'll use what we learn to reorganize our Text Adventure game to allow us to expand more easily in the coming chapters.

Source and Header Files

C++ supports the ability to separate code out into separate source and header files to better organize programs. The header files of a project contain declarations of data types and functions that can then be used in source files. Source files contain the definitions of functions that are built by the compiler. Listing 7-1 shows the source code contained in a file named HelloWorld.cpp.

Listing 7-1. HelloWorld.cpp

```
#include <iostream>

using namespace std;

void HelloWorld()
{
        cout << "Hello World!";
}
```

This very basic example shows that we can declare functions inside code files. This file itself does not do anything interesting; it does not contain the entry point to our program. We would like to be able to call this function from other places in our code base. To be able to do this we must create a header file that contains a function declaration. Listing 7-2 shows our HelloWorld.h file.

Listing 7-2. HelloWorld.h

```
#pragma once

void HelloWorld();
```

The header file is very simple and contains our function declaration.

The #pragma once is necessary in header files to inform the compiler that we only want to include this file a single time. If we do not have this line at the beginning of our header file we will suffer from compile errors as the function definitions will occur more than once.

> **Note**   #pragma once is a modern compiler directive that is not supported by older compilers. In the past, header files would have include guards instead. Include guards use #ifndef, #define, and #endif to wrap header files and prevent the code from being included more than once. This is less efficient than #pragma once, which can tell the compiler to skip opening the file and reduce compile times if it has been processed before.

Now that we have a header file and a source file we will be able to use this to call our function from other files. Listing 7-3 shows how we can do this.

Listing 7-3. Calling HelloWorld from _tmain

```
#include "stdafx.h"
#include "HelloWorld.h"

int _tmain(int argc, _TCHAR* argv[])
{
        HelloWorld();

        return 0;
}
```

We can see from this example that our source files can now be kept in a much neater and more maintainable state. We simply include the HelloWorld.h file and we have access to the function that it contains. As we move forward we will be using source and header files extensively. This simple example covers all of the necessary details to be able to use these in our projects.

Creating Namespaces

Namespaces allow us to group functionality from multiple files into a single named code unit. This allows us to keep our functions and data types together. It also has the added benefit of keeping our new type and function names out of the *global namespace*. Usually we can only use a function name a single time, so by using namespaces we can use the same function and type names in a different context. Listing 7-4 shows an example that creates and uses two different namespaces.

Listing 7-4. Creating Namespaces

```
#include "stdafx.h"
#include <iostream>

namespace Player
{
        void PrintName()
        {
                std::cout << "My name is Bruce!" << endl;
        }
}

namespace Vehicle
{
        void PrintName()
        {
                std::cout << "I am a car!" << endl;
        }
}

using namespace Player;

int _tmain(int argc, _TCHAR* argv[])
{
        PrintName();

        Vehicle::PrintName();

        return 0;
}
```

This example shows the creation of two different namespaces, one named Player and another named Vehicle. Both of these namespaces contain a function named PrintName. If these were not contained within a namespace they would be required to have different names. Because they are contained within namespaces their usage in the code must be *qualified*. We can qualify our use of items contained in namespaces in two ways.

The first example is the Player namespace. We use the using namespace directive to inform all of the following code that any type and function within the namespace can be used. You can see this in the first line of the _tmain function, which can call PrintName directly.

The second example is where we call `Vehicle::PrintName`. This form of qualification is more explicit. This is the form of qualification I would recommend in this situation where we would be calling the same named function from two different namespaces. The explicit qualification makes it clear which of the namespace functions we would like to use.

This is also as complicated as we need namespaces to be for now. We will now rewrite the Text Adventure example from the previous chapter to use multiple source files and namespaces.

Updating Text Adventure with Source Files, Header Files, and Namespaces

By the end of Chapter 6 our Text Adventure game consisted of five functions, an enum `class`, and a `struct`. The number of these elements will only increase as we flesh out the functionality of our game. It would not take very long for our only source file to consist of thousands of lines of code and be unmanageable.

In this section we are going to split the code we created in Listing 6-12 into separate files. We will also use a `namespace` to group our game loop functions together. We begin by taking a look at the `Chapter7-TextAdventure.cpp` file in Listing 7-5, which is included with the sample accompanying this chapter.

Listing 7-5. Chapter7-TextAdventure.cpp

```
#include "stdafx.h"
#include "Player.h"
#include "GameLoop.h"

int _tmain(int argc, _TCHAR* argv[])
{
        Player player;
        GameLoop::WelcomePlayer(player);

        bool isPlaying = true;
        while (isPlaying)
        {
                isPlaying = GameLoop::RunGame();
        }

        return 0;
}
```

Our source file is now much shorter and much easier to read. The major differences to the function when comparing it to the version in Listing 6-12 are the uses of the `GameLoop` namespace qualifier on the `WelcomePlayer` and the `RunGame` function calls.

You can see at the top of the file that we now include two new header files, `Player.h` and `GameLoop.h`. We'll take a look at `Player.h` in Listing 7-6.

Listing 7-6. Player.h

```cpp
#pragma once

#include <string>

struct Player
{
        std::string m_name;
};
```

This file is very simple. All we have here is the definition of the Player struct. This might seem like a waste, but I can assure you that this struct will grow in size as we build out our game.

Listing 7-7 shows the code contained in GameLoop.h.

Listing 7-7. GameLoop.h

```cpp
#pragma once

#include "Player.h"
#include "PlayerOptions.h"

namespace GameLoop
{
        void WelcomePlayer(Player& player);

        void GivePlayerOptions();

        void GetPlayerInput(std::string& playerInput);

        PlayerOptions EvaluateInput(std::string& playerInput);

        bool RunGame();
}
```

We have created a namespace called GameLoop to contain our functions. This will prevent any name clashes that might occur with functions in other files in the future. You might notice that the header only contains the declarations for our functions. This is an important feature, as it provides an optimization for the compiler and also makes the code easier to read for other programmers. The compiler can build source files that call functions from this header file faster when it does not need to read and compile the entire function declarations. Programmers can use the functions faster by simply looking at the parameters the function takes and the types that they return. Other programmers do not necessarily need to know exactly how the function operates internally.

The actual function definitions are contained in the GameLoop.cpp file shown in Listing 7-8.

Listing 7-8. GameLoop.cpp

```cpp
#include "GameLoop.h"
#include <iostream>

using namespace std;
```

```cpp
namespace GameLoop
{
        void WelcomePlayer(Player& player)
        {
                cout << "Welcome to Text Adventure!" << endl << endl;
                cout << "What is your name?" << endl << endl;

                cin >> player.m_name;

                cout << endl << "Hello " << player.m_name << endl;
        }

        void GivePlayerOptions()
        {
                cout << "What would you like to do? (Enter a corresponding number)"
                        << endl << endl;
                cout << "1: Quit" << endl << endl;
        }

        void GetPlayerInput(string& playerInput)
        {
                cin >> playerInput;
        }

        PlayerOptions EvaluateInput(string& playerInput)
        {
                PlayerOptions chosenOption = PlayerOptions::None;

                if (playerInput.compare("1") == 0)
                {
                        cout << "You have chosen to Quit!" << endl << endl;
                        chosenOption = PlayerOptions::Quit;
                }
                else
                {
                        cout << "I do not recognize that option, try again!"
                                << endl << endl;
                }

                return chosenOption;
        }

        bool RunGame()
        {
                bool shouldEnd = false;

                GivePlayerOptions();
```

```
            string playerInput;
            GetPlayerInput(playerInput);

            shouldEnd = EvaluateInput(playerInput) == PlayerOptions::Quit;

            return !shouldEnd;
        }
}
```

Our functions have not changed since Listing 6-12. The main difference to pay attention to is the `namespace` wrapping the function calls. Our `GameLoop` `namespace` has been extended to include the function definitions, if we had not done this, the compiler would complain that it could not find our functions when building.

`PlayerOptions.h` is our last new file and is shown in Listing 7-9.

Listing 7-9. PlayerOptions.h

```
#pragma once

enum class PlayerOptions
{
        Quit,
        None
};
```

This file is very simple and contains our `enum` `class`.

Hopefully this example will give you a feel for how we use multiple source and header files to manage our source code. Make sure to download the sample accompanying this chapter from the following web site `http://www.apress.com/9781430264576`.

Summary

This chapter has introduced concepts that C++ provides to help manage large software projects. Video games definitely qualify as large and complex projects and productive development is only going to happen through the proper use of header and source files and namespaces.

Header files allow us to create function declarations that can be included for use in multiple source files. This is necessary to allow the compiler to optimize its processes and to allow programmers to use functions without concerning themselves with the implementation details.

Having separate source files allows us to simplify the code. Having smaller source files makes them more readable and also allows us to group functions with functionality that is similar to others into the same source files. This concept of grouping functions related to similar concepts will be expanded on in later in this book when we look at object-oriented programming.

Namespaces are another essential source code management technique. Where source files allow us to group similar functions into files, namespaces provide a method for communicating these types of groupings to the compiler. It is more common for namespaces to span multiple files and be used to contain the functionality needed to represent an entire *module* of code. Code modularity is an important concept that we will look at more and more as we progress.

This chapter brings us to the end of our look at procedural programming in the C style using C++. The next part of the book covers object-oriented programming and specifically looks at the concept of classes, how they are created and used, how we inherit from classes, and how we can use polymorphism.

Part 2

Object-Oriented Programming

Procedural programming can allow you to write full programs without any more features being required. However, C++ was built using C as its foundation, which means that you can write programs in different ways.

Object-oriented programming introduces the concept of programming with objects. C++ allows you to create blueprints for your objects in the form of classes. Classes allow you to express the design of your programs in terms of collections of data contained within classes along with the operations that can be applied to that data. Years of research has led to best practice being applied in object-oriented programming, including the correct use of features such as polymorphism and designing programs to fully utilize encapsulation, minimize coupling, and promote cohesion.

This part of the book introduces you to the features of C++ that enable you to use objects in your programs as well as lay the foundations for you to be able to design programs following best practices.

Object-Oriented Programming with Classes

The preceding part of this book covered a programming paradigm known as procedural programming. This part introduces the concept of object-oriented programming (OOP). Procedural programming was the major paradigm supported by the C programming language. The C++ programming language was conceived to support OOP in the same syntax as a C programming language.

This chapter covers the major techniques behind designing OOP-based programs and then takes a look at the class.

Object-Oriented Programming

Writing computer programs in the OOP style involves thinking about our programs at a high level. So far you have been looking at low-level programming concepts such as deciding on which variables to use and how to split your program into functions. Designing OOP involves considering how objects will interact before deciding exactly which variables and methods will be used. You will usually begin writing your program with a design document. This design might be long and complex or short and to the point; this will depend on the requirements of the program you are working on. The following short paragraph covers the design of our Text Adventure game so far.

> *The game begins by welcoming the user. This welcome state will ask the player to enter their name so that we can personalize their gameplay experience. The game then enters the game loop that continuously asks players to enter their input choice. The quit option should always be available to the player and, when selected, exits the program.*

It is your job as a programmer to turn the design created by a game designer into a working implementation. If you were using the OOP paradigm, you would take this design and break it down into distinct objects in the program. We do this by looking for the nouns that exist in the design, as they are ideal candidates to be turned into classes. Classes form a blueprint from which you can create the individual objects in your program. The following nouns are present in the design and could be considered suitable for being turned into classes:

- Game
- User
- Player
- Name
- Game loop

At this point you need to consider which of these really are suitable candidates for being turned into classes. Game seems like an obvious choice for a class, as it can be the object that represents the entire game. User might not be a good candidate for a class in our program. The user is the person interacting with our program and does not need to be represented in the program itself; however, a Player class would be useful to represent the current state of the players in our game. Name appears to be data related to the player. You've seen so far that we can represent strings in the game using the C++-supplied string class, which means we don't have to create our own class for the player name. The game loop from Listing 7-7 was created using a namespace and a set of functions. In this chapter we look at how we can represent this using a class rather than a namespace to group the functionality.

This section has given you a brief introduction to the OOP design process. The rest of this chapter looks at how we can build programs out of classes in C++.

Encapsulation

One of the main questions that comes up with programmers who are new to OOP is "Why do we even use classes?" There are many answers to this question, making it a complicated topic to explain. We cover more of the advanced features provided by classes in C++ as we work through this chapter. The first major benefit for the new programmer is the concept of encapsulation. Classes in C++ allow us to group together data in the form of variables and functions, known as methods, that operate on this data. The classes allow us to mark some of these variables and methods as being hidden from the rest of the program.

This concept of data hiding is known as encapsulation. Encapsulation is a desirable feature of OOP because it allows us to operate loosely on the basis of contracts in our programs. The classes we write will have a *public interface* that other classes can expect to behave in a certain manner. This interface will remain consistent to allow us to create easily maintainable programs; however, the private data and methods can be changed as often as we need them to. This is another concept that can be difficult to understand, so we will work through a class listing to see how this works in practice. Listing 8-1 shows the code for our first class, Player.

Listing 8-1. The Player Class

```
#pragma once

#include <string>

class Player
{
        std::string m_name;
};
```

The Player class in Listing 8-1 might look familiar. It is almost exactly the same as the Player struct from Listing 7-6. All we have done is change the struct keyword to the class keyword. If you were to do this in our Text Adventure example from the previous chapter, the code would no longer compile. When you try to compile in Visual Studio you receive the following error:

```
Error   1     error C2248: 'Player::m_name' : cannot access private member declared in class 'Player'
```

This error occurs thanks to the encapsulation features of C++. Listing 8-2 shows why this is the case.

Listing 8-2. class vs. struct Encapsulation

```
class Player
{
private:
        std::string m_name;
};

struct Player
{
public:
        std::string m_name;
};
```

The code in Listing 8-2 makes the distinction between a class and a struct in C++ explicit. By default all member variables and functions in a class are private. In a struct all members and methods are public.

> **Note** A traditional C style struct cannot contain any methods (member functions). However, these are allowed in C++, which means that the difference between a class and a struct in C++ is simply the default access to member variables and functions.

The error thrown by the compiler is caused by the following line of code:

```
cin >> player.m_name;
```

When using public access, this line of code is allowed, which is why our program compiled without errors in Chapter 7. We could fix the compile error by changing our class to code shown in Listing 8-3.

Listing 8-3. A public Class

```
class Player
{
public:
        std::string m_name;
};
```

There is a problem caused by having public member variables in C++: It breaks our encapsulation. We might decide later to separate the player's first name and surname into separate strings, for example, and then code that relies on our Player class supplying a single name would break. The proper way to fix the problem is to provide accessor methods. Listing 8-4 shows the Player class with accessors for the name variable.

Listing 8-4. A Player Class with Accessors

```
class Player
{
private:
        std::string m_name;

public:
        void SetName(const std::string& name)
        {
                m_name = name;
        }

        const std::string& GetName() const
        {
                return m_name;
        }
};
```

You now have a class that respects the rules of encapsulation. The code that refused to compile earlier can now be fixed using the following code.

```
string name;
cin >> name;
player.SetName(name);
```

This section has shown why you would use classes in C++ and how to create a basic class that uses the benefits of encapsulation. To recap, the public specifier tells the compiler that any of the following member variables and methods are accessible to code outside of the class. The private access specifier informs the compiler that the following member variables and methods are only accessible from inside the class; that is, from within public or private methods that make up the class. The rest of this chapter looks at how we use classes properly in our code base.

Constructors and Destructors

When you use the class keyword, you are actually informing the compiler to create a new type in the C++ language. When you create a variable of a given type in C++ the first task to be completed is generally initialization. C++ provides methods called constructors that are called when our classes are initialized. Listing 8-5 adds a constructor to our Player class.

Listing 8-5. The Player Class Constructor

```cpp
class Player
{
private:
        std::string m_name;

public:
        Player(const std::string& name)
                : m_name(name)
        {
        }

        void SetName(const std::string& name)
        {
                m_name = name;
        }

        const std::string& GetName() const
        {
                return m_name;
        }
};
```

The bold code in Listing 8-5 shows the class constructor. The constructor is a special method in C++ classes. It does not contain a return type as it can never return a value and it also contains an initializer list. The initializer list is used to call the constructors on our member variables and Listing 8-5 shows that we have called the string class constructor on m_name before the constructor function itself is executed. We would use a comma if we had more variables to add to the initializer list:

```cpp
Player(const std::string& name, int anotherVariable)
        : m_name(name)
        , m_anotherVariable(anotherVariable)
{
}
```

If you try to execute this code after adding this constructor you will see that there is another compile error in the code.

Error   1   error C2512: 'Player' : no appropriate default constructor available

There are several implications to this error:

- All classes must have a constructor.

- The compiler will create a default constructor if you do not specify one. This default constructor calls the default constructors of all member functions if they have them. Built-in types such as int do not have default constructors and are therefore uninitialized. Default constructors do not take any parameters.

- The compiler will not generate a default constructor if you specify a constructor.

Our class no longer has a default constructor once we specified the constructor that takes the string parameter, which means that we cannot create a class without passing a string to player. The following line is the offending code:

```
Player player;
```

You can fix this in two ways, either by passing a string parameter:

```
Player player("defaultName");
```

or by adding your own default constructor to the Player class, as shown in Listing 8-6.

Listing 8-6. Adding a Default Constructor to Player

```
class Player
{
private:
        std::string m_name;

public:
        Player()
        {
        }

        Player(const std::string& name)
                : m_name(name)
        {
        }

        void SetName(const std::string& name)
        {
                m_name = name;
        }

        const std::string& GetName() const
        {
                return m_name;
        }
};
```

Whether you add default constructors to your classes will depend on whether it is valid to do so. Not all classes make sense when they are not passed values to initialize them. Class constructors are called when objects of our class type are being created; class destructors are called when our objects are being destroyed. Objects can be destroyed in a number of ways, but our code currently only destroys objects when they are going *out of scope*. Listing 8-7 shows an example.

Listing 8-7. Going out of Scope

```
int _tmain(int argc, _TCHAR* argv[])
{
        Player player;
        GameLoop::WelcomePlayer(player);

        bool isPlaying = true;
        while (isPlaying)
        {
                isPlaying = GameLoop::RunGame();
        }

        return 0;
}
```

The Player constructor is called when the player variable is created. This code is calling the default constructor. The player variable goes out of scope once the function that contains it returns. This means that the destructor is called automatically after the return call is executed. Listing 8-8 shows the Player class with a destructor added.

Listing 8-8. The Player Class destructor

```
class Player
{
private:
        std::string m_name;

public:
        Player()
        {
        }

        Player(const std::string& name)
                : m_name(name)
        {
        }

        ~Player()
        {
        }

        void SetName(const std::string& name)
        {
                m_name = name;
        }
```

```
        const std::string& GetName() const
        {
                return m_name;
        }
};
```

The destructor function also doesn't specify a return type and does not return a value. The destructor is created by having a function that is named the same as the class itself but with a ~ prepended. All classes have destructor methods but again, the compiler will create a default destructor if we do not. You do not have any code to put into your destructor at the moment; however, we will look at how they can be used to greater effect in later chapters.

> **Note**   When we are talking about the code that makes up a class we are talking about classes. When we talk about variables that are of a class type, we refer to them as objects. That means the class is the type, and an object is an instance of the class.

This section has shown you how to specify the methods that are called when objects are created and destroyed. The rest of this chapter covers some more advanced features that will be useful as we move through the rest of the book.

Method Overloading

C++ allows you to *overload* methods. This actually means that you can create methods of the same name but that take different input parameters. You can see an example of this in Listing 8-9.

Listing 8-9. Overloading Player::SetName

```
class Player
{
private:
        std::string m_name;

public:
        Player()
        {
        }

        Player(const std::string& name)
                : m_name(name)
        {
        }

        ~Player()
        {
        }
```

```
        void SetName(const std::string& forename, const std::string& surname)
        {
                m_name = forename;
                m_name.append(" ");
                m_name.append(surname);
        }

        void SetName(const std::string& name)
        {
                m_name = name;
        }

        const std::string& GetName() const
        {
                return m_name;
        }
};
```

Your Player class now contains two methods called SetName. You can call either of these methods using the following lines:

```
player.SetName("Bruce Sutherland");
player.SetName("Bruce", "Sutherland");
```

The compiler automatically works out which of the two methods to call based on the parameters being passed in. The first line here would call the method that simply assigns the string to m_name; the second line would call the function that assigns the first name then appends a space before appending the surname. Both functions result in m_name storing the same string value.

Methods can only be overloaded by having different parameter types. Methods with different names are not overloaded, but the code will still compile. Methods that only have different return types are not allowed. Listing 8-10 shows an example of this.

Listing 8-10. SetName with Different Return Types

```
void SetName(const std::string& name)
{
        m_name = name;
}

bool SetName(const std::string& name)
{
        m_name = name;
        return true;
}
```

If you try this in Visual Studio, you will see the following error:

```
error C2556: 'bool Player::SetName(const std::string &)' : overloaded function differs only by
return type from 'void Player::SetName(const std::string &)'
```

Methods aren't the only things that C++ allows us to overload. We can also overload operators, which allows us to use our classes like the built-in types.

Operator Overloading

Listing 8-11 shows our player class with an overloaded += operator.

Listing 8-11. Overloading Player's += Operator

```cpp
class Player
{
private:
        std::string m_name;

public:
        Player()
        {
        }

        Player(const std::string& name)
                : m_name(name)
        {
        }

        ~Player()
        {
        }

        void SetName(const std::string& forename, const std::string& surname)
        {
                m_name = forename;
                m_name.append(" ");
                m_name.append(surname);
        }

        void SetName(const std::string& name)
        {
                m_name = name;
        }

        void operator+=(const std::string& name)
        {
                m_name.append(name);
        }

        const std::string& GetName() const
        {
                return m_name;
        }
};
```

Our += operator is an assignment operator, which means we want to use it to modify our object. You can see this in our operator method where we append the name string onto the object's m_name member variable. We can use this in the following manner:

```
player.SetName("Bruce");
player += " Sutherland";
```

Sometimes you might not want to modify the object, but instead would like to add the name to the passed string and store a returned value. It might make more sense to overload the + operator in this instance. Listing 8-12 shows an example of this.

Listing 8-12. The Overloaded + Operator

```
std::string operator+(const std::string& name)
{
        std::string output(m_name);
        output.append(name);
        return output;
}
```

This function appends the passed string parameter to the m_name member and returns the new string that was created to store the result. We can use this operator in the following way.

```
player.SetName("Bruce");
string fullName = player + " Sutherland";
```

These examples are not the most useful and are being created just to show you how you can incorporate operator overloading into your future classes. There's also a drawback to the examples we have looked at: We cannot chain the operators together. Listing 8-13 shows an assignment operator that allows chaining.

Listing 8-13. Operator Chaining

```
const Player& operator=(const Player& player)
{
        m_name = player.name;
        return *this;
}
```

The major new keyword being used in this example is this. The this pointer is a built-in keyword that C++ supplies. It is a pointer that stores the address of the current object. Our = operator returns a constant reference to the current Player object. Listing 8-14 alters our WelcomePlayer method to show how this allows operator chaining in practice.

Listing 8-14. Operator Chaining

```
void WelcomePlayer(Player& player)
{
        cout << "Welcome to Text Adventure!" << endl << endl;
        cout << "What is your name?" << endl << endl;
```

```
        string name;
        cin >> name;
        player.SetName("Bruce");
        Player player1, player2, player3, player4;
        player1 = player2 = player3 = player4 = player;

        cout << endl << "Hello " << player.GetName() << endl;
}
```

Operator chaining has allowed us to assign the value from player to all of the temporary Player objects we have created. You can think of these statements being operated in the following order.

```
player4 = player;
player3 = player4;
player2 = player3;
player1 = player2;
```

Chaining makes sense for the assignment operator; however it might not make a lot of sense in other areas. You will see examples of practical uses for operator overloading and chaining as we move through the remaining chapters of the book.

Updating Text Adventure to Use Classes

Now that you have a grasp of what classes are and how they can be used, we will update the Text Adventure game to be based around the principles of OOP. The first change you will make will be to remove the GameLoop namespace and create a Game class. Listing 8-15 shows this new Game class.

Listing 8-15. The Game Class

```
class Game
{
private:
        Player m_player;

        void WelcomePlayer();
        void GivePlayerOptions();
        void GetPlayerInput(std::string& playerInput);
        PlayerOptions EvaluateInput(std::string& playerInput);

public:
        void RunGame();
};
```

Our Game class contains a private member variable representing our player and private methods to update the game state. These methods are listed in the corresponding source file shown in Listing 8-16.

Listing 8-16. Game.cpp

```cpp
#include "Game.h"
#include <iostream>

using namespace std;

void Game::WelcomePlayer()
{
        cout << "Welcome to Text Adventure!" << endl << endl;
        cout << "What is your name?" << endl << endl;

        string name;
        cin >> name;
        m_player.SetName(name);

        cout << endl << "Hello " << m_player.GetName() << endl;
}

void Game::GivePlayerOptions()
{
        cout << "What would you like to do? (Enter a corresponding number)"
                << endl << endl;
        cout << "1: Quit" << endl << endl;
}

void Game::GetPlayerInput(string& playerInput)
{
        cin >> playerInput;
}

PlayerOptions Game::EvaluateInput(string& playerInput)
{
        PlayerOptions chosenOption = PlayerOptions::None;

        if (playerInput.compare("1") == 0)
        {
                cout << "You have chosen to Quit!" << endl << endl;
                chosenOption = PlayerOptions::Quit;
        }
        else
        {
                cout << "I do not recognize that option, try again!" << endl << endl;
        }

        return chosenOption;
}
```

```
void Game::RunGame()
{
        WelcomePlayer();

        bool shouldEnd = false;
        while (shouldEnd == false)
        {
                GivePlayerOptions();

                string playerInput;
                GetPlayerInput(playerInput);

                shouldEnd = EvaluateInput(playerInput) == PlayerOptions::Quit;
        }
}
```

The examples so far in this chapter had all defined the class methods inside the class declaration. Our Game class now declares the methods in the header file and creates the declarations in a source file. You can see how we achieve this by prepending the class name to the method name like this:

```
void Game::WelcomePlayer()
```

Another change made to the methods when comparing them to the functions in Chapter 7 is that they can now access the m_player object as a member variable rather than requiring that it be passed into the methods. You can also see that we have moved our entire game loop into the RunGame method. This is the change that has allowed you to make all of the other methods that make up the Game class private. This is a good example of encapsulation, as any other code that now uses the Game class can only ask it to run. All of its implementation details have been hidden behind its public interface.

We have been altering our Player class as we moved through this chapter, and the final result is shown in Listing 8-17.

Listing 8-17. The Player Class

```
class Player
{
private:
        std::string m_name;

public:
        void SetName(const std::string& name)
        {
                m_name = name;
        }

        const std::string& GetName() const
        {
                return m_name;
        }
};
```

Our Player class has gone back to being very basic. At the moment, the default constructor and destructor do everything we need for the class and the overloaded methods and operators that we looked at in this chapter were purely instructional and actually don't make much sense for the player object. The player object will still grow over time; however, for now, storing the user's name is all we need it to do.

The last changes that you need to make to the code from Chapter 7 involve the main function. The new main function is shown in Listing 8-18.

Listing 8-18. The main Function

```
int _tmain(int argc, _TCHAR* argv[])
{
    Game game;
    game.RunGame();

    return 0;
}
```

main is now very basic. It creates an instance of the Game class and then calls the only public method that is exposed, RunGame. The player object is now a private member of Game, as are the functions we had created to make the game loop more readable. We can now refer to those variables and members generally as the implementation details of the class, and RunGame is part of the Game class's public interface.

Summary

This chapter has introduced you to the class concept of C++. Classes were the first feature that set C++ apart from the C programming language. Adding classes to C allowed a new way of thinking about computer programming to be used in C-style programs, object-oriented programming. In this chapter you looked at how you can think about OOP from a high level and how you can turn a basic design into a class design for a program by finding the nouns.

You then learned how to use classes effectively in C++ by creating them in a manner that helps encourage encapsulation in your programming. You learned that by hiding data and methods inside classes it is possible to create code that is more easily maintainable in the future. This is possible because the details of how a class is implemented can be changed so long as the public methods remain consistent and carry out their intended operations.

You've seen that classes are essentially a way for you to add your own user-defined types to the C++ language and that C++ also provides features such as method and operator overloading to make those types blend in with others. These features make writing code with classes simpler for other programmers, but they rely on you to ensure that the operations that overloaded methods and operators perform are consistent with how they have been used in other places in the C++ language.

The next chapter is going to shed some more light on some of the keywords that help make classes more secure, make them faster, and to allow them to share data. We have already seen examples of the const keyword and you've already created some implicitly inline methods without even realizing it. The next chapter will make these concepts clearer.

Chapter

Controlling Data with Access Modifiers

C++ allows you to control how data in variables can be accessed by using different access modifiers. There are modifiers that tell the compiler that a variable should be shared among classes or that the program cannot change the value of the variable after it has been initialized. Unfortunately some of the keywords supplied by C++ are reused and mean different things in different circumstances. I'll cover the use of the `static`, `const`, `mutable`, and `friend` keywords in C++, and their multiple uses in this chapter.

The static Keyword

The `static` keyword has four major uses in C++ programs:

- It is used within functions to indicate that a variable should remember its value each time the function is called.

- It is used within classes to tell the compiler that each object created from the class should share the same variable.

- It is used within classes to tell the compiler that a method can be called without having an object instance.

- It is used to tell the compiler that a variable declared outside of a class or function should have file scope rather than global scope.

These completely different uses for the `static` keyword make it difficult to master or even just to remember which effect the word will have when you use it in your code. The following section provides examples of each case to help you understand how `static` behaves in everyday usage.

Creating static Local Variables

The static local variable is the simplest version of static to understand. A normal local variable will lose its value each time a function returns and will reset to the initialized value the next time the function is called. Listing 9-1 shows an example of a normal local variable in action.

Listing 9-1. A Normal Local Variable

```
void NormalLocalVariable()
{
        int x = 0;
        std::cout << x++ << std::endl;
}
```

With the function source in Listing 9-1 the console will have the value 0 added every time we call the function NormalLocalVariable. This is because the variable is re-created each time the function is called. Listing 9-2 shows the code for a static local variable.

Listing 9-2. A static Local Variable

```
void StaticLocalVariable()
{
        static int x = 0;
        std::cout << x++ << std::endl;
}
```

This time you have told the compiler that you would like the variable x to be static. When you do this, the compiler creates a variable in a location in memory that prevents it from being overwritten each time the function is called (you will learn more about C++ memory management in Chapter 26). The effect of this is that the value stored in the variable is preserved and will increase with each call. The non-static variable in Listing 9-1 always contained 0 when it was printed out, whereas the variable in Listing 9-2 will print 0 on the first call, 1 on the second call, and so on.

The use of static local variables is a practice I wouldn't recommend for normal code as it encourages you to take shortcuts in the design of your code. These shortcuts almost always cause you more difficult problems in the longer term. You'll see how private member variables can be used instead when we cover classes. It can be useful to use static variables to count the number of times a function has been called or to time how long the execution of those function calls takes, but static local variables are rarely the best design choice for standard game code.

Using static class Member Variables

The static keyword can also be used with class member variables. Listing 9-3 shows an example class that contains a static member variable.

Listing 9-3. A static Member Variable

```cpp
class StaticCounter
{
private:
        static int m_counter;

public:
        void IncrementCounter()
        {
                ++m_counter;
        }
        void Print()
        {
                std::cout << m_counter << std::endl;
        }
};

int StaticCounter::m_counter = 0;
```

Using the static keyword on a member variable has a similar effect as using it on a local variable. The variable will be created in static memory rather than within the memory space for the object itself. You should pay special attention to the final line of this listing. Member variables that we declare to be static must be defined and this usually occurs in the source file that accompanies a header file for the class. A clear example of this is shown in the source code sample that accompanies this chapter and can be downloaded from this book's accompanying web site: http://www.apress.com/9781430264576. This causes all objects created from this class type to share the same static variable, which in Listing 9-4 is the m_counter variable. The source code in Listing 9-4 shows how we can call these functions.

Listing 9-4. Using the StaticCounter Class

```cpp
StaticCounter counter1;
counter1.Print();
counter1.IncrementCounter();
counter1.Print();

StaticCounter counter2;
counter2.Print();
counter2.IncrementCounter();
counter2.Print();
```

These lines of code in a program would output 0, 1, 1, then 2. This happens because both counter1 and counter2 are sharing the same m_counter variable. Another way you could see this in action would be to look at the address of the m_counter variable. Listing 9-5 shows how you can do this.

Listing 9-5. Getting the Address of m_counter

```cpp
void Print()
{
        std::cout << m_counter << std::endl;
        int* address = &m_counter;
}
```

If you were to run this code in your debugger you would be able to set a breakpoint on the line containing the closing brace for the function block. Your debugger should have two variables shown in the local variables window. Figure 9-1 shows the local variable window from a Visual Studio integrated development environment (IDE).

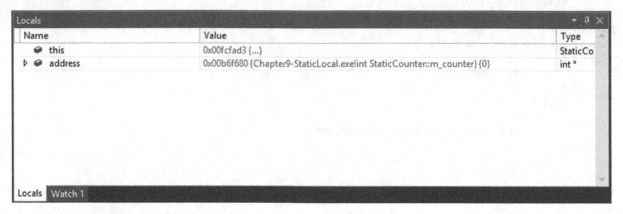

Figure 9-1. The counter1 *this address*

Figure 9-1 shows the state of the debugger when execution stops in the Print method that has been called on the counter1 object. You can see that the address of counter1 is stored in the this pointer and is 0x00fcfad3. The address variable that stores the address of m_counter holds the address 0x00b6f680. Figure 9-2 shows the same variables when Print is called on the counter2 object.

Locals			▾ ⱷ ×
Name	Value		Type
ⱷ this	0x00fcfac7 {...}		StaticCo
▷ ⱷ address	0x00b6f680 {Chapter9-StaticLocal.exe!int StaticCounter::m_counter}{1}		int *

Locals Watch 1

Figure 9-2. The counter2 *this address*

You can see in Figure 9-2 that the value stored in this has changed. The Visual Studio debugger has helpfully displayed the value in red to show that the value has changed. Both values in Figure 9-1 are red as they were both new values that were being shown. The address of counter2 is now stored in the this pointer and is 0x00fcfac7. Despite the change in the object address, the address of m_counter has stayed exactly the same and is a direct result of using the static keyword on the member variable of the StaticCounter class. Every instance of the StaticCounter class would now use the exact same m_counter variable and any change to this variable will be shared.

Using static Member Methods

Listing 9-3 contained the IncrementCounter method, which we called on the counter1 and counter2 objects in Listing 9-5. This method was a standard method that relied on an existing object to be usable. C++ also allows us to create static member methods that do not rely on an object to be callable. Listing 9-6 shows an updated version of the StaticCounter class that uses a static member method.

Listing 9-6. Using a static Member Method

```
class StaticCounterMethod
{
private:
        static int m_counter;

public:
        static void IncrementCounter()
        {
                ++m_counter;
        }

        static void Print()
        {
                std::cout << m_counter << std::endl;
                    int* address = &m_counter;
        }
};

int StaticCounterMethod::m_counter = 0;
```

You can see in Listing 9-6 that the only changes that we make to turn our methods into static methods is to add the static keyword at the beginning of their method signature. Listing 9-7 shows how you can use these static methods.

Listing 9-7. Using static Methods

```
StaticCounterMethod::Print();
StaticCounterMethod::IncrementCounter();
StaticCounterMethod::Print();

StaticCounterMethod::Print();
StaticCounterMethod::IncrementCounter();
StaticCounterMethod::Print();
```

You can see in Listing 9-7 that we can now call these static methods in a different way than non-static methods. First you use the name of the class, which is followed by the scope resolution operator (::) and the name of the static function we would like to call. You have already used the scope resolution operator when accessing variable and function names that exist inside of namespaces. In this instance we are simply letting the compiler know that we'd like to access the global variables or methods that are contained within the class.

Using static to Alter Global Scope

The last use of the static keyword allows you to tell the compiler that you would like a variable to exist within the scope of a single file rather than in the global scope. Global variables are generally frowned on as they break encapsulation in object-oriented programs and we won't be using any in our Text Adventure game that hold game data. You might come across these in production code, though, so it's good to know how to work with them. Listing 9-8 shows an example of a globally scoped and a file scoped variable.

Listing 9-8. Globally Scoped and File Scoped Variables

```
#include "stdafx.h"
#include <iostream>
#include "extern.h"

int globalVariable = 0;
static int fileVariable = 0;

int _tmain(int argc, _TCHAR* argv[])
{
        IncrementGlobalCounters();
        std::cout << globalVariable << std::endl;

        return 0;
}
```

Listing 9-8 defines a global variable named globalVariable and a file variable named fileVariable. The declaration of the function IncrementGlobalCounters is contained in the extern.h header file. Listing 9-9 shows the contents of this basic file.

Listing 9-9. extern.h

```
#pragma once

void IncrementGlobalCounters();
```

The function definition is in extern.cpp, shown in Listing 9-10.

Listing 9-10. extern.cpp

```
#include "extern.h"

void IncrementGlobalCounters()
{
        extern int globalVariable;
        ++globalVariable;

        // Error - will not compile as fileVariable is not global!
        extern int fileVariable;
        ++fileVariable;
}
```

Listing 9-10 introduces the extern keyword. You use extern to tell the compiler that it can search the global scope for a variable of this name. In this case the variable will be found in the file containing _tmain. Trying to use extern with fileVariable will cause an unresolved external symbol error when you try to build. The variable is unresolved because fileVariable has been declared as static, which means that it can only be used from within the file where it was declared.

This use of static to limit variables to file scope is deprecated. That means it is still supported but no longer the recommended method for achieving file scoped variables. A more modern approach is to use an anonymous namespace. Listing 9-11 alters Listing 9-8 to use an anonymous namespace instead of a static variable.

Listing 9-11. Anonymous namespaces

```
#include "stdafx.h"
#include <iostream>
#include "extern.h"

int globalVariable = 0;

namespace
{
        int fileVariable = 0;
}

int _tmain(int argc, _TCHAR* argv[])
{
        IncrementGlobalCounters();
        std::cout << globalVariable << std::endl;

        return 0;
}
```

The anonymous namespace is simply a namespace that is not given a name. Any of the variables, functions, or classes that you include inside the namespace will be accessible inside the file that contains the anonymous namespace.

This section should have given you an idea of just how overloaded the static keyword is. The next section covers the const keyword, which is not quite as overloaded but still confusing.

The const Keyword

A constant in C++ is a variable that cannot be changed. Constants are useful to store values that you know at compile time, for passing values into methods that you don't want to be able to change, and for marking methods in classes that should not be allowed to change member variables. I'll cover these uses in the following sections.

Constant Variables

Constant variables are used to avoid having magic numbers in our code and to generally represent values that we know at compile time and will never change during execution. Classic examples in game programming are constant values used to represent pi or the values used to convert angles in degrees to angles in radians and vice versa. Listing 9-12 shows how we can create some constant variables to reference in our code.

Listing 9-12. Example Constant Variables

```
#include "stdafx.h"
#include <iostream>
#include "extern.h"

int globalVariable = 0;

namespace
{
        const unsigned int MAX_LOOPS = 10;
}

int _tmain(int argc, _TCHAR* argv[])
{
        for (unsigned int i = 0; i < MAX_LOOPS; ++i)
        {
                IncrementGlobalCounters();
                std::cout << globalVariable << std::endl;
        }
}
```

We have added a const unsigned int variable named MAX_LOOPS to our code from Listing 9-11. The benefit of using a constant is that if you use the same variable in multiple places, you would only have to change the value in a single place to ensure that the value is changed everywhere it is used. You can see this benefit in Listing 9-13.

Listing 9-13. Using a const Variable in Multiple Places

```
unsigned int arrayOfValues[MAX_LOOPS];
for (unsigned int i = 0; i < MAX_LOOPS; ++i)
{
        arrayOfValues[i] = i;
        IncrementGlobalCounters();
        std::cout << globalVariable << std::endl;
        std::cout << fileVariable << std::endl;
}
```

If you fail to use a constant variable and instead use the value 10 in the array definition and in the loop, you run the risk of introducing bugs. If the array was reduced to contain 5 elements and the loop remained at 10 then the loop would overrun the end of the array and overwrite memory used to store values in other variables.

Constant Pointers

Pointers can also be made to be constant; however, the logic is a little more involved. Listing 9-14 shows the different types of pointer constant that we can create.

Listing 9-14. Three Types of Constant Pointer

```
const char* const     NAME = "Bruce Sutherland";
const char*           BOOK = "Learn C++ Game Development";
char* const           YEAR = "2014";
```

The first example shows the type const char* const. When dealing with constant pointers we read the type keywords from right to left so this first example gives us a constant pointer to a character constant. In practice this means that you cannot change the address to which the pointer points or the data that it points at.

The second example is a pointer to a character constant. You cannot change the text data but you can change the address pointed to, so adding the following line would be valid.

```
BOOK = NAME;
```

This would result in both BOOK and NAME pointing to the string "Bruce Sutherland".

The remaining example is a constant pointer to character data. You can't change the pointer but you can change the data pointer to it, so you can do the following.

```
YEAR[0] = '3';
```

The array operator would not have compiled if it was used on either NAME or BOOK, as the character data was constant.

Constant Parameters

It is a straightforward task to make parameters constant. Listing 9-15 shows a function with constant parameters.

Listing 9-15. Constant Parameters

```
bool ConstParams(const int numLetters, const char* const stringData)
{
        return strlen(stringData) == numLetters;
}
```

This example uses a C-style string just for the purposes of the example. As you can see, we can pass constant built-in types or constant pointers to functions or class member methods.

Constant Member Methods

This last section on constants will show you how to create constant member methods. Listing 9-16 shows an example.

Listing 9-16. A const Member Method

```
class ConstantExample
{
private:
        int     m_counter;

public:
        ConstantExample() : m_counter(0) {}
        int GetCounter() const  { return m_counter; }
        void IncrementCounter() { ++m_counter; }
};
```

You can create a const method by adding const to the end of the method signature. The implication of this goes hand in hand with const variables. Listing 9-17 gives an example.

Listing 9-17. A const Reference

```
ConstantExample example;
const ConstantExample& constRefExample = example;
constRefExample.IncrementCounter();
constRefExample.GetCounter();
```

If you try to compile the code in Listing 9-17 you will receive an error. We cannot call IncrementCounter using the const reference, as it is not a constant member method. You also cannot call non-const members on constant pointers or on constant variables.

You will receive a compile error if you try to alter any member variables in const member methods. Listing 9-18 shows how we can use the mutable keyword to tell the compiler that a member variable can be changed in const member methods.

Listing 9-18. The mutable Keyword

```
class ConstantExample
{
private:
        int     m_counter;
        mutable int m_countGets;

public:
        ConstantExample() : m_counter(0), m_countGets(0) {}
        int GetCounter() const  { ++m_countGets; return m_counter; }
        void IncrementCounter() { ++m_counter; }
};
```

Listing 9-18 shows a good example of the mutable keyword. It is best used sparingly and usually for debug information as the keyword technically goes against the normal usage of const member methods. The code in Listing 9-18 allows us to count how many times the GetCounter method is called even though is it a const member method and shouldn't be able to change any member values.

Two More Keywords

Whereas static and const have several uses and will be common in your code, there are another two keywords that make an appearance in C++ but don't have such obvious effects. The first is the inline keyword and the second is the friend keyword.

The inline Keyword

At different times in your programming journey you will have to consider different goals. Sometimes you will need to write code that executes as quickly as possible and at others you will have to write code that uses as little memory as possible. The inline keyword and inline member methods allow us to ask the compiler to help us with this.

When you inline a method the compiler will skip the instructions it needs to call the method; instead, the function body will be duplicated every time you call the method. This duplication of instructions reduces the length of time it takes to call the method, but increases the amount of memory used by duplicating the method throughout the code. For methods that are called many times, this duplication could be significant. Listing 9-18 contained two functions, GetCounter and IncrementCounter.

The compiler will attempt to inline these methods because the definitions are contained within the class definition. You could achieve the same thing explicitly by making the changes shown in Listing 9-19.

Listing 9-19. The inline Keyword

```
class ConstantExample
{
private:
        int     m_counter;
        mutable int m_countGets;

public:
        ConstantExample() : m_counter(0), m_countGets(0) {}
        int GetCounter() const;
        void IncrementCounter();
};

inline int ConstantExample::GetCounter() const
{
        ++m_countGets;
        return m_counter;
}

inline void ConstantExample::IncrementCounter()
{
        ++m_counter;
}
```

You might find that your code is more readable if you move the method definitions out of the body of the class. This is where the `inline` keyword helps. Now that you know how to make inline methods you might be wondering why you would do this. Each time we call a function or method, the compiler inserts code to set up the parameters, handle the return value, and ensure that the code can carry on where it left off when the method returns. For simple methods this plumbing code can take more time than the code contained in the method. You can use `inline` to avoid the cost of this setup code. Compare the code in Listings 9-20 and 9-21.

Listing 9-20. A Non-inline Method

```
ConstantExample example;
const ConstantExample& constRefExample = example;

int count = constRefExample.GetCounter();
```

Listing 9-21. The Result of Using inline

```
ConstantExample example;
const ConstantExample& constRefExample = example;

++constRefExample.m_countGets;
int count = constRefExample.m_counter;
```

Listing 9-21 shows how the code would look if we had public access to the member variables of `constRefExample`. This is how the compiler would write your code if you define `GetCounter` as an inline method.

> **Note**   The `inline` keyword is just a compiler hint. The compiler can choose to ignore the keyword or it can inline functions that do not have the keyword. This is especially true for inline methods that call other methods or functions.

The friend Keyword

The `friend` keyword allows us to write classes that can access the `private` member variables and methods of another class. You can see this in action in Listing 9-22.

Listing 9-22. The friend Keyword

```
class ConstantExample
{
        friend class ConstantExampleFriend;

private:
        int     m_counter;
        mutable int m_countGets;

        int GetCounter() const;
```

```
public:
        ConstantExample() : m_counter(0), m_countGets(0) {}
        void IncrementCounter();
};

inline int ConstantExample::GetCounter() const
{
        ++m_countGets;
        return m_counter;
}

inline void ConstantExample::IncrementCounter()
{
        ++m_counter;
}

class ConstantExampleFriend
{
public:
        int GetCounter(const ConstantExample& constantExample)
        {
                return constantExample.GetCounter();
        }
};
```

The ConstantExample::GetCounter method is private in Listing 9-22. This means that we would not be able to access this method from an object of this type. I have added a line to ConstantExample to inform the compiler that ConstantExampleFriend is a friend class of ConstantExample. Listing 9-23 shows how we can use this class to access the private ConstantExample::GetCounter method.

Listing 9-23. Using a friend class

```
ConstantExample example;
ConstantExampleFriend exampleFriend;
int count = exampleFriend.GetCounter(example);
```

Listing 9-23 shows that the count value contained in example can be accessed via an instance of ConstantExampleFriend.

Summary

This chapter has covered a few utility keywords in the C++ language. The static, const, extern, inline, and friend keywords allow you to control how variables are accessed and more important allow you to communicate the intent of your code more clearly. Data that is to be shared and remain consistent across multiple function calls can be made static. Variables that are never meant to be changed can be marked as const.

The concepts that were introduced in this chapter can take some time to become second nature. You will see several examples of inline and friend as we go through this book. I would recommend that you avoid using inline, friend, and extern until you are more confident in your programming.

A good modern compiler will `inline` functions that it believes will benefit from the performance boost automatically and the other two keywords can be a sign of code that might be better written in a different way. The `extern` keyword is particularly rare in modern code as it generally goes against the aim of object-oriented code to keep data and implementations behind interfaces using encapsulation.

The next chapter will introduce you to inheritance. Inheritance allows us to create hierarchies of classes and is particularly important for game development. The Text Adventure game you are developing will become much more interesting in the next chapter as you create rooms, items, and commands that allow a player to interact with the game world.

Building Games with Inheritance

Being a productive video game developer involves writing well-organized code that can be reused as often as possible. C++ classes provide a feature named inheritance that helps us achieve both of these goals. Inheritance allows us to create generalized base classes that can be *derived* from to create classes with a more specific purpose. In this chapter you learn how this allows us to share behavior among classes.

Inheriting from a Base Class

The classic example used to explain inheritance to new programmers is that of motor vehicles. There are multiple categories of vehicles, including cars, motorbikes, and trucks. All of these things can be thought of as vehicles and therefore can be included in a vehicle category. All have common features such as wheels, engines, and lights but all are obviously very different. If we were to make a game that included vehicles we could easily represent these in a class hierarchy. Figure 10-1 shows how we can visualize our class structure.

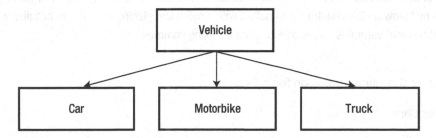

Figure 10-1. *The vehicle class hierarchy*

The simple diagram in Figure 10-1 shows that we will have a base class named Vehicle and that there will be three derived classes, one named Car, one named Motorbike, and one named Truck. Listing 10-1 shows the code for the Vehicle class.

Listing 10-1. The Vehicle Class

```
class Vehicle
{
private:
        unsigned int m_numberOfWheels;

public:
        Vehicle();

        unsigned int GetNumberOfWheels() const;
};

Vehicle::Vehicle()
        : m_numberOfWheels(0)
{

}

unsigned int Vehicle::GetNumberOfWheels() const
{
        return m_numberOfWheels;
}
```

The Vehicle class contains a private variable that stores the number of wheels the vehicle has. The variable is private and the Vehicle class does not provide a method to set it. Instead, classes that derive from Vehicle will set their own number of wheels in their own constructor.

> **Note**   The constructor for the Vehicle class uses an *initializer list* to initialize its variables. An initializer list ensures that the variables' values are set before any of the code contained within the constructor is executed and is the preferred method for initializing class member variables. You can use an initializer list in your class constructors by following the constructor signature with a colon and placing the value to initialize within brackets. Subsequent variables can be added to the list using commas.

Listing 10-2 shows the class definition for a Car.

Listing 10-2. The Car Class

```
class Car : public Vehicle
{
public:
        Car();
};

Car::Car()
{
        m_numberOfWheels = 4;
}
```

The Car class is inheriting from Vehicle using public inheritance. You can inherit one class from another by following the class name with a colon, followed by public then the name of the class you wish to derive from. Listing 10-2 shows that we have derived Car from Vehicle.

If you enter the code from Listing 10-2 into your integrated development environment (IDE) and try to compile you will be given a compiler error. The compiler cannot access m_numberOfWheels in the Car constructor as it is a private member of Vehicle. One option would be to make m_numberOfWheels a public variable; however, this would break our encapsulation and allow the variable to be accessed from anywhere in our code. A better option is to use the protected keyword. Listing 10-3 updates the Vehicle class with the protected keyword.

Listing 10-3. Using protected in Vehicle

```
class Vehicle
{
protected:
        unsigned int     m_numberOfWheels;

public:
        Vehicle();

        unsigned int     GetNumberOfWheels() const;
};
```

The protected keyword makes variables behave as though they are private to outside code; that is, they still cannot be accessed directly by calling code. The key difference to private member variables is that they can be accessed by derived classes. By declaring m_numberOfWheels as protected in the Car class we can now access it directly in Car and set the number of wheels to 4. Listing 10-4 shows some code to print the number of wheels each vehicle type contains.

Listing 10-4. Printing the Number of Wheels

```
void PrintNumberOfWheels()
{
        Vehicle vehicle;
        Car      car;

        std::cout << vehicle.GetNumberOfWheels() << std::endl;
        std::cout << car.GetNumberOfWheels() << std::endl;
}
```

This function will result in 0 being printed followed by the number 4. It's important that you note what this function has achieved. The Car class defined in Listing 10-2 does not contain a GetNumberOfWheels method, nor does it have a variable to store a number of wheels. The Car class has inherited these from the Vehicle class. Listing 10-5 shows how you can inherit another class from Vehicle, this time Motorcycle.

Listing 10-5. The Motorcycle Class

```
class Motorcycle : public Vehicle
{
public:
        Motorcycle();
};

Motorcycle::Motorcycle()
{
        m_numberOfWheels = 2;
}
```

You can see that we add our new class to `PrintNumberOfWheels` in Listing 10-6.

Listing 10-6. Adding Motorcycle to PrintNumberOfWheels

```
void PrintNumberOfWheels()
{
        Vehicle vehicle;
        Car     car;
        Motorcycle motorcycle;

        std::cout << vehicle.GetNumberOfWheels() << std::endl;
        std::cout << car.GetNumberOfWheels() << std::endl;
        std::cout << motorcycle.GetNumberOfWheels() << std::endl;
}
```

`Motorcycle` inherits from `Vehicle`, just as `Car` does, but it sets the number of wheels to 2 and this is printed out when we call the `PrintNumberOfWheels` function.

You now understand the basics of how to create classes that inherit behaviors from base classes. Now I'll move on to show you how this works in practice.

Constructors and Destructors in Derived Classes

In the previous section you saw that we can set values in member variables belonging to our parent class if the variables were declared as `protected` or `public`. Listing 10-7 shows the constructors from the `Vehicle`, `Car`, and `Motorbike` classes.

Listing 10-7. Your Vehicle, Car, and Motorbike Constructors

```
Vehicle::Vehicle()
        : m_numberOfWheels(0)
{

}

Car::Car()
{
        m_numberOfWheels = 4;
}
```

```
Motorcycle::Motorcycle()
{
        m_numberOfWheels = 2;
}
```

The Vehicle class constructor sets m_numberOfVehicles to 0 in an initializer list. Car and Motorbike assign the values directly as an initializer list cannot be used on nonmember variables from our base class. What you might be surprised to hear is that the Vehicle constructor is called automatically when we create a Car or Motorbike object. You can see this in practice by adding some logging code to the constructors, which we do in Listing 10-8.

Listing 10-8. Adding Logging to Your Constructors

```
Vehicle::Vehicle()
        : m_numberOfWheels(0)
{
        std::cout << "Vehicle Constructed" << std::endl;
}

Car::Car()
{
        m_numberOfWheels = 4;

        std::cout << "Car Constructed" << std::endl;
}

Motorcycle::Motorcycle()
{
        m_numberOfWheels = 2;

        std::cout << "Motorcycle Constructed" << std::endl;
}
```

If you execute the PrintNumberOfVehicles function from Listing 10-6 once more you will see that we have some new text in the output. It should read:

```
Vehicle Constructed
Vehicle Constructed
Car Constructed
Vehicle Constructed
Motorcycle Constructed
0
4
2
```

Vehicle Constructed is printed three different times. That is because the Vehicle constructor is being called each time any class that derives from Vehicle is instantiated. The order of the constructors is important: The constructors of parent classes are called before the constructors of derived classes. You can see this in action where the Vehicle Constructed output text is printed before both Car Constructed and Motorcycle Constructed.

C++ supplies classes with a destructor as well as a constructor. Listing 10-9 shows what destructors for the Vehicle, Car, and Motorcycle classes could look like.

Listing 10-9. Vehicle, Car, and Motorcycle Destructors

```
Vehicle::~Vehicle()
{
        std::cout << "Vehicle Destructed" << std::endl;
}

Car::~Car()
{
        std::cout << "Car Destructed" << std::endl;
}

Motorcycle::~Motorcycle()
{
        std::cout << "Motorcycle Destructed" << std::endl;
}
```

Destructors are defined in a similar manner to constructors. They do not have a return value and they use the name of the class. A destructor is shown to be different from a constructor by having the ~ symbol added to its name.

If you execute the PrintNumberOfWheels function again with these destructors in place you will see the following output:

```
Vehicle Constructed
Vehicle Constructed
Car Constructed
Vehicle Constructed
Motorcycle Constructed
0
4
2
Motorcycle Destructed
Vehicle Destructed
Car Destructed
Vehicle Destructed
Vehicle Destructed
```

You can deduce a few things from this output. First, you can see that any local variables that are created from classes are automatically destroyed when the function returns. This is known as going out of scope. Second, you can see that destructors are called automatically when locally instantiated objects go out of scope. Third, you can see that the destructors for the base classes are also called; that is, ~Vehicle is called for both Car and Motorcycle. Finally, you should note that the objects are destroyed in the reverse order in which they were created. The motorcycle object is destroyed before car, which is destroyed before vehicle. This is a useful feature that we use to our advantage later in this book.

Method overriding is the final feature of class inheritance you'll learn in this chapter.

Method Overriding

Earlier in this chapter, you saw how we can change the number of wheels in derived classes by changing the value of a variable in the derived class's constructor. Although that is a more correct method for achieving this, I will show you how we could have achieved a similar outcome using method overriding in this chapter. To use method overriding we will create a `GetNumberOfWheels` method in each of our three classes. Listing 10-10 shows these methods.

Listing 10-10. Overriding `GetNumberOfWheels`

```
unsigned int Vehicle::GetNumberOfWheels() const
{
        return 0;
}

unsigned int Car::GetNumberOfWheels() const
{
        return 4;
}

unsigned int Motorcycle::GetNumberOfWheels() const
{
        return 2;
}
```

Now each of your classes has a method with an identical name. In the `PrintNumberOfWheels` method so far, each call to `GetNumberOfWheels` called `Vehicle::GetNumberOfWheels`, which returned the value stored in m_numberOfWheels. With method overriding the compiler will call the `GetNumberOfWheels` method for the appropriate class; therefore, we will see calls to `Car::GetNumberOfWheels` and `Motorcycle::GetNumberOfWheels` in the proper place in our `PrintNumberOfWheels` function.

Updating Text Adventure

The Text Adventure game you are building has fairly limited functionality at this point. In this chapter we are going to add some rooms to the game and update `Player` to be inherited from a class named `Entity`.

Creating an Entity Class

`Entity` will be our game's base class for all objects that exist in the game world. Listing 10-11 shows the code for `Entity`.

Listing 10-11. The `Entity` Class

```
class Entity
{
public:
        void Update()    {}
};
```

Our Entity class at the moment is very straightforward; all we want it to do is provide our inherited classes with an Update method. The Update method can be important when developing game software, as your program will likely be *updating* your objects once per frame.

Adding Inheritance to the Player Class

Your Player class can now be changed to inherit from Entity. The new Player class can be seen in Listing 10-12.

Listing 10-12. Inheriting Player from Entity

```cpp
class Player
        : public Entity
{
private:
        std::string m_name;

public:
        Player()
        {
        }

        void SetName(const std::string& name)
        {
                m_name = name;
        }

        const std::string& GetName() const
        {
                return m_name;
        }
};
```

You will see what the Player class's Update method will look like once we have added some rooms for the player to move through.

Adding Rooms

To be able to have the player move through rooms in the game you will need to create a Room class, and the code for this is shown in Listing 10-13.

Listing 10-13. The Room Class

```cpp
class Room
        : public Entity
{
public:
        enum class JoiningDirections
        {
                North = 0,
                East,
```

```
                South,
                West,
                Max
        };

private:
        Room* m_pJoiningRooms[JoiningDirections::Max];

public:
        Room();

        void AddRoom(JoiningDirections direction, Room* pRoom);
        Room* GetRoom(JoiningDirections direction) const;
};

Room::Room()
{
        for (unsigned int i = 0;
                i < static_cast<unsigned int>(JoiningDirections::Max);
                ++i)
        {
                m_pJoiningRooms[i] = nullptr;
        }
}

void Room::AddRoom(Room::JoiningDirections direction, Room* pRoom)
{
        m_pJoiningRooms[static_cast<unsigned int>(direction)] = pRoom;
}

Room* Room::GetRoom(Room::JoiningDirections direction) const
{
        return m_pJoiningRooms[static_cast<unsigned int>(direction)];
}
```

For now, a Room is a simple object. We have inherited from Entity and have created an array to store pointers to connecting rooms. There is an enum class that is used to enumerate the four different directions in which rooms can be connected to the current room. The value of North is set to 0 in our enum class as we will be using these values to index into our array of Room pointers. You can see this in action in the method Room::AddRoom where we must static_cast the value of direction to be able to index into our array and assign the passed Room* to the correct array member. The final method in Room is GetRoom, which will allow us to get the pointer to a room adjoining any given room for the supplied direction.

Now that you have a room class you will be able to add some rooms to our Game class. You can see how this is done in Listing 10-14.

Listing 10-14. Adding a Room Array to Game

```cpp
class Game
{
private:
        static const unsigned int m_numberOfRooms = 4;
        Room m_rooms[m_numberOfRooms];

        Player m_player;

        void InitializeRooms();
        void WelcomePlayer();
        void GivePlayerOptions() const;
        void GetPlayerInput(std::string& playerInput) const;
        PlayerOptions EvaluateInput(std::string& playerInput) const;
public:

        void RunGame();
};
```

The Game class now has an array that stores all of the Room objects our game requires. We can increase the number of rooms by increasing the value stored in the static const variable m_numberOfRooms. The new method, InitializeRooms, is shown in Listing 10-15 and is responsible for creating the connections between the different Room objects.

Listing 10-15. Game::InitializeRooms

```cpp
void Game::InitializeRooms()
{
        // Room 0 heads North to Room 1
        m_rooms[0].AddRoom(Room::JoiningDirections::North, &(m_rooms[1]));

        // Room 1 heads East to Room 2, South to Room 0 and West to Room 3
        m_rooms[1].AddRoom(Room::JoiningDirections::East, &(m_rooms[2]));
        m_rooms[1].AddRoom(Room::JoiningDirections::South, &(m_rooms[0]));
        m_rooms[1].AddRoom(Room::JoiningDirections::West, &(m_rooms[3]));

        // Room 2 heads West to Room 1
        m_rooms[2].AddRoom(Room::JoiningDirections::West, &(m_rooms[1]));

        // Room 3 heads East to Room 1
        m_rooms[3].AddRoom(Room::JoiningDirections::East, &(m_rooms[1]));
}
```

It is important to make sure that any Room that connects to another also has that Room connect back or the player might be able to get into a Room and not able to get back out. Listing 10-16 shows an option for where you can call InitializeRooms.

Listing 10-16. Calling InitializeRooms from Game::RunGame

```
void Game::RunGame()
{
        InitializeRooms();

        WelcomePlayer();

        bool shouldEnd = false;
        while (shouldEnd == false)
        {
                GivePlayerOptions();

                string playerInput;
                GetPlayerInput(playerInput);

                shouldEnd = EvaluateInput(playerInput) == PlayerOptions::Quit;
        }
}
```

Now that you have some Room objects in the game, you will need to keep track of which Room the player is currently in. You can do this by adding a pointer to a Room to the Player object. Listing 10-17 shows how this can be achieved.

Listing 10-17. Adding a Room Pointer to Player

```
class Room;

class Player
        : public Entity
{
private:
        const Room* m_pCurrentRoom;
        std::string m_name;

public:
        Player()
        {
        }

        void SetName(const std::string& name)
        {
                m_name = name;
        }

        const std::string& GetName() const
        {
                return m_name;
        }
```

```
        void SetCurrentRoom(const Room* pCurrentRoom)
        {
                m_pCurrentRoom = pCurrentRoom;
        }

        const Room* GetCurrentRoom() const
        {
                return m_pCurrentRoom;
        }
};
```

The Player class contains a pointer to a Room object and accessor methods to set and retrieve the current Room.

> **Note**   We did not have to include Room.h in the Player.h file to add a pointer to the Player class. What you see in Listing 10-17 is known as a forward declaration. A forward declaration can be used when only a pointer or reference to an object is used in a header file and not the object itself. You are only required to include the full class definition if you were going to call a method on an object or instantiate a class in any given file.

I've added another line to InitializeRooms to set the Player's current Room pointer in Listing 10-18.

Listing 10-18. Setting m_player's Current Room

```
void Game::InitializeRooms()
{
        // Room 0 heads North to Room 1
        m_rooms[0].AddRoom(Room::JoiningDirections::North, &(m_rooms[1]));

        // Room 1 heads East to Room 2, South to Room 0 and West to Room 3
        m_rooms[1].AddRoom(Room::JoiningDirections::East, &(m_rooms[2]));
        m_rooms[1].AddRoom(Room::JoiningDirections::South, &(m_rooms[0]));
        m_rooms[1].AddRoom(Room::JoiningDirections::West, &(m_rooms[3]));

        // Room 2 heads West to Room 1
        m_rooms[2].AddRoom(Room::JoiningDirections::West, &(m_rooms[1]));

        // Room 3 heads East to Room 1
        m_rooms[3].AddRoom(Room::JoiningDirections::East, &(m_rooms[1]));

        m_player.SetCurrentRoom(&(m_rooms[0]));
}
```

Now that you have rooms and a way to store which room the player is in, you should add some options to allow the player to move through those rooms.

Moving Through Rooms

Listing 10-19 updates the Game::RunGame method to store the user's selected option and call a new UpdateOnOption method.

Listing 10-19. Updating Game::RunGame

```
void Game::RunGame()
{
        InitializeRooms();

        WelcomePlayer();

        bool shouldEnd = false;
        while (shouldEnd == false)
        {
                GivePlayerOptions();

                string playerInput;
                GetPlayerInput(playerInput);

                PlayerOptions selectedOption = EvaluateInput(playerInput);
                shouldEnd = selectedOption == PlayerOptions::Quit;
                if (shouldEnd == false)
                {
                        UpdateOnOption(selectedOption);
                }
        }
}
```

RunGame now stores the result from EvaluateInput and calls UpdateOnOption if the player has not chosen to quit. Before I show you the code for UpdateOnOption we will look at the updated GivePlayerOptions and EvaluateInput methods in Listing 10-20.

Listing 10-20. Updating GivePlayerOptions and EvaluateInput

```
void Game::GivePlayerOptions() const
{
        cout << "What would you like to do? (Enter a corresponding number)"
                << endl << endl;
        cout << "1: Go North" << endl << endl;
        cout << "2: Go East" << endl << endl;
        cout << "3: Go South" << endl << endl;
        cout << "4: Go West" << endl << endl;
        cout << "5: Quit" << endl << endl;
}

PlayerOptions Game::EvaluateInput(string& playerInput) const
{
        PlayerOptions chosenOption = PlayerOptions::None;
```

```
        if (playerInput.compare("1") == 0)
        {
                cout << "You have chosen to Go North!" << endl << endl;
                chosenOption = PlayerOptions::GoNorth;
        }
        else if (playerInput.compare("2") == 0)
        {
                cout << "You have chosen to Go East!" << endl << endl;
                chosenOption = PlayerOptions::GoEast;
        }
        else if (playerInput.compare("3") == 0)
        {
                cout << "You have chosen to Go South!" << endl << endl;
                chosenOption = PlayerOptions::GoSouth;
        }
        else if (playerInput.compare("4") == 0)
        {
                cout << "You have chosen to Go West!" << endl << endl;
                chosenOption = PlayerOptions::GoWest;
        }
        else if (playerInput.compare("5") == 0)
        {
                cout << "You have chosen to Quit!" << endl << endl;
                chosenOption = PlayerOptions::Quit;
        }
        else
        {
                cout << "I do not recognize that option, try again!" << endl << endl;
        }

        return chosenOption;
}
```

Your player will now see options 1 through 5 to choose which room to move to or whether he or she would like to quit. The last task required is to move the m_player object to the new selected Room. Listing 10-21 shows how you can achieve this in the new UpdateOnOption method.

Listing 10-21. Moving the Player in UpdateOnOption

```
void Game::UpdateOnOption(PlayerOptions selectedOption)
{
        if (selectedOption == PlayerOptions::GoNorth ||
            selectedOption == PlayerOptions::GoEast  ||
            selectedOption == PlayerOptions::GoSouth ||
            selectedOption == PlayerOptions::GoWest)
        {
                Room::JoiningDirections directionToMove
                        = Room::JoiningDirections::North;
```

```
switch (selectedOption)
{
case PlayerOptions::GoEast:
{
        directionToMove = Room::JoiningDirections::East;
}
break;

case PlayerOptions::GoSouth:
{
        directionToMove = Room::JoiningDirections::South;
}
break;

case PlayerOptions::GoWest:
{
        directionToMove = Room::JoiningDirections::West;
}
break;
}

const Room* pPlayerCurrentRoom = m_player.GetCurrentRoom();
const Room* pNewRoom = pPlayerCurrentRoom->GetRoom(directionToMove);
if (pNewRoom != nullptr)
{
        m_player.SetCurrentRoom(pNewRoom);
}
else
{
        const char* strDirection = "North";
        switch (selectedOption)
        {
        case PlayerOptions::GoEast:
        {
                strDirection = "East";
        }
        break;

        case PlayerOptions::GoSouth:
        {
                strDirection = "South";
        }
        break;

        case PlayerOptions::GoWest:
        {
                strDirection = "West";
        }
        break;
        }
```

```
                    cout << "There is no room to the "
                         << strDirection << endl << endl;
              }
       }
}
```

The UpdateOnOption method can be broken down into three main sections. First it works out which direction the player would like to move in from the supplied option. It does this using the first switch statement in the method. It then updates the current Room pointer stored by m_player so long as the Room we are trying to move to is valid and not a nullptr. If the chosen Room is a nullptr, the method then outputs to the player that there is no room in the direction in which he or she tried to move.

You now have the ability to move through the game world. Congratulations! We could stop learning about C++ at this point and have the ability to write a full-text adventure game with everything you have learned so far; however, your code would be very long and you would find yourself repeating certain code over and over again. The rest of this book will try to expand your knowledge of C++ and show you how some more advanced features of the language can be used to cut down on the amount of code you have to write.

Summary

This chapter has introduced you to the concept of class inheritance. The inheritance you've seen in this chapter is useful for sharing behavior and code between objects that can be logically grouped together. Vehicles are a classic example used to introduce new programmers to inheritance, as it is a simple set of objects to group logically and they have simple features that can be used to show differences between different members of the set.

You've seen in this chapter that the *access specifier* (public, protected, and private) used when declaring class member variables has an important part to play in sharing data between base classes and their derived children. You've also learned that constructors and destructors play an important role in the creation and destruction of objects and in which order they are called. Finally you learned that it's possible to alter the behavior of a derived class by overriding methods that exist in a parent class by defining a method with the same signature in the derived class.

The following chapter is going to introduce you to the concept of polymorphism. Polymorphism allows us to create class interfaces and abstract out class implementations. This is a very powerful technique that you will find used in game play, engine, and cross-platform game programming. The code you have seen in this chapter for the Text Adventure game will be rewritten once you understand the concepts behind polymorphism and you will see how much simpler and clean-looking your code can be.

Designing Game Code with Polymorphism

You saw how inheritance can be used to design reusable code in the last chapter. In this chapter you will learn how the power of inheritance can be unlocked in much more useful ways through the power of polymorphism. C++ supports the ability to access classes of different types through pointers to a base class, known as polymorphism. The program can determine the type of the object at runtime and call the correct method. The mechanism supplied by C++ to tell the compiler that a method can be different in the base class to any derived classes is the virtual method.

Virtual Methods

You have seen that methods in class hierarchies can be overridden, which allows the compiler to call a given method for a class type rather than call the version from the base class when accessing an object of a given type. When you use polymorphism, the compiler cannot tell what the actual type of the object is and therefore we must write our methods in a different manner. Listing 11-1 shows how the Vehicle class can be modified to turn the GetNumberOfWheels method into a virtual method.

Listing 11-1. Creating a Virtual Method

```
class Vehicle
{
public:
        Vehicle();

        ~Vehicle();

        virtual unsigned int GetNumberOfWheels() const
        {
                return 0;
        }
};
```

You create virtual methods by adding the virtual keyword to the beginning of the method signature. The method GetNumberOfWheels is now a virtual method. To get the benefit of this, Listing 11-2 updates the Car and Motorcycle classes to make their GetNumberOfWheels methods virtual.

Listing 11-2. Making GetNumberOfWheels Virtual in Car and Motorcycle

```cpp
class Car : public Vehicle
{
public:
        Car();
        ~Car();

        virtual unsigned int GetNumberOfWheels() const
        {
                return 4;
        }
};

class Motorcycle : public Vehicle
{
public:
        Motorcycle();
        ~Motorcycle();

        virtual unsigned int GetNumberOfWheels() const
        {
                return 2;
        }
};
```

The code in Listing 11-2 completes our updates to the GetNumberOfWheels methods in the Vehicle, Car, and Motorcycle classes. Listing 11-3 modifies the PrintNumberOfWheels method to make use of polymorphism.

Listing 11-3. Using Polymorphism in PrintNumberOfWheels

```cpp
void PrintNumberOfWheels()
{
        Vehicle vehicle;
        Car     car;
        Motorcycle motorcycle;

        Vehicle* pVehicle = &vehicle;
        std::cout << pVehicle->GetNumberOfWheels() << std::endl;

        pVehicle = &car;
        std::cout << pVehicle->GetNumberOfWheels() << std::endl;

        pVehicle = &motorcycle;
        std::cout << pVehicle->GetNumberOfWheels() << std::endl;
}
```

The code in PrintNumberOfWheels now accesses the GetNumberOfWheels methods of Vehicle, Car, and Motorcycle through a pointer to the Vehicle class. The output from this program is still correct. The first std::cout will print 0, the second will print 4, and the third will print 2. This is a perfect example of polymorphism in action: This code calls the Car::GetNumberOfWheels and Motorcycle::GetNumberOfWheels methods through a Vehicle pointer.

Once you begin to write more complex polymorphic programs you will find you'll need to cast to the proper derived types in certain circumstances. C++ provides the dynamic_cast for these situations.

Downcasting and Upcasting with dynamic_cast

Moving between different types at runtime is usually an unsafe operation. In complex code it can sometimes be difficult to be sure where pointers have come from, what they point to, and which other classes exist in the class hierarchy for a given type. You should use dynamic_cast in these situations to be sure that your code does not crash when converting between types. Listing 11-4 adds some code to PrintNumberOfWheels to show you how dynamic_cast can be used.

Listing 11-4. Using dynamic_cast to Downcast

```
void PrintNumberOfWheels()
{
        Vehicle vehicle;
        Car        car;
        Motorcycle motorcycle;

        Vehicle* pVehicle = &vehicle;
        std::cout << pVehicle->GetNumberOfWheels() << std::endl;

        pVehicle = &car;
        Car* pCar = dynamic_cast<Car*>(pVehicle);
        if (pCar != nullptr)
        {
                std::cout << pCar->GetNumberOfWheels() << std::endl;
        }

        pVehicle = &motorcycle;
        pCar = dynamic_cast<Car*>(pVehicle);
        if (pCar != nullptr)
        {
                std::cout << pCar->GetNumberOfWheels() << std::endl;
        }
}
```

Listing 11-4 has two dynamic_cast calls to convert the current value stored in pVehicle to a pointer to a Car object. The result of a dynamic_cast can either be a valid pointer to the requested class or nullptr. This means that we must ensure that the result of a dynamic_cast is valid before trying to dereference the resulting pointer or our application can crash. The first cast in Listing 11-4 results in a valid pointer and therefore the number of wheels for a car will be printed out. The second cast will fail and return nullptr. Both of these casts were attempts at a downcast. You can visualize a class hierarchy as having the base class at the top and all child classes below that. Casting from a higher class to a lower class is a downcast and the opposite is an upcast. The code in Listing 11-5 is safer than the code in Listing 11-4, as we use dynamic_cast to upcast to the Vehicle pointer.

Listing 11-5. Upcasting

```
void PrintNumberOfWheels()
{
        Vehicle vehicle;
        Car     car;
        Motorcycle motorcycle;

        Vehicle* pVehicle = dynamic_cast<Vehicle*>(&vehicle);
        std::cout << pVehicle->GetNumberOfWheels() << std::endl;

        pVehicle = dynamic_cast<Vehicle*>(&car);
        Car* pCar = dynamic_cast<Car*>(pVehicle);
        if (pCar != nullptr)
        {
                std::cout << pCar->GetNumberOfWheels() << std::endl;
        }

        pVehicle = dynamic_cast<Vehicle*>(&motorcycle);
        pCar = dynamic_cast<Car*>(pVehicle);
        if (pCar != nullptr)
        {
                std::cout << pCar->GetNumberOfWheels() << std::endl;
        }
}
```

The upcasts to Vehicle in Listing 11-5 are all much safer than the previous implicit casts. This would not matter too much in this example code, as we know all of the objects derive from Vehicle, but in production code you might not be able to guarantee that a given pointer derives from a specific base class.

Creating Interfaces with Pure Virtual Methods

The Vehicle class has a value to return for GetNumberOfWheels. In a proper program it would be unlikely that we would want to be able to create basic Vehicle objects as we are more likely to want to create instances of Car or Motorcycle. It also makes little sense for a Vehicle to have any number of wheels, even none. We can turn Vehicle into an interface by making its GetNumberOfWheels class a pure virtual method. Listing 11-6 shows how to do this.

Listing 11-6. Making Pure Virtual Methods

```
class Vehicle
{
public:
        virtual unsigned int GetNumberOfWheels() const = 0;
};
```

Pure virtual methods are created by adding = 0 to the end of the method declaration. The method then does not contain a body, as we do not wish to have any code associated with the method in this class. Adding a pure virtual method to a class turns the class into an abstract class. Abstract classes cannot be *instantiated,* which means we can no longer create Vehicle objects. You will need to remove the instance of Vehicle in PrintNumberOfWheels. Listing 11-7 shows a version of the function with this removed.

Listing 11-7. Removing Vehicle from PrintNumberOfWheels

```
void PrintNumberOfWheels()
{
        Car        car;
        Motorcycle motorcycle;

        Vehicle* pVehicle = dynamic_cast<Vehicle*>(&car);
        Car* pCar = dynamic_cast<Car*>(pVehicle);
        if (pCar != nullptr)
        {
                std::cout << pCar->GetNumberOfWheels() << std::endl;
        }

        pVehicle = dynamic_cast<Vehicle*>(&motorcycle);
        pCar = dynamic_cast<Car*>(pVehicle);
        if (pCar != nullptr)
        {
                std::cout << pCar->GetNumberOfWheels() << std::endl;
        }
}
```

Another effect of the pure virtual method is that it turns Vehicle into an interface class. Interface classes are usually simply referred to as interfaces. Any pure virtual methods in a parent class must be overridden in a class that you wish to be able to instantiate. You might recall that the notion of contracts was touched on in Chapter 8 when we discussed OOP. Using interfaces is one method that you can use to define these contracts. You can try commenting out the GetNumberOfWheels methods from the Car and Motorcycle classes to see the compiler errors that are generated.

Using Polymorphism in Text Adventure

The options that have been supplied to the player in Text Adventure have so far been coded procedurally. You can make it much easier to add new options by using a more object-oriented approach to the system. Listing 11-8 shows the Option interface that you can use to create future options.

Listing 11-8. The Option Class

```
class Option
{
protected:
        PlayerOptions   m_chosenOption;
        std::string     m_outputText;
        std::string     m_optionText;
```

```
public:
        Option(PlayerOptions chosenOption, const std::string& outputText)
                : m_chosenOption(chosenOption)
                , m_outputText(outputText)
        {
        }

        void Option::SetOptionText(const std::string& optionText)
        {
                m_optionText = optionText;
        }

        const std::string& GetOutputText() const
        {
                return m_outputText;
        }

        PlayerOptions GetChosenOption() const
        {
                return m_chosenOption;
        }

        virtual bool Evaluate(const std::string& optionText, Player& player) = 0;
};
```

The Option class stores the PlayerOption value that it represents as well as the text that is output to the player and a string to compare to the text the player enters. You can then derive specific classes from Option, the MoveOption and QuitOption classes. Listing 11-9 shows the MoveOption class and Listing 11-10 shows the QuitOption class.

Listing 11-9. The MoveOption Class

```
class MoveOption
        :         public Option
{
private:
        Room::JoiningDirections m_directionToMove;

public:
        MoveOption(Room::JoiningDirections joiningDirection,
                PlayerOptions chosenOption,
                const std::string& outputText)
                : Option(chosenOption, outputText)
                , m_directionToMove(joiningDirection)
        {
        }

        virtual bool Evaluate(const std::string& optionText, Player& player);
};
```

```
bool MoveOption::Evaluate(const std::string& optionText, Player& player)
{
        bool handled = false;

        if (m_optionText.compare(optionText) == 0)
        {
                const Room* pPlayerCurrentRoom = player.GetCurrentRoom();
                const Room* pNewRoom = pPlayerCurrentRoom->GetRoom(m_directionToMove);
                if (pNewRoom != nullptr)
                {
                        player.SetCurrentRoom(pNewRoom);
                        std::cout << "You have chosen to "
                                << m_outputText << std::endl << std::endl;
                }
                else
                {
                        const char* strDirection = "North";
                        switch (m_chosenOption)
                        {
                        case PlayerOptions::GoEast:
                        {
                                strDirection = "East";
                        }
                        break;

                        case PlayerOptions::GoSouth:
                        {
                                strDirection = "South";
                        }
                        break;

                        case PlayerOptions::GoWest:
                        {
                                strDirection = "West";
                        }
                        break;
                        }

                        std::cout << "There is no room to the "
                                << strDirection << std::endl << std::endl;
                }

                handled = true;
        }

        return handled;
}
```

The MoveOption class now contains all of the code necessary to work out if the player has chosen
to move to another room and the code necessary to change the Player class Room pointer to the
appropriate Room object.

Listing 11-10. The QuitOption Class

```cpp
class QuitOption
        : public Option
{
private:
        bool m_shouldQuit;

public:
        QuitOption(const std::string& outputText)
                : Option(PlayerOptions::Quit, outputText)
                , m_shouldQuit(false)
        {
        }

        bool ShouldQuit() const { return m_shouldQuit; }
        virtual bool Evaluate(const std::string& optionText, Player& player);
};

bool QuitOption::Evaluate(const std::string& optionText, Player& player)
{
        m_shouldQuit = m_optionText.compare(optionText) == 0;

        if (m_shouldQuit == true)
        {
                std::cout << "You have chosen to quit!" << std::endl << std::endl;
        }

        return m_shouldQuit;
}
```

The QuitOption determines whether the player has chosen to quit the game. Listing 11-11 shows how you can add these options to the Game class.

Listing 11-11. Adding the New Options to Game

```cpp
class Game
{
private:
        static const unsigned int m_numberOfRooms = 4;
        Room m_rooms[m_numberOfRooms];

        Player m_player;

        MoveOption m_moveNorthOption;
        MoveOption m_moveEastOption;
        MoveOption m_moveSouthOption;
        MoveOption m_moveWestOption;
        QuitOption m_quitOption;

        static const unsigned int m_numberOfOptions = 5;
        Option* m_options[m_numberOfOptions];
```

```
        void InitializeRooms();
        void WelcomePlayer();
        void GivePlayerOptions() const;
        void GetPlayerInput(std::string& playerInput) const;
        PlayerOptions EvaluateInput(std::string& playerInput);
public:
        Game();

        void RunGame();
};
```

There are four MoveOption instances, one QuitOption instance, and an array of Option pointers.
The constructor of the class is also new. Listing 11-12 shows the constructor for Game.

Listing 11-12. The Game Class Constructor

```
Game::Game()
        : m_moveNorthOption(Room::JoiningDirections::North,
                PlayerOptions::GoNorth,
                "Go North")
        , m_moveEastOption(Room::JoiningDirections::East,
                PlayerOptions::GoEast,
                "Go East")
        , m_moveSouthOption(Room::JoiningDirections::South,
                PlayerOptions::GoSouth,
                "Go South")
        , m_moveWestOption(Room::JoiningDirections::West,
                PlayerOptions::GoWest,
                "Go West")
        , m_quitOption("Quit")
{
        m_options[0] = dynamic_cast<Option*>(&m_moveNorthOption);
        m_options[1] = dynamic_cast<Option*>(&m_moveEastOption);
        m_options[2] = dynamic_cast<Option*>(&m_moveSouthOption);
        m_options[3] = dynamic_cast<Option*>(&m_moveWestOption);
        m_options[4] = dynamic_cast<Option*>(&m_quitOption);
}
```

The Game class constructor initializes the Option class objects and the array of pointers. Next you
need to update the Game::GivePlayerOptions method. You can see how this is done in Listing 11-13.

Listing 11-13. Updating Game::GivePlayerOptions

```
void Game::GivePlayerOptions() const
{
        cout << "What would you like to do? (Enter a corresponding number)"
                << endl << endl;
        for (unsigned int i = 0; i < m_numberOfOptions; ++i)
        {
                Option* option = m_options[i];
                const unsigned int chosenOption = i + 1;
                cout << chosenOption << ": " << option->GetOutputText() << endl << endl;
```

```
                std::ostringstream chosenOptionString;
                chosenOptionString << chosenOption;
                option->SetOptionText(chosenOptionString.str());
        }
}
```

The GivePlayerOptions method loops over the array of Option pointers, displays the options that the user can select for each option, and sets the option text on the Option object. This method now does not have to be changed as we add new options to the option array. The user input option will automatically update as we change the array and the output text that we enter into the Option constructors. The EvaluateInput method also gets an update in Listing 11-14.

Listing 11-14. The EvaluateInput Method

```
PlayerOptions Game::EvaluateInput(string& playerInput)
{
        PlayerOptions chosenOption = PlayerOptions::None;

        for (unsigned int i = 0; i < m_numberOfOptions; ++i)
        {
                Option* option = m_options[i];
                bool handled = option->Evaluate(playerInput, m_player);
                if (handled == true)
                {
                        chosenOption = option->GetChosenOption();
                        break;
                }
        }

        if (chosenOption == PlayerOptions::None)
        {
                cout << "I do not recognize that option, try again!" << endl << endl;
        }

        return chosenOption;
}
```

The EvaluateInput method has been simplified. It now also loops over the Option array and calls Evaluate on each Option object. The last method to get an update is RunGame in Listing 11-15.

Listing 11-15. The RunGame Method

```
void Game::RunGame()
{
        InitializeRooms();

        WelcomePlayer();

        bool shouldEnd = false;
```

```
        while (shouldEnd == false)
        {
                GivePlayerOptions();

                string playerInput;
                GetPlayerInput(playerInput);

                PlayerOptions selectedOption = EvaluateInput(playerInput);
                shouldEnd = selectedOption == PlayerOptions::Quit;
        }
}
```

The UpdateOnOption method from Chapter 10 has been removed, as the code from that method has been moved into the MoveOption class. This allows you to remove the call to that method from the RunGame class.

Summary

This chapter has introduced polymorphism. This allows you to write code that is more flexible and reusable. You have seen that base class pointers combined with virtual methods allow a programmer to create interfaces and code that allows programs to evaluate their behavior at runtime for the correct course of action. You have also seen how the dynamic_cast allows you to ensure that you can safely move from one type of object pointer to another. Pure virtual functions were then introduced, along with an example of how you can create abstract classes that enforce specific methods to be overridden in classes that derive from that class.

The chapter ended with a practical example of how you can use polymorphism to improve your code in a number of ways. The Option class creates a simple interface for in-game options. The MoveOption and QuitOption classes show how you can use virtual methods to create types to represent specific actions. Finally, you saw that polymorphism can be used to write methods that are reusable and easily maintainable. New options can be added to Text Adventure without the need to alter the Game GivePlayerOptions and EvaluateInput methods.

Chapter 12

Copying and Assigning Data to Objects

You have seen how we can pass data into functions by value, by reference, or by pointer. If you choose to pass a class object into a function by value, C++ will make a copy of the class. This copy operation happens automatically or *implicitly*. This chapter is going to show you some of these implicit operations that can occur when using classes in your programs and the ways in which you can alter and manage these implicit operations.

Copy Constructors

Classes in C++ can use constructors and destructors to initialize and clean up the objects that you use in your programs. C++ also allows you to specify a copy constructor that is called when an object is being copied into a new instance of an object. Listing 12-1 shows a simple copy constructor.

Listing 12-1. A Copy Constructor

```
class Player
      : public Entity
{
private:
      const Room* m_pCurrentRoom;
      std::string m_name;

public:
      Player()
      {
      }
```

```
        Player(const Player& originalPlayer)
        {
                m_pCurrentRoom = originalPlayer.m_pCurrentRoom;
                m_name = originalPlayer.m_name;
        }

        void SetName(const std::string& name)
        {
                m_name = name;
        }

        const std::string& GetName() const
        {
                return m_name;
        }

        void SetCurrentRoom(const Room* pCurrentRoom)
        {
                m_pCurrentRoom = pCurrentRoom;
        }

        const Room* GetCurrentRoom() const
        {
                return m_pCurrentRoom;
        }
};
```

The copy constructor in Listing 12-1 is a constructor method that takes a constant reference to an object of the same type of class; in this case the Player copy constructor takes a constant reference to another Player object. Copy constructors are an added cost when passing objects into functions. Usually you would be better served by passing a constant reference into the function instead. Copy constructors are mostly useful when you wish to return a new instance of an object from a function. When you do this, the object you are returning will go out of scope and be destroyed after the function has returned. Returning objects by value ensures that you are not exposed to bugs caused by trying to return references to local variables that no longer exist. Listing 12-2 shows two different functions that take a player by value and by constant reference.

Listing 12-2. Passing by Value and const Reference

```
void CopyPlayer(Player player)
{

}

void PassPlayerByConstReference(const Player& player)
{

}
```

Any code that you could place inside these methods would be identical and all of the data contained by both would also be the same. The major difference between the two methods is the length of time it takes to execute the two. Passing player by value would invoke the copy constructor, whereas passing a constant reference does not. Using a constant reference therefore avoids the time taken to call the copy constructor method and the length of time it takes to execute a full copy of the class.

Passing by a constant reference also helps protect programmers against another more subtle problem. The first method has passed the class by value and therefore the player parameter is a copy of the original object. If you then called any methods that set values on the parameter, that data would be lost when the function returns. You can get around this by declaring the copied object as const; however, at that point there's no reason why you wouldn't also use a reference. Using const variables with copied objects will cause the compiler to throw errors if you try to call public methods on the object, which helps to avoid a source of errors and bugs in your games.

Assignment Operators

Although copy constructors will be invoked when passing objects by value into functions or methods, assignment operators are invoked when using the = operator on objects. Listing 12-3 shows how you can overload an assignment operator on the Player class.

Listing 12-3. The Player Assignment Operator

```
class Player
        : public Entity
{
private:
        const Room* m_pCurrentRoom;
        std::string m_name;

public:
        Player()
        {
        }

        Player(const Player& originalPlayer)
        {
                m_pCurrentRoom = originalPlayer.m_pCurrentRoom;
                m_name = originalPlayer.m_name;
        }

        Player& operator=(const Player& originalPlayer)
        {
                m_pCurrentRoom = originalPlayer.m_pCurrentRoom;
                m_name = originalPlayer.m_name;
                return *this;
        }
```

```
        void SetName(const std::string& name)
        {
                m_name = name;
        }

        const std::string& GetName() const
        {
                return m_name;
        }

        void SetCurrentRoom(const Room* pCurrentRoom)
        {
                m_pCurrentRoom = pCurrentRoom;
        }

        const Room* GetCurrentRoom() const
        {
                return m_pCurrentRoom;
        }
};
```

An assignment operator is passed a constant reference to the object that is being assigned from. This allows you to copy all of the relevant fields to the object being assigned to. There is a major difference between a copy constructor and an assignment operator. A copy constructor is invoked when a new object is being created and can be initialized by copying from an existing object. The assignment operator is invoked when assigning to an already existing object. Listing 12-4 shows an example.

Listing 12-4. Invoking an Assignment Operator

```
Player newPlayer;
newPlayer = m_player;
```

You can now use general arithmetic assignment operators with your classes so long as you remember to overload the assignment operator appropriate for assigning to your class as in Listing 12-3.

Move Semantics

Move semantics are useful when dealing with some more complex C++ code. We'll cover some cases where move semantics are useful later in this book, but for now I'll show you how you can add move constructors and move assignment operators to your classes. Move semantics differ from normal copy constructors and assignment operators in that they operate on rvalue references. An rvalue reference is denoted in C++ using a double ampersand. These rvalue references can only be used when working with temporary objects, which can be created under many circumstances in C++, such as when returning objects from functions by value. Listing 12-5 shows a move constructor for the Player class.

Listing 12-5. The Player Move Constructor

```
Player(Player&& tempPlayer)
{
        m_pCurrentRoom = tempPlayer.m_pCurrentRoom;
        m_name = tempPlayer.m_name;

        tempPlayer.m_pCurrentRoom = nullptr;
        m_name.clear();
}
```

The double reference symbol in a move constructor means that the reference being passed in is an *rvalue reference*. rvalue references occur when passing temporary objects into methods. This occurs often when using STL containers, which we'll be looking at in Part 3 of this book. It's also important to clear the data from the object passed into the move constructor, and you'll see why this is the case when we look at memory management in Part 5. A move assignment operator can also be added to your classes. Listing 12-6 shows how to do this.

Listing 12-6. A Move Assignment Operator

```
Player& operator=(Player&& tempPlayer)
{
        if (this != &tempPlayer)
        {
                m_pCurrentRoom = tempPlayer.m_pCurrentRoom;
                m_name = tempPlayer.m_name;

                tempPlayer.m_pCurrentRoom = nullptr;
                m_name.clear();
        }

        return *this;
}
```

Summary

This short chapter has introduced you to the methods that can be added to classes to allow you to pass data around in your programs. These are not particularly useful as stand-alone procedures, but they will be very useful in the next part of this book when we look at the STL. The STL provides us with containers to store many objects in data structures and we will be using copy constructors, assignment operators, and move semantics liberally throughout that entire part of the book.

You have seen how copy constructors allow you to make copies of classes. This occurs most often when passing objects into functions by value; however, you will usually be satisfied with passing most objects by a const reference to avoid the cost of invoking the copy constructor. You've also seen how you can overload assignment operators to copy data from one object to another preexisting object. Finally, you saw how move semantics can be added to your classes. You'll see better how these are useful later in this book.

Part 3

The STL

Modern programming languages come with many features, data structures, and algorithms out of the box. C++ is no exception. The Standard Template Library (STL) provides interfaces to a preexisting library of functionality that will allow you to write better programs faster.

The STL provides you with tools to manage collections of objects, execute algorithms on those collections, and learn how to best structure the data in your applications.

This part of the book will help you learn the differences between the different STL containers and when to use each in your programs. You'll also see the string class in action, which will help you work with strings in a much easier manner than using raw C strings.

The STL also provides excellent exposure to the syntax required to use templates in your programs. This will be very useful in the next part of the book when you learn how to create your own templates.

Chapter 13

The STL String Class

The next few chapters of this book are going to introduce you to the Standard Template Library (STL). The STL contains classes that you can use to manipulate strings, store objects, and access them using several different patterns. The STL also provides iterators to traverse collections and algorithms for carrying out different types of operations on your data sets. You have already been using the STL `string` class throughout this book. This chapter looks at the different methods that the STL provides for working with classes and points out some of the reasons why using this class is more desirable than dealing with raw C strings.

Standard string and basic_string

The STL should give you a brief clue that we will be using templates of classes to create concrete types. You'll learn how to create your own templates in Part 4 of this book when we cover the Generic Programming Paradigm. For now, all you need to know is that templates behave exactly as their name suggests and provide a blueprint for the compiler to create specific classes.

The `string` class is implemented in exactly this way. The template `basic_string` is used to generate four different types of standard strings. Listing 13-1 shows how the STL uses type aliases to generate these types.

Listing 13-1. The STL basic_string Aliases

```
using string = basic_string<char>;
using u16string = basic_string<char16_t>;
using u32string = basic_string<char32_t>;
using wstring = basic_string<wchar_t>;
```

There are a few operations happening here, so I'll talk you through the important parts. The first thing to notice is how you can create template specializations. The `basic_string<char>` is creating a specialization of the `basic_string` template using the `char` data type. As you have seen, a `char` is a data type that can store a single byte of data. Listing 13-1 also creates specializations of `basic_string` using `char16_t`, `char32_t`, and the `wchar_t` data types. Two bytes are generally used to store `wchar_t` data types and always used to store `char16_t` and four bytes are used to store `char32_t` data.

147

The other important aspect of the lines in Listing 13-1 is the fact that they create type aliases. You've been using the `string` alias already in this book. What the alias has done is allow you to use the `string` keyword when declaring `string` variables rather than having to type the full typename, which would be `basic_string<char>`.

The concepts of template specialization and type aliases are all you need to understand about templates to be able to use the functionality provided by the STL.

> **Note** Type aliases are a modern feature of C++11. If your compiler does not support type aliases, you can use an older style. The code `typedef basic_string<char> string;` would serve a similar purpose.

Constructing Strings

The `basic_string` template provides many different types of constructors for creating instances of strings. Listing 13-2 shows how to create empty strings.

Listing 13-2. An Empty String

```
string emptyString;
```

Listing 13-3 shows how you can create strings from a C-style string literal.

Listing 13-3. A Literal String

```
string literalString{ "This is a literal string!" };
```

You can also use a copy constructor to copy a string as shown in Listing 13-4.

Listing 13-4. Copying a String

```
string copiedString{ literalString };
```

This example has copied the `literalString` from Listing 13-3 into `copiedString`. This means that both `literalString` and `copiedString` contain the literal "This is a literal string!". They are both still discrete copies, so any changes you make to one do not affect the other.

It's also possible to initialize new strings from substrings; that is, to specify the specific start position and optionally the number of characters you wish to copy. Listing 13-5 shows the possible substring initializers.

Listing 13-5. Initializing Strings with Substrings

```
string listerStartPosition{ "This is a literal string!", 5 };
string listerStartPositionAndNumber{ "This is a literal string!", 5, 4 };
```

This example will result in `literalStartPosition` containing "is a literal string!" and `literalStartPositionAndNumber` will contain "is a". This is because the start position 5 is passed into both and in the second line we also specify that we would only like to copy the next four characters.

Working with Strings

Once you have your data in a string object there are many different methods provided by basic_string that operate on the internal string data. The first set of useful functions allows you to ask and alter the string's size and capacity. Table 13-1 shows the different methods supplied to work with the size of your string data.

Table 13-1. basic_string Capacity Methods

Method	Description
n=str.size()	The number of letter elements in the string.
n=str.length()	Returns the same value as size().
n=str.max_size()	The maximum possible string length.
str.resize(n, c)	Resizes the string. If the size is shorter than before, trailing characters are lost. If the size is longer than before, the new elements are initialized to the supplied character.
str.resize(n)	Calls str.resize(n, '\0')
n=str.capacity()	Returns the amount of memory allocated to store the string.
str.reserve(n)	Asks the string to increase the capacity to at least the supplied value.
str.shrink_to_fit()	Asks the string to reduce the capacity to just large enough to fit the size of the string. Some implementations of basic_string allocate more memory than is needed in case you try to add more to the string later.
str.clear()	Removes the current string data and reduces size to 0 but might leave capacity unchanged.
b=str.empty()	Returns true if size() == 0.

Note: str is a string, n is a number, c is a single character, and b is a boolean.

This set of methods allows you to determine the size of your strings and the amount of memory being used by your string data. They also allow you to modify the memory requirements of your strings. Table 13-2 shows the methods you can use to modify your strings.

Table 13-2. basic_string Modifiers

Method	Description
str&=str.append(str)	Append a string to the current string.
str&=str.append(str, pos, n)	Append a substring starting at pos and n length to a string.
str&=str.append(cstr*)	Append a C-style string literal to a string.
str&=str.append(cstr*, n)	Append n characters from a C-style string.

Note: str is a string, cstr is a C-style string, c is a single character, and n is a number.

The methods in Table 13-2 show how you can append data to the end of an existing string. Each of the types also have a corresponding overloaded += operator, meaning that you can append to a string using code that resembles a normal arithmetic equation.

The same types are also supported by the assign methods. Where append adds the supplied text to the end of your strings, assign replaces the data in your string with the supplied text. The assign methods are also implemented as the overloaded = operators.

It's also possible to access individual characters in our string using the array operator. str[0] would return the first character of a given string. It's rare that you'll want to access string data in this manner, and the next section covers a more useful way of traversing string data.

Accessing String Data Through Iterators

Iterators are going to become second nature to you as you work with the STL. All of the data containers supplied by the STL use the iterator pattern to supply you access to their individual elements. In the case of a string, an iterator gives access to a single character in your string. You can use iterators to traverse the data structure forward and backward. Listing 13-6 shows how you can loop over a string and print out the individual characters using iterators.

Listing 13-6. Looping over a String

```
void StringIterators()
{
        using namespace std;

        string myString{ "This is my string!" };
        for (string::iterator iter = myString.begin(); iter != myString.end(); ++iter)
        {
                cout << *iter << endl;
        }
}
```

The type for a string iterator is string::iterator. The methods begin and end return iterators that represent the beginning and end of our string data. The iterator we declare is named iter and we can move to the next element in the string using the increment operator. You can see that we must *dereference* iter to gain access to the data that is contained at the current position in the string. It's also possible to decrement string::iterator and you can see this in action in Listing 13-7.

Listing 13-7. Decrementing string::iterator

```
for (string::iterator iter = myString.end()-1; iter != myString.begin(); --iter)
{
        cout << *iter << endl;
}
```

A better way to move backward through a string from end to beginning is to use string::reverse_ iterator, which you can see in Listing 13-8.

Listing 13-8. string::reverse_iterator

```
for (string::reverse_iterator iter = myString.rbegin(); iter != myString.rend(); ++iter)
{
        cout << *iter << endl;
}
```

The reverse_iterator is used with the methods rbegin and rend. Listing 13-9 shows the const versions of the iterators.

Listing 13-9. Const Iterators

```
for (string::const_iterator iter = myString.cbegin(); iter != myString.cend(); ++iter)
{
        cout << *iter << endl;
}

for (string::const_reverse_iterator iter = myString.crbegin();
        iter != myString.crend();
        ++iter)
{
        cout << *iter << endl;
}
```

Constant iterators are different from normal iterators in that you cannot modify the data to which they are pointing. Listing 13-10 shows how you could have modified the data pointed to by an iterator.

Listing 13-10. Using Iterators to Alter Data

```
for (string::iterator iter = myString.begin(); iter != myString.end(); ++iter)
{
        *iter = 'a';
        cout << *iter << endl;
}
```

This simple example shows how you can modify data through an iterator dereference. Trying to assign through a const_iterator would result in a compile error. If your loops are designed to only read from your collection using an iterator you should prefer a const_iterator to ensure that no mistakes are made that can alter your data.

There is also a more modern way of looping over all of the elements in an STL collection, the range-based for loop. You can use a range-based for loop with any C++ type that has a begin and end method; this includes classes that you write yourself. Listing 13-11 shows a range-based for loop with our string.

Listing 13-11. Range-Based for

```
for (char &letter : myString)
{
        cout << letter << endl;
}
```

This for loop allows you to alter the data at each element as the element is accessed through a reference variable. You can avoid this by making the type a const variable as shown in Listing 13-12.

Listing 13-12. Range-Based for with Constant Access

```
for (const char &letter : myString)
{
        cout << letter << endl;
}
```

A better way to write your range-based for loops might be to use the auto keyword as in Listing 13-13.

Listing 13-13. Using auto in Range-Based for Loops

```
for (auto &letter : myString)
{
        letter = 'a';
        cout << letter << endl;
}

for (const auto &letter : myString)
{
        cout << letter << endl;
}
```

If you were to do this, you would change the type of string template specialization without being required to change all of your range-based for loops. Listing 13-14 shows how auto can also be useful for standard for loops.

Listing 13-14. Using auto with Standard for Loops

```
for (auto iter = myString.begin(); iter != myString.end(); ++iter)
{
        cout << *iter << endl;
}

for (auto iter = myString.cbegin(); iter != myString.cend(); ++iter)
{
        cout << *iter << endl;
}
```

The auto keyword in these examples automatically detects if the iterator is constant or not. This saves you from having to use the correct type of iterator in your definitions, makes it easier to switch between string types, and still gives const correctness when using cbegin and cend.

Searching Within Strings

The C++ STL supplies methods to allow you to search for data within strings. Listing 13-15 gives you an example of the find method in action.

Listing 13-15. The `string::find` *Method*

```
string myString{ "This is my string!" };
void FindInString(string myString)
{
        size_t found = myString.find("is");
        if (found != string::npos)
        {
                cout << "\" is\" found at position: " << found << endl;
        }

        found = myString.find("is", found+1);
        if (found != string::npos)
        {
                cout << "is found at position: " << found << endl;
        }
}
```

The example in Listing 13-15 shows two different versions of found. The first finds the first instance of "is" in the `string` and returns the index where it can be found. This first call will return 2 for the is that makes up part of This. The `find` method will return the constant value `string::npos` if it fails to find the supplied data. We can then call `find` again and pass in the start position for the search. In our example we pass in the position of the previously found instance and add 1 to skip over it. This second call returns 5 when it finds the word is. The `rfind` method will carry out the same operation but search backward through the string and `myString.rfind("is")` would return 5. `rfind` can also take a position value to start working back from.

It's also possible to search for a single character in a supplied set using `find_first_of`. Listing 13-16 shows this method in action.

Listing 13-16. The `string::find_first_of` *Method*

```
found = myString.find_first_of("msg");
if (found != string::npos)
{
        cout << "is found at position: " << found << endl;
}
```

This method does not look for the entire phrase *msg*; instead it looks for *m, s,* and *g* individually. In our example the first of these characters is the s in This and therefore the method returns 3. There are also complementary methods `find_last_of`, `find_first_not_of`, and `find_last_not_of`. These methods behave as you would expect: `find_last_of` finds the last character in the supplied set, `find_first_not_of` finds the first character not in the set, and `find_last_not_of` finds the last character not in the set.

Formatting Data with stringstream

If you've used the C or C++ programming languages in the past, you might be familiar with the `printf` method for formatting string data. Even today many C++ programmers still use this older C-style method of formatting data for use within strings. This book, however, covers the more modern method for formatting string data, using `iostream` *modifiers*. You have already seen some examples of `iostream` modifiers in action. One of the most common modifiers is `std::endl` and earlier in the book you also used the `std::hex` and `std::showbase` modifiers with `cout`. Listing 13-17 shows a method that uses a `stringstream` to format data into a `string`.

Listing 13-17. stringstream Modifiers

```
#include <iostream>
#include <sstream>
#include <iomanip>
#include <ios>
void StringStreamExample()
{
        stringstream myStringStream;

        myStringStream << "Hi" << endl;

        cout << "width: " << myStringStream.width() << endl;
        myStringStream << 123 << endl;
        myStringStream << setw(10) << 123 << endl;
        myStringStream << setw(0) << 123 << endl;

        myStringStream << 123.567 << endl;
        myStringStream << setprecision(4) << 123.567 << endl;
        myStringStream << fixed << setprecision(2) << 123.567 << endl;
        myStringStream << defaultfloat << setprecision(0) << 123.567 << endl;

        myStringStream << 110 << endl << showbase;
        myStringStream << hex << 110 << endl;
        myStringStream << oct << 110 << endl;
        myStringStream << dec << 110 << endl << noshowbase;

        string myString = myStringStream.str();
        cout << myString;
}
```

You can see in Listing 13-17 that you can use a `stringstream` object in the same way we have been using the cout object to write to the console window. This means that all of the modifiers that are available to cout are also available to `stringstream` and later in the book you'll see how they're also available when writing and reading files.

The specific examples of modifiers that you can see in Listing 13-17 are the setw, setprecision, fixed, defaultfloat, showbase, noshowbase, hex, oct, and dec modifiers. The setw modifier ensures that the number specified is the minimum number of characters written to the stream. In this case we will write the value 123 and 7 padding characters, in this case spaces, into the stream. We clear the width by setting the value of the width back to 0.

The setprecision modifier is used to round numbers. This will round floating point values. The value of 4 in the example will round 123.567 to 123.6. When we use the fixed modifier, we are telling the stream to fix the number of decimal places using the value set by setprecision. Therefore << fixed << setprecision(2) will round our number to 123.57. The last line related to floating point values removes the fixed modifier by reinstating the defaultfloat setting and setting the precision back to its default value of 0.

We can also alter the way decimal numbers are represented by outputting them as hexadecimal values, octal values, or back to decimal values. We can also use the `showbase` and `noshowbase` to include or remove the 0x appendage on hexadecimal numbers or the 0 appendage on octal numbers.

The last operation shown with the stringstream is to obtain a string representation of the data we have created. This is necessary, as we cannot use a `stringstream` object as an input to `cout`. The `str` method is provided by the `stringstream` class for this purpose.

Summary

This chapter has given you an introduction to the STL string library. This is the first time you have had to consider how C++ uses templates to specialize generic code into specific implementations. This process is used throughout the STL and the `string` class is a perfect introduction to this concept. You've used strings in the examples contained in this book from the very beginning, which goes to show the flexibility and power of the ability of C++ ability to have generic code be hidden from programmers. Understanding how templates can be used in such a manner will give you an advantage over many programmers, as there are many who believe templates are too complex to be used in day-to-day code.

You've seen in this chapter how you can access and manipulate string data in C++ programs using the methods provided by STL rather than using the older C-style string methods. This can lead to your code being more robust, as the string class is a first class type in C++. As you've seen, C-style strings are nothing more than arrays that end with a null terminator and rely on convention to ensure that they are implemented properly. The `string` class avoids this problem by enforcing the proper null termination of strings without requiring the user to remember to accommodate them.

Another advantage to C++ strings is that the storage for string data is automatically handled by the class. When appending C-style strings, you would be responsible for allocating new arrays large enough to hold both strings and ensuring that the data are copied properly, deleted properly, and null terminated properly. This can lead to length functions when a single line of C++ code can carry out the same operation. Thanks to the nature of C++ and the STL we do not need to look at memory management topics until much later in this book.

You've also seen in this chapter that STL containers can be accessed through iterators. This is a common design pattern in C++ and all STL containers use the same access method. You will see this in action throughout the rest of this book, including in the next chapter, where we look at the STL `array` and `vector` containers.

Chapter 14

STL Array and Vector

You saw in Chapter 13 that the STL provides different types of `string` classes by specializing a template to create different implementations. This is where the template part of the STL comes from. The STL `string` classes are what we call *containers*, because they store string data. In this chapter you will see two more of the STL's containers in the `array` and `vector` templates.

STL's array class can be used in place of the built-in array types that you have seen earlier in this book. This allows you to use arrays in the same way you would use other STL containers; for example, the STL array template provides `iterator` access to the array elements. The size of an STL array is still determined at compile time. Sometimes you might not know how many elements you will need to store in your collection, and this is where the `vector` template is useful. A `vector` stores any number of elements and can dynamically grow and shrink to accommodate more or less items at runtime. Let's take a look at how these templates can be used.

The STL Array Template

Before we get into STL arrays, it is worth remembering how to define a traditional C-style array in C++, as shown in Listing 14-1.

Listing 14-1. A Traditional C-Style Array

```
const unsigned int ARRAY_SIZE = 5;
int oldArray[ARRAY_SIZE] = { 0, 1, 2, 3, 4 };
```

Hopefully you find that familiar. Listing 14-2 shows how you can construct an array holding the same values using a C++ STL array container.

Listing 14-2. An STL array Container

```
const unsigned int ARRAY_SIZE = 5;
std::array<int, ARRAY_SIZE> newArray = { 0, 1, 2, 3, 4 };
```

As you can see, the syntax changes a bit when using an STL array. You can see the now familiar template specialization syntax at work. The first template parameter tells the compiler that you would like to use the int type for storing the values in our array. The second parameter then tells the compiler how many elements we would like our array to hold. Now that you know how to create arrays using the STL array template, I can show you some examples of why this is desirable over using standard C-style arrays. Listing 14-3 shows several examples of different ways you can use to find elements in an array.

Listing 14-3. Searching in an array

```
using MyArray = std::array<int, ARRAY_SIZE>;
void FindInArray(MyArray myArray)
{
        for (unsigned int i = 0; i < ARRAY_SIZE; ++i)
        {
                if (myArray[i] == 2)
                {
                        cout << "Found: " << myArray[i]
                                << " at position: " << i << endl;
                }
        }

        for (auto iter=myArray.begin(); iter!=myArray.end(); ++iter)
        {
                if (*iter == 2)
                {
                        cout << "Found: " << *iter << endl;
                }
        }

        for (auto& number : myArray)
        {
                if (number == 2)
                {
                        cout << "Found : " << number << endl;
                }
        }

        MyArray::iterator found = find(myArray.begin(), myArray.end(), 2);
        if (found != myArray.end())
        {
                cout << "Found : " << *found << endl;
        }
}
```

The very first line in Listing 14-3 creates a *type alias* for our array type. You get a benefit when using type aliases with template specializations in two ways. First it means that you do not have to type out the full template specialization each time you wish to refer to that type. It also means that if you need to change the type that you only have to change it in the type alias and it will apply to all of the places where the type alias is used. The alias MyArray can now be used in place of std::array<int, ARRAY_SIZE> everywhere in our code.

The first for loop in Listing 14-3 shows the standard method for looping through array elements. This syntax is the same whether looping over a C-style array or when using the STL array template.

The second loop uses iterators in the same manner as you saw when looping over the characters in your strings in Chapter 13. You can then also see the range-based for loop used.

The last example is something a little different: It uses an STL *algorithm* to find the element we would like in the array. You have already seen that the STL provides containers that you can use to store elements and now you can see that the STL also provides algorithms that operate on those containers. This algorithm is the find and it works by taking an iterator marking the beginning of a range and an iterator marking the end of a range as well as the value we wish to search for. The beginning and end iterators supplied to find do not have to be the beginning and end iterators from your collection; they could have been the second and third iterators from our array. The find function returns an iterator to the first element that matches the supplied value. If no values match, it returns the end iterator that you passed in. You can see this result tested in the if statement following the find call.

The STL Vector Class

The STL array takes a size parameter that tells the compiler exactly how big we need the array to be before our program ever runs. However, we might not always know how many elements we will need. When this is the case, we can use the STL vector template. Listing 14-4 shows how you can specialize vector.

Listing 14-4. Specializing STL vector

```
using namespace std;
using MyVector = vector<int>;
MyVector myVector = { 0, 1, 2 };
myVector.push_back(3);
myVector.push_back(4);
```

Listing 14-4 shows that you can add new values to a vector even after it has been initialized. The vector automatically resizes itself if it needs more memory to store the new element. You can also insert elements into other places in a vector and erase elements. Listing 14-5 shows how this is done.

Listing 14-5. vector insert and erase

```
MyVector::const_iterator iter = myVector.cbegin() + 1;
myVector.insert(iter, 5);
myVector.erase(iter);
```

The insert and erase methods take a constant iterator to the position where we would like the insert and remove operator to take place. The insert shown in Listing 14-5 would result in our vector storing the values 0, 5, 1, 2, 3, 4 in that order, and the erase would remove from the same location, which would remove the 5. It does not remove the 1, as the iterator points to the second location in the vector, which is occupied by 5 after the insert. Each element after that location has moved one position to the right.

You'll be glad to know that thanks to the standardization of the STL, the loops we looked at in Listing 14-3 with the STL array also work in exactly the same way for the vector template. Listing 14-6 shows these vector loops.

Listing 14-6. Finding Values in a vector

```
void FindInVector(MyVector myVector)
{
        for (unsigned int i = 0; i < myVector.size(); ++i)
        {
                if (myVector[i] == 2)
                {
                        cout << "Found: " << myVector[i]
                                << " at position: " << i << endl;
                }
        }

        for (auto iter = myVector.begin(); iter != myVector.end(); ++iter)
        {
                if (*iter == 2)
                {
                        cout << "Found: " << *iter << endl;
                }
        }

        for (auto& number : myVector)
        {
                if (number == 2)
                {
                        cout << "Found : " << number << endl;
                }
        }

        MyVector::iterator found = find(myVector.begin(), myVector.end(), 2);
        if (found != myVector.end())
        {
                cout << "Found : " << *found << endl;
        }
}
```

Sorting Arrays and Vectors

The STL provides many different algorithms that can operate on your data, and one of the more useful is sort. This algorithm does exactly what you think it might: It sorts elements into order. The sort function takes an iterator to the first and last elements of the range we would like to sort and can optionally take a function to determine the sort order. Listing 14-7 shows this in action.

Listing 14-7. std::sort

```
bool Descending(int first, int second)
{
        return first > second;
}

void SortVector()
{
        MyVector myVector = { 0, 1, 2, 3, 4 };

        sort(myVector.begin(), myVector.end(), Descending);
        for (auto& value : myVector)
        {
                cout << value << endl;
        }

        sort(myVector.begin(), myVector.end());
        for (auto& value : myVector)
        {
                cout << value << endl;
        }
}
```

The first call to sort reverses the order of our vector. This is achieved by the Descending function. If this supplied function returns true, the elements are left in the current order; if it returns false, the elements are switched. A practical example would be the elements 0 and 1. When these two numbers are compared, 0 > 1 is false; therefore the elements would be switched to 1, 0, which is what we want.

The second sort call does not take a comparison function as a parameter, so by default this would use the comparison first < second.

Summary

The fact that the code in Listings 14-3 and 14-6 is identical other than for the types passed into the function is a perfect example of the flexibility of the STL. The STL containers are written to be interchangeable and the correct container should be used for the correct purpose.

You have seen in this chapter that you can replace your use of C-style arrays with STL array with no impacts on any of the code you are writing. You can still use the [ ] operator to access values. However, the STL implementation of array also allows you to use the powerful iterators and algorithms that it supplies to coexist with the container classes.

The array should be used any time you have a collection of values to store and you know the exact number you will need at compile time. If you need a collection that can grow or shrink as your program runs, you should use the vector.

Both of these containers are excellent at storing sets of data that you plan to access in a linear fashion as the data is stored together in memory. They do have some drawbacks, however. The array container cannot be resized, which means you need to know at compile time how many elements you would like to store. The vector stores its data internally inside an array. When you add elements and the vector requires more room it will create another array, usually double the size of the current array and copy all of the elements from the old array to the new array. In the next chapter we will look at another linear STL container, the List, which can be used when you need to add and remove elements to a linear collection often without having to worry about the resize performance required by a vector.

Chapter 15

STL List

The STL `list` template is another linear data collection. The previous chapter briefly mentioned the difference between `array`, `vector`, and `list`, and this chapter goes into more detail about why and when you would use these different collections. The main point to remember is that you should always use the correct tool for the job at hand. Video games rely on extracting the most performance possible from the target hardware, and access times to data in collections is a major bottleneck with modern processors. This chapter shows you how to build your own `list` class in an effort to help you understand the difference between arrays and linked lists.

Understanding Array and List Memory Layouts

An array is a very efficient method for storing a fixed number of elements. The compiler will pack each of the elements in your array into a *contiguous* block of memory. You can see this contiguous memory in action when you work with pointers to arrays and you move between array elements using pointer arithmetic. As integers are usually 4 bytes in size, you can move from one integer to the next in an array by adding 4 bytes to the current memory address for the element you have a pointer to. The same happens when we are working with arrays of any given type: The compiler can automatically work out the number of bytes required to represent the type and move between elements efficiently.

This contiguous memory access suits modern processors due to their use of cache memory. A processor can calculate arithmetic and other instructions at a much faster rate than it can read from memory. To combat this, processors read from memory in blocks known as cache lines into an on-die fast memory. It's not uncommon for processors to read in blocks of 64 or 128 bytes. Even if you need to read only 4 bytes of memory to access an integer, the processor will read a full cache line. This means that array accesses are very efficient on modern processors because whole chunks of an array can be read into the processor's cache when you access the first element in the array.

The problem with arrays arises when you do not know exactly how many elements you need at compile time. Compilers require you to inform them of how many elements will be in your array so that they can allocate the proper memory for storage. The vector class provides a resizable array, but this is a little bit of a trick. The vector works by providing more storage than you actually need when the vector is initialized. If you add more elements than the vector currently has capacity for, the template requests a new array from the operating system, which is usually double the size of the current capacity. The vector then copies all of the elements from the old array into the new array. If you are doing this resizing often, a vector can prove to be a fairly slow container.

A linked list, on the other, hand does not store its elements in a contiguous block of memory. Instead each element in the list stores a pointer to the next and previous elements in order. This provides a container that is resizable and can provide for fast inserting and removal of elements in the list. However, because the list is noncontiguous in memory, the processor cannot use its cache as effectively when traversing the list. Many C++ courses like to teach the list, as it's a good introduction to data structures. Unfortunately for game developers, the list is rarely a good choice for code that you would like to perform as efficiently as possible due to the cache implications. This chapter shows you how to create your own list and how to use the STL list, but you should always keep the memory and cache implications in mind.

Building a List Class

Building a linked list is a fairly straightforward process once you understand how to use pointers. If you need to recap what pointers are and how they work, I suggest that you reread Chapter 4 before continuing. Listing 15-1 shows the ListNode class.

Listing 15-1. ListNode

```cpp
class ListNode
{
private:
        void* m_Data = nullptr;
        ListNode* m_Last = nullptr;
        ListNode* m_Next = nullptr;

public:
        ListNode(void* data)
        : m_Data{data}
        {
        }

        void* GetData()
        {
                return m_Data;
        }

        void SetLast(ListNode* last)
        {
                m_Last = last;
        }
```

```
        ListNode* GetLast()
        {
                return m_Last;
        }

        void SetNext(ListNode* next)
        {
                m_Next = next;
        }

        ListNode* GetNext()
        {
                return m_Next;
        }
};
```

Listing 15-1 represents a very basic implementation of a double linked list. A single linked list would only have pointers to the next element in the list, but our `ListNode` class has pointers to both the next and the previous nodes. `ListNode` also stores a `void*` to the data that the node represents. A better way to implement this would have been to create our own templates, and I'll begin to cover how to do this in Part 4 of this book. You'll get a better appreciation of how the class operates by looking at some code that puts it to use, such as in Listing 15-2.

Listing 15-2. Using ListNode

```
void OurList()
{
        unsigned int firstData = 1;
        ListNode first(&firstData);

        unsigned int secondData = 2;
        ListNode second(&secondData);

        unsigned int thirdData = 3;
        ListNode third(&thirdData);

        first.SetNext(&second);

        second.SetLast(&first);
        second.SetNext(&third);

        third.SetLast(&third);

        for (ListNode* iter = &first; iter != nullptr; iter = iter->GetNext())
        {
                unsigned int* number = static_cast<unsigned int*>(iter->GetData());
                cout << *number << endl;
        }
}
```

The OurList function creates three nodes to add to our list, each storing an unsigned int to illustrate the result when we loop over the list. What you can see is that the m_Next pointer of first is set to point to the ListNode second. In turn second points back to first and forward to third and third points back to second.

The for loop in the function then traverses the list and prints the value stored by each. It does this by faking an iterator to the list. In fact, all we do is get a pointer to first, then have the iter pointer be updated to iter->GetNext() each time the loop iterates. Eventually we get to third's m_Next pointer, which will be set to nullptr, and the loop ends. At this point you could delve deeper into implementing your own lists; however, I would recommend sticking to the STL list template. All of the features you might like in a list have already been implemented and the STL list is compatible with all of the iterator types and algorithms that also support other STL containers.

The STL List Template

You will not be surprised to hear that STL's list syntax is very similar to that of vector. You can see this in Listing 15-3.

Listing 15-3. STL list

```
using namespace std;
using MyList = list<int>;

MyList myList = { 0, 1, 2 };
myList.push_back(3);
myList.push_back(4);
MyList::const_iterator iter = myList.cbegin();
++iter;
Iter = myList.insert(iter, 5);
myList.erase(iter);
```

There is only a single difference between this code when using a list compared to using a vector: list iterators cannot be modified using the + and - operators. Instead we get the iterator and then use the ++ or -- operators to move to the position in the list where we would like to insert or erase elements. The iterator we have also remains pointing to the same element after we insert into myList. To be able to remove the correct element we had to catch the new iterator returned by the insert method.

The last major difference in usage between list and vector is that the [] operator is not supported by list. This makes sense if you think back to the way that these containers store their elements in memory. Generally vector is implemented using arrays internally, which means that it's easy to use the [] operator and pointer arithmetic to offset into the array to get the proper element for a given index. This operation doesn't make any sense for a list where the underlying implementation does not store elements contiguously in memory.

STL's list implementation supports all of the same iterator types and the find algorithm that we looked at in Chapter 14. The sort function is a little different and is implemented as a method rather than a stand-alone function. Listing 15-4 shows the list::sort method in action.

Listing 15-4. `list::sort`

```
bool Descending(int first, int second)
{
        return first > second;
}

void SortList()
{
        MyList myList = { 0, 1, 2, 3, 4 };
        myList.sort(Descending);
        for (auto& value : myList)
        {
                cout << value << endl;
        }

        cout << endl;

        myList.sort();
        for (auto& value : myList)
        {
                cout << value << endl;
        }
}
```

The implication of this difference is that you cannot sort ranges of values within the list; you can only sort the entire list at once.

Summary

This chapter has shown you how you can use the STL list template. I began by discussing the differences between the way array, vector, and list store their elements in memory, along with a basic explanation of how these differences affect the performance of the different containers.

I then covered how you could create your own very basic list implementation to help you understand how the list behaves differently than an array or vector at a code level. Finally we looked at how the STL list shares some iterator and algorithm types with array and vector, but also how it differs with respect to the array operator and the sort method.

The next chapter covers four more STL containers: set, map, unordered_set, and unordered_map. These containers provide slight variations on the binary search tree and hash map data structures and are very useful when you need to sort and access very large sets of data.

Chapter 16

STL's Associative Containers

All of the STL containers you have seen so far have stored individual data elements. In this chapter you will be introduced to associative containers. These containers associate a key with the data values that you are inserting. In the case of the map and unordered_map containers, you are required to supply a value to use as the key, whereas the set and unordered_set containers automatically generate keys from the data you supply. I'll explain the differences between each of these containers as I work through some examples in this chapter, beginningwith the set container.

The STL set Container

You won't be surprised to find out that a set is a template class and you are required to specialize the set container to store the types you require. Listing 16-1 gives an example of how you can specialize the set template.

Listing 16-1. Specializing set

```
using namespace std;
using MySet = set<int>;
```

Once you have specialized a set template you can initialize a container in the same manner as other STL containers. Listing 16-2 shows how you can create and add values to a set.

Listing 16-2. Initializing and Adding to set Containers

```
MySet mySet = { 2, 1, 0 };
mySet.emplace(4);
mySet.insert(3);
```

There are two important aspects of Listing 16-2 to which you should pay particular attention. The first is the emplace method used. This method has the same result as the insert method in that the value will be added to the set. However, emplace is actually faster at achieving this than insert in some circumstances. It achieves this speed improvement by avoiding a copy construction when using a set with class types. You should always use emplace rather than insert with all containers when it is available.

The second important aspect is the values we are adding to the set. The first curious feature is that the numbers are not in order. A set will automatically sort the values as they are added, which is one of the reasons you might consider using a set rather than an array, vector, or list. After the final line that inserts the value 3, the set will contain the numbers 0, 1, 2, 3, and 4 in order. The other important feature of the values is that they are all unique. If we had tried to add duplicate values to the set, they would be ignored. This is important to remember and is different to the behavior of array, vector, and list, which would allow you to add duplicate values.

The sample code that accompanies this chapter shows examples of using a set with iterators and the STL find algorithm. This code is identical to the iterator-based and range-based for loops that you have seen with previous containers in Chapters 14 and 15. Hopefully you have begun to get the hang of how to access elements in STL containers.

The next container I will show you is map. A map is conceptually similar to a set, but it requires that you provide a key along with your data.

The STL map Container

All of the containers you have seen so far take a single value and store these individual values at discrete locations. The map container is different: It requires that you supply a key along with the value to be stored. You then use this key to retrieve the value from the map. When inserting elements into a map, you are required to supply the values using the pair template. Listing 16-3 shows the template specializations for the map and pair templates.

Listing 16-3. Specializing map and pair

```
using namespace std;
using MyMap = map<int, string>;
using MyPair = pair<int, string>;
```

The map and the pair templates are supplied matching parameters to ensure that we are adding the correct types to the map. If we tried to supply the wrong types to a map, the compiler would generate an error.

You can see in Listing 16-4 just how we add elements to our map.

Listing 16-4. Adding Elements to a map

```
MyMap myMap = { { 2, "Two" }, { 1, "One" }, { 0, "Zero" } };

MyPair node{ 4, "Four" };
myMap.insert(node);

myMap.emplace( 3, "Three" );
```

The definition of a map can take a list of pairs that should be in the map at the time of its creation. In this example we have added pairs representing the values Zero, One, and Two, along with their respective integer representations as keys.

The insert method requires the use of our pair template to add values to myMap. You can see that we first construct the MyPair object node with the key 4 and value Four. After this, I've added an example of the emplace method. You can see how it can be more efficient to use emplace compared with insert in this example. You can leave out the creation of the pair object and a subsequent copy from the pair into the map by using emplace. The map shares a property with set: Both containers sort their values as they are entered. A map container will sort the keys into order as the elements are entered. This is the reason you would use a map rather than a set. If you have a complex class that you would like to store objects of in a map then the sorting and retrieval of these objects would be more efficient if you supplied simple data types such as integers as keys. It would also be possible to store two objects that are identical into a map by giving both objects different keys, as only the keys in a map are required to be unique.

Unsurprisingly, a map cannot be iterated with exactly the same code as some of the other containers, as it stores elements as key–value pairs and our loops must take this into account. Listing 16-5 shows an example of how we can loop over all of the elements stored in a map.

Listing 16-5. Looping over a map

```
for (const auto& node : myMap)
{
        cout << "First: " << node.first << " Second: " << node.second << endl;
}
```

The for loop itself is the same and C++ has allowed us to abstract out the MyPair type by using the auto keyword in its place. You can access the key and value stored in a pair using the first and second variables. The first variable stores the key and second stores the value.

The find method also supplies an iterator to a map that represents a pair element, as you can see in Listing 16-6.

Listing 16-6. Using map::find

```
MyMap::iterator found = myMap.find(2);
if (found != myMap.end())
{
        cout << "Found First: " << found->first << " Second: " << found->second << endl;
}
```

To find a value in a map you can use the find method on the map itself, not the stand-alone find algorithm. The find method takes the key you wish to search for as a parameter and if that key does not exist, the end element of the map is returned.

Binary Search Trees

At this point we have covered five different STL containers. In the previous chapter I explained the difference between the way a list and a vector are implemented. set and map are also implemented differently to the linear containers. The map and set containers are implemented as binary search trees.

A node in a binary search tree stores pointers to two nodes, one to the left and one to the right. Figure 16-1 shows a visual representation of a tree.

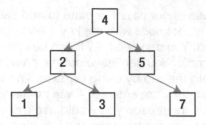

Figure 16-1. A binary search tree

The binary search tree stores the tree in a sorted order to make it a very efficient structure when looking up nodes. The *head* node of the tree in Figure 16-1 stores the value 4. If we were looking for the node that stores the value 2, we would begin by comparing 2 against the value at the head, which is 4. If our search value is equal to the current node, we have found our value. If it is lower we move to the left node; if it is higher we move to the right node. As 2 is less than 4, in our example we would move to the left node. We would then repeat this process at the new node. We compare first to the value of the node, and 2 equals 2, so we know that we have found the node we were searching for.

The process of repeating the same operation over and over like this is known as *recursion*. We generally implement recursive algorithms using functions that call themselves. Listing 16-7 shows an implementation of a simple `TreeNode` class that can be used to recursively search a binary tree structure.

Listing 16-7. A simple `TreeNode`

```
class TreeNode
{
private:
int m_value;

TreeNode* m_pLeft = nullptr;
TreeNode* m_pRight = nullptr;
public:
TreeNode(int value)
: m_value{value}
{}

TreeNode* Find(int searchValue)
{
TreeNode* pResult = nullptr;

if (m_value == searchValue)
{
pResult = this;
}
else if (m_pLeft != nullptr && m_value > searchValue)
{
pResult = m_pLeft->Find(searchValue);
}
else if (m_pRight != nullptr && m_value < searchValue)
```

```
{
pResult = m_pRight->Find(searchValue);
}

return pResult;
}
};
```

All of the code you need to search for a value inside a binary search tree is contained within the Find method in Listing 16-7. If you imagine that we have used this class to represent the tree in Figure 16-1, then you would have a pointer to the tree *head* node stored in our program. You can then call Find on this node and pass it a value to search for.

If we pass in 1, the first if statement in Find would fail. The second if statement would pass so we would return the result of m_pLeft->Find. This call to find would follow the same process: The first if would fail and we would return the result of m_pLeft->Find. This call to find will see the first if statement pass, so we do not call another function; we simply return this. At this point, all of our function calls will unwind. Our last call to Find returns this to the second call to Find, which returns the pointer to the first call to Find, which finally returns it back to the variable being assigned.

Searching for values in a binary tree is, generally, a faster operation than searching through an array, vector, or list. In those collections you would have to potentially compare against every element if the value you were looking for was at the very end of the collection. A binary search tree is much more efficient. In Figure 16-1 we would only ever have to make 3 comparisons to search against 7 different values. If we were to add another level to the tree, we would have 4 comparisons to make against 15 different values, and another layer would be 5 comparisons for 31 values. You can see how quickly these numbers are rising for each level in a binary search tree.

> **Note**   Recursion can be a complicated topic for beginning programmers to understand as it ties in with the concept of the program stack. We'll cover more about this stack in Chapter 22.

The other major algorithm for traversing a collection is called *iteration.* You have already seen multiple examples of iteration in action and the iterator types you have seen in use take their name from this algorithm. Iterating a binary search tree involves visiting each node in turn, and you can use iterators on a set and a map to visit each element in order.

Binary search trees are one way to store data in associative containers, and another is to use a hash map.

Fast Data Access Using a Hash Map

A binary search tree structure provides fast access to sorted data. The tree is automatically sorted when adding data and you've seen how a search of that data can be done very quickly. It is possible to use an even faster structure than a binary search tree when you do not need to iterate over sorted data. A hash map has a constant time insert and retrieval of a value. This means that it will take the same length of time to insert the first element as it will to insert the tenth or the millionth. It also has a constant time retrieval of data. This means that finding data in a container does not increase the time elapsed along with the number of elements the container holds.

Hash maps achieve this by turning the key into a hash value and then using that hash to store the data in an appropriate bucket. The process of writing a hash map is a complicated task, but luckily for us the STL provides us with two ready-made hash map containers, the unordered_set and the unordered_map.

STL `unordered_set` and `unordered_map`

The code for unordered_set and unordered_map is going to look very familiar. Listing 16-8 shows how you can specialize these templates.

Listing 16-8. Specializing unordered_set and unordered_map

```
using namespace std;
using MyUnorderedSet = unordered_set<int>;
using MyUnorderedMap = unordered_map<int, string>;
using MyPair = pair<int, string>;
```

The unordered_set and unordered_map container templates take the same parameters as the set and map containers. The unordered_set stores a value and calculates the key automatically for the value,whereas the unordered_map requires that you specify the type to use for the key followed by the type for the value.

You can then initialize and add elements to these containers in the same way you did before, as Listing 16-9 shows.

Listing 16-9. Initializing and Adding to unordered_set and unordered_map

```
MyUnorderedSet myUnorderedSet = { 2, 1, 0 };
myUnorderedSet.emplace(4);
myUnorderedSet.insert(3);

MyUnorderedMap myUnorderedMap = { { 2, "Two" }, { 1, "One" }, { 0, "Zero" } };
myUnorderedMap.emplace(3, "Three");
MyPair node{ 4, "Four" };
myUnorderedMap.insert(node);
```

The code to find elements in an unordered_set is similar to what you have seen previously, either using the find algorithm or the find method. Listing 16-10 shows both versions.

Listing 16-10. Using find with unordered_set

```
MyUnorderedSet::iterator found = find(myUnorderedSet.begin(), myUnorderedSet.end(), 2);
if (found != myUnorderedSet.end())
{
cout << "Found : " << *found << endl;
}

found = myUnorderedSet.find(2);
if (found != myUnorderedSet.end())
{
cout << "Found : " << *found << endl;
}
```

Values in an unordered_map are accessed a little differently. You will have to use either the [ ] operator or the at method. Both are shown in Listing 16-11.

Listing 16-11. Using [ ] and at

```
string& myString = myUnorderedMap[2];
cout << "Found : " << myString << endl;

myString = myUnorderedMap.at(2);
cout << "Found : "<< myString << endl;
```

These methods differ in a very significant way. The [ ] operator can be used to insert or retrieve values from an unordered_map. If the key 2 had not existed in myUnorderedMap, a new string would have been added to the map and its reference returned. If the key did already exist, the current string would have been returned. The at method never adds a new element to our unordered_map, instead it throws an exception. Listing 16-12 shows how you can update the at call to handle exceptions.

Listing 16-12. Handling Exceptions

```
try
{
string& myString = myUnorderedMap.at(5);
cout << "Found : " << myString << endl;
}
catch (const std::out_of_range& outOfRange)
{
cout << "Out of range error: " << outOfRange.what() << endl;
}
```

Your program would have crashed with an unhandled exception error if you had called this code without the try...catch block. Throwing your own exceptions is as easy as using the throw keyword, as you can see in Listing 16-13.

Listing 16-13. Throwing Exceptions

```
void ExceptionExample()
{
if (true)
{
throw -1;
}
}
```

Catching an exception from this method is shown in Listing 16-14.

Listing 16-14. Catching Exceptions

```
try
{
ExceptionExample();
}
catch (int errorValue)
{
cout << "Error: " << errorValue << endl;
}
```

> **Note**   You'll see the unordered_map put to practical use in Chapter 21, which covers an EventManager class that stores Event objects keyed by a unique ID value.

Summary

This chapter has introduced you to STL containers based on binary search trees and the hash maps. These containers provide alternatives to the other containers, which are of particular benefit when you are dealing with large sets of data. The set and map containers are useful when you need to have data that is regularly iterated over and you need to be in order, but you also need to find individual elements regularly. The unordered_set and unordered_mapcontainers are useful when you need to know that inserting and retrieving values will always take the same length of time to execute and you do not need the data to be sorted.

The next chapter introduces you to the stack and queue containers. These containers are more specialized versions of existing data structures. Stacks can be used to add and remove elements from the top of the container, whereas queues act in a first in, first out manner.

Chapter 17

STL's Stack and Queue

The STL containers you have seen so far have all provided options for storing and retrieving values and are suited to different circumstances. The stack and queue containers are designed for different reasons. Although they do store values, their behavior is much more important. I'll show you exactly how these containers behave in this chapter.

> **Note** The game examples in this book don't use these containers, but I didn't want to leave them out. You might find a stack useful in a game where you are building a UI system and want to track the path to the current screen. I've also found a queue to be useful in event systems where you wish to process events in the exact order in which they were received.

The STL stack Container

The stack container is used when you would like a container that can only be accessed in a last in, first out behavior. You can think of this like a tower of blocks. When you place a block onto a tower, that is the only block you can then remove. Hopefully you can see how this container is useful more for its behavior than for its ability to contain values. Listing 17-1 shows how you can specialize the stack container.

Listing 17-1. Specializing the stack Container

```
using namespace std;
using MyStack = stack<int>;
```

You should be growing comfortable with the syntax used when specializing templates. Listing 17-2 shows how we can create an instance of a stack and add values to it.

Listing 17-2. Creating a stack and Adding Values

```
MyStack myStack;
myStack.emplace(0);
myStack.push(1);
myStack.push(2);
```

The stack provides a push method to push values onto the top of the stack. Once again you can see that this container also has the more optimal emplace method, which provides a faster way to place elements onto the top.

Now that you have values in a stack, you cannot access the data using array operators or iterators, as that would break the last in, first out behavior the stack provides. Instead the stack provides the top method, which you can see in use in Listing 17-3.

Listing 17-3. Using stack::top

```
cout << "Top of the stack: " << myStack.top() << endl;
```

The code in Listing 17-3 would print the number 2. When you decide that you no longer need the value on the top of the stack, you use the pop method to remove the top element from the stack. This is shown in Listing 17-4.

Listing 17-4. Using stack::pop

```
myStack.pop();

cout << "Top of the stack: " << myStack.top() << endl;
```

The cout call in Listing 17-4 would print the number 2 to your console. You can push and pop values to and from a stack as often as you deem necessary. The last remaining important call on a stack is the empty method. A call to myStack.empty() would return a boolthat when true means that your stack contains no values.

That's all there is to know about the stack container. The queue container is very similar but provides first in, first out access to its elements.

The STL queue Container

Whereas the stack provides last in, first out access, the queue container provides first in, first out access. You can visualize this as being like a conveyor belt. The first item you place onto the belt will be the first item to reach the end of the belt and each subsequent added item will arrive in that order. Listing 17-5 shows all of the code you need to use a queue container.

Listing 17-5. The queue Container

```
using namespace std;
using MyQueue = queue<int>;

MyQueue myQueue;
myQueue.emplace(0);
myQueue.emplace(1);
myQueue.emplace(2);

cout << "Front of the queue: " << myQueue.front() << endl;

myQueue.pop();
```

The call to front in Listing 17-5 would print 0 to the console. After the call to pop, a call to front would result in 1 being returned. The queue class also provides a back method to retrieve the last element in a queue, but you cannot remove this element. I haven't shown this method in action, as I have never found much use for it. The queue container is used for its first in, first out properties.

Summary

This chapter was short and sweet. The stack and queue containers are much more limited than other containers. Although their purpose is to store elements in a manner similar to the other containers provided by the STL, they are actually designed to provide restrictions on how you can access their elements.

The stack provides a last in, first out access pattern, whereas the queue provides a first in, first out pattern.

The next chapter covers the last type of STL container you will see in this book, the bitset.

Chapter 18

STL's bitset

The last STL container type object that I cover is the `bitset`. I say STL *type* because the `bitset` is not strictly a container. It does not support iterators, the range-based `for` loops, or STL's algorithms. A `bitset` is used for tracking individual `boolean` values in a combined set. A traditional method for achieving the same result are *flags* implemented using bitwise operators and shifts.

Creating bitset Objects

A `bitset` is yet another template provided by the STL. A major difference between a `bitset` and other STL containers is that you are not required to specify a type for the `bitset`. You can see in Listing 18-1 that the only parameter taken by the template is the number of bit flags we would like the `bitset` to contain.

Listing 18-1. Specializing bitset

```
#include <bitset>

using namespace std;

namespace
{
        const unsigned int NUMBER_OF_BITS = 5;
}

using MyBitset = bitset<NUMBER_OF_BITS>;
```

This code allows us to create `bitset`s that consist of 5 bits. We could create a `bitset` containing more or fewer bits by altering the value passed into the template.

Listing 18-2 shows the different constructors you can use to initialize bitsets.

Listing 18-2. bitset Constructors

```
MyBitset defaultConstructor;
MyBitset unsignedLongConstructor{ 0x17 };
MyBitset stringConstructor{ string{ "11011" } };
```

There are three constructors you can use. The first is the default constructor, which initializes all bits to zero. The second constructor uses an unsigned long to initialize the bits. In this example, I have used a literal value to pass into the constructor. The last constructor takes a string containing 1s and 0s representing the value you wish each bit to contain.

Working with bitsets

A bitset provides methods to carry out several different operations. These can be split into methods that query the current state of the bitset and methods that are used to alter the bits. Listing 18-3 shows the methods you can use to gather information about your bitset.

Listing 18-3. Querying bitsets

```
cout << boolalpha;

cout << "Size of the bitset: " << stringConstructor.size() << endl;
cout << "Number of set bits: " << stringConstructor.count() << endl;

cout << "Is any bit set? " << stringConstructor.any() << endl;
cout << "Are all bits set? " << stringConstructor.all () << endl;
cout << "Are no bits set? " << stringConstructor.none() << endl;

for (unsigned int i = 0; i < stringConstructor.size(); ++i)
{
        cout << "Bit " << i << " value: " << stringConstructor[i] << endl;
        cout << "Bit " << i << " test: " << stringConstructor.test(i) << endl;
}
```

The bitset template provides methods to query the size and count of a bitset. The size method should return the size you passed into the template and count will return the number of bits that you have set to true. Figure 18-1 shows the output you can expect to see when you execute the code from Listing 18-3.

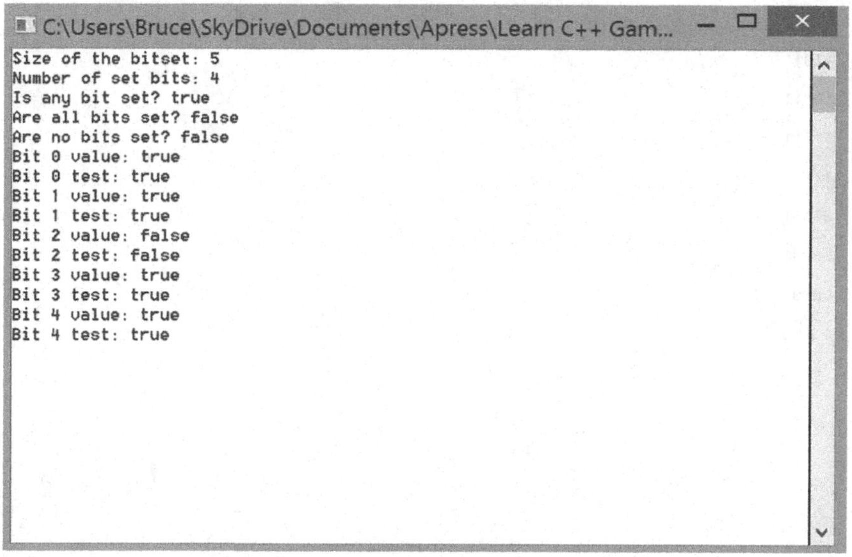

```
C:\Users\Bruce\SkyDrive\Documents\Apress\Learn C++ Gam...   –   ☐   ✕
Size of the bitset: 5
Number of set bits: 4
Is any bit set? true
Are all bits set? false
Are no bits set? false
Bit 0 value: true
Bit 0 test: true
Bit 1 value: true
Bit 1 test: true
Bit 2 value: false
Bit 2 test: false
Bit 3 value: true
Bit 3 test: true
Bit 4 value: true
Bit 4 test: true
```

Figure 18-1. The output generated by executing the code in Listing 18-3

There are also helper methods that can tell you if any, all, or none of the bits are set. Finally you can see two methods to query the status of individual bits. You can either use the array operator and index or you can use the test method.

There are three methods supplied that allow you to alter the values stored in the bitset. These are shown in Listing 18-4.

Listing 18-4. Altering Bits

```
stringConstructor.set(1, false);
stringConstructor.set(1);
stringConstructor.set();

stringConstructor.reset(0);
stringConstructor.reset();

stringConstructor.flip(4);
stringConstructor.flip();
```

The three methods are set, reset, and flip. Figure 18-2 shows the results of these lines of code in the order in which they appear in Listing 18-4.

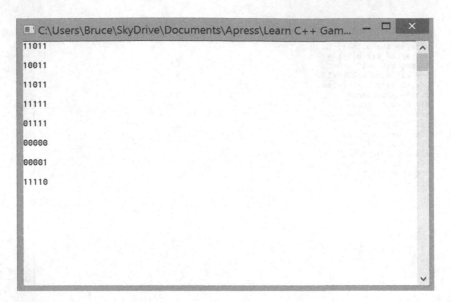

Figure 18-2. The results from the code in Listing 18-4

The set method has been overloaded to provide different functionality. The first example takes a bit index and a value to set the bit to. The second takes just an index, and this method will then set the given bit to 1. The final version of set will make all of the bits in the set 1.

The reset method has similar behavior. It can be passed an index that will reset the given bit to 0 or it can be used without parameters, which sets all bits to 0. The flip method also has two versions: When given an index it will change the given bit from true to false or false to true and when given no parameters it flips the values of all bits.

Summary

The bitset template is a simple object provided by the STL to give programs an easy and reusable bit flag implementation. Bitsets can be used in game development in a number of situations. I have seen them used particularly often in multiplayer development, where transmitting the state of an object over the Internet requires that programmers pack data into as small a location as possible. Packing boolean values into individual bits is as small as you can possibly get.

This was our last chapter looking at the containers provided by the STL. The next chapter covers a full implementation of the Text Adventure game. The examples of the game you have seen so far have been compromised by the fact that we had not yet covered STL containers. Game programming involves a lot of data object management and storing objects in appropriate data structures is essential. Now that you have seen the different containers the STL provides, you'll be in a better position to see how we can write a game in a more structured manner.

Chapter 19

Using the STL in Text Adventure

So far you have seen how a game can be built using classes, member variables, and C-style arrays. In this chapter you will see how you can use some of the STL classes covered in this part of the book to simplify the code you have been creating. This chapter uses polymorphism to store pointers to base classes in our STL containers. If you need a recap on polymorphism and how it is used, you should read over Chapter 11.

Some gameplay elements are also added to this chapter. Our Text Adventure game now has an end state. There are two enemies in the game world and the player must find and kill both of these enemies. Before the player will be able to attack the enemies, they must be armed with a weapon. This gameplay logic is relatively simple and there are still only a handful of rooms in the world. This is to help keep the code size small so you can get a good grasp on how to write a complete game.

Using STL array to Store Room Pointers

When you last saw the code for the Text Adventure game it was using a standard C-style array in the Game class to store the Room objects. In this chapter we switch over to using an STL array. Listing 19-1 shows the STL array code.

Listing 19-1. Using an STL array to Store Rooms

```
class Game
{
private:
        static const unsigned int m_numberOfRooms = 4;
        using Rooms = std::array<Room, m_numberOfRooms>;
        Rooms m_rooms;
};
```

Here you can see a const unsigned int that stores the number of rooms our game contains. The game will have the same T layout for the game rooms that we used in Chapter 12. The second line uses a type alias to reduce the amount of typing we would need to reference the type of the array in other places in the code. We then use the alias to create the array of rooms.

The rest of the code to deal with the Rooms array remains the same. This is one of the main reasons you should switch from old C-style arrays to newer style arrays. The newer style arrays can be used with other STL algorithms and also provide iterator support, which C-style arrays do not.

The Rooms array change is relatively straightforward, but the changes to the Options are much more substantial.

Using a vector and a map to Store Options

In Chapter 11 the Option pointers were stored in a C-style array in the Game class. This chapter reworks the Option storage entirely. The first significant change is that the Option pointers are no longer stored in the Game class. Each Room object stores pointers to the relevant options instead. This allows us to do some things a little differently. One drawback of the previous solution was that all of the options were presented for every room. In this chapter, we only show options that have a logical action. This means the player will never see an option to move east if the current Room does not have a Room joining to the east. This is a general improvement in usability.

The options for moving between rooms and for quitting the game are constant operations that never change. Our new gameplay logic also includes operations that can only be performed once. These are the options to open a chest and the option to attack an enemy. For simplicity's sake, the enemies in our game are currently killed in a single attack and a chest can only be opened once. When players carry out these actions, they will not be shown them a second time. This gives us two different classes of options, dynamic options and static options.

We will be storing the dynamic options in a vector. This would allow us to have as many dynamic options as necessary and allow us to add new options as the game progresses. Our static options will be stored in a map. The map allows the Option pointers to be associated with a key. The key will be used to access the Option pointer quickly regardless of how many static options we add.

While we're looking at the Room class you can also see that the JoiningRooms array has been updated to an STL array, as shown in Listing 19-2.

Listing 19-2. Using STL Containers in the Room Class

```
class Room
        : public Entity
{
public:
        enum class JoiningDirections
        {
                North = 0,
                East,
                South,
                West,
                Max
        };
```

```
private:
        using JoiningRooms = std::array<Room*, static_cast<size_t>(JoiningDirections::Max)>;
        JoiningRooms m_pJoiningRooms;

        using StaticOptions = std::map<unsigned int, Option*>;
        StaticOptions m_staticOptions;
        unsigned int m_staticOptionStartKey{ 1 };

        using DynamicOptions = std::vector<Option*>;
        DynamicOptions m_dynamicOptions;
};
```

A type alias is created for all three of the STL containers in use. The JoiningRooms alias uses a static_cast to convert the JoiningDirections::Max enum element into a usable size for the STL array. The compiler would give you a specialization error because it cannot implicitly cast an enum class value, and the static_cast avoids this error. There are additional type aliases, one for the map to store static options and one for the vector that stores the dynamic options.

The map is keyed by unsigned integers that will allow us to use the numbers entered by the user to access the relevant pointer for the selected option. They keys are set automatically by the Room class as the Options are added so we set the initial key to 1.

> **Note**   Initializing m_staticOptionStartKey in this manner is using a new C++11 feature. Before C++11 only static constants that were declared using built-in types could be initialized inside a class. C++11 added the ability to initialize members where they are declared to reduce the size of constructors.

Listing 19-3 shows the new methods that have been added to the Room class to add dynamic and static options.

Listing 19-3. Adding Dynamic and Static Options to Room

```
void Room::AddStaticOption(Option* option)
{
        assert(option != nullptr);
        m_staticOptions[m_staticOptionStartKey++] = option;
}

void Room::AddDynamicOption(Option* option)
{
        assert(option != nullptr);
        m_dynamicOptions.push_back(option);
}
```

The static options are added to the map using the map using the [ ] operator. The key being used is postincremented on each insert call. The AddDynamicOption method uses the vector::push_back method to push the new option into the vector. Both methods have a call to assert in their first line that will trigger if the Option pointer being added is a nullptr. This will allow you to track down invalid options while your program is running.

Now that the options are stored within a Room instance, the class is required to have a method to print the available options to the player, which is shown in Listing 19-4.

Listing 19-4. Printing the Available Options

```
void Room::PrintOptions() const
{
        for (unsigned int i = 0; i < m_dynamicOptions.size(); ++i)
        {
                const Option* option = m_dynamicOptions[i];
                std::cout << i + 1 << ": " << option->GetOutputText() << std::endl << std::endl;
        }

        for (StaticOptions::const_iterator iter = m_staticOptions.cbegin();
                iter != m_staticOptions.cend();
                ++iter)
        {
                const Option* option = iter->second;
                const unsigned int chosenOption = iter->first + m_dynamicOptions.size();
                std::cout << chosenOption << ": "
                        << option->GetOutputText() << std::endl << std::endl;
        }
}
```

The PrintOptions method must print out all of the dynamic options followed by the static options. Each option is preceded by an index number that the player will then be asked to enter. A for loop is used to track the option number to be printed for the dynamic options, and you can see this in the cout statement where we add 1 to i when printing.

Constant iterators are used to loop over the static options. Each static option is keyed starting from 1 so we can add the size of m_dynamicOptions to each key to find the appropriate index for each static option. The iterators represent key–data pairs with the key stored in the first member of the pair and the Option pointer stored in second.

The Room class will also be responsible for evaluating the player's input. Listing 19-4 shows the Room::EvaluateInput method.

Listing 19-5. Room::EvaluateInput

```
Option* Room::EvaluateInput(unsigned int playerInput)
{
        Option* option = nullptr;
        const unsigned int numDynamicOptions = m_dynamicOptions.size();
        if (playerInput <= numDynamicOptions)
```

```
        {
                unsigned int dynamicIndex = playerInput - 1;
                option = m_dynamicOptions[dynamicIndex];
                m_dynamicOptions.erase(m_dynamicOptions.begin() + dynamicIndex);
        }
        else
        {
                option = m_staticOptions.at(playerInput - numDynamicOptions);
        }
        return option;
}
```

The player has been presented options that could include dynamic and static options. The static options have been offset by the number of dynamic options, so EvaluateInput must account for this offsetting. It does this by determining if the entered number is less than the number of dynamic options. If it is then the chosen options can be used as an index into the m_dynamicOptions vector after subtracting 1.

> **Note** We must subtract 1 because the vector indexes begin at 0; however, we have shown the player choices beginning at 1, because not many nonprogrammers like to begin counting from 0.

If the player's input was greater than the number of dynamic options, we can calculate the key for the map of static options by subtracting the number of dynamic options from the player's input. This will work when there are no dynamic options, as the subtraction will remove 0 from the player input and we do not need to subtract 1 from the key as we initialized the map's keys beginning at 1.

The most important part of this method to pay attention to is the line that calls erase on m_dynamicOptions. This is the line that makes these options dynamic, as it ensures that each dynamic option can only be called once and it means that the options presented to the player after the option has been executed will be different. This is less than ideal from a usability perspective, as the user will be presented different numbers to choose the same actions; however, I felt it was a useful exercise in showing how a vector can be used for dynamic data sets.

Adding Gameplay to Text Adventure

Now that we have a mechanism in place to add dynamic and static options to Room instances, it's time to look at a couple of gameplay elements. The first gameplay element will be the ability to open chests and retrieve their contents. To do this we will need a Chest class. Listing 19-6 shows the class definition.

Listing 19-6. The Chest Class

```
class Chest
        : public Entity
{
private:
        const Item* m_item;
        bool m_isOpen{ false };
```

```
public:
        Chest(const Item* item);
        void Update();

        bool IsOpen() const
        {
                return m_isOpen;
        }

        const Item* Open()
        {
                m_isOpen = true;
                return m_item;
        }
};
```

The Chest class inherits from Entity. This makes sense, as a Chest will be an object that exists in the game world in its own right. Chest has two member variables, one to store a pointer to an Item and a bool to track if the Chest is open.

The Open method sets m_isOpen to true and returns the pointer to the stored Item to the caller. The Item class is shown in Listing 19-7.

Listing 19-7. The Item Class

```
class Item
{
private:
        std::string m_name;

public:
        Item(const std::string& name)
                : m_name{ name }
        {

        }

        virtual ~Item() {}

        const std::string& GetName() const
        {
                return m_name;
        }
};
```

The only useful functionality provided by the Item class is to store a string that contains the Item's name. This allows us to print the name of the Item to the player when they pick it up. This means that we need an Item that the player can collect. Listing 19-8 shows the Sword class.

Listing 19-8. The Sword Class

```
class Sword
        : public Item
{
public:
        Sword()
                : Item("Sword")
        {

        }
};
```

The Sword class does not do anything particularly exciting; its only method is a constructor that is used to pass the string "Sword" through to the Item parent class constructor.

The interesting work is done by our new OpenChestOptions class, which derives from Option, shown in Listing 19-9.

Listing 19-9. The OpenChestOption Class

```
class OpenChestOption
        : public Option
{
private:
        Chest* m_chest;

public:
        OpenChestOption(Chest* chest, const std::string& outputText)
                : m_chest{chest}
                , Option(PlayerOptions::OpenChest, outputText)
        {

        }

        virtual void Evaluate(Player& player);
};
```

The OpenChestOption class stores a pointer to the Chest object on which it will operate. It also overrides the Evaluate method from the Option parent class. The Evaluate method is shown in Listing 19-10.

Listing 19-10. OpenChestOption::Evaluate

```
void OpenChestOption::Evaluate(Player& player)
{
        if (m_chest->IsOpen() == false)
        {
                const Item* item = m_chest->Open();
                player.AddItem(item);

                std::cout << "You picked up a " << item->GetName() << " from the chest!"
                        << std::endl << std::endl;
        }
}
```

The Evaluate method is where the Chest::Open call is made. The method first checks to see if the Chest is closed; if it is, then the Open call is made and the Item pointer is passed to Player::AddItem. The last task is to print a message informing the player which Item was obtained from the Chest.

The Evaluate method brings us nicely to our next example of STL containers in our game. The Player class requires storage for the Item objects that the user can obtain. You can see in Listing 19-11 that a vector<Item*> has been added to the Player class.

Listing 19-11. The Player Class's Item vector

```cpp
class Player
        : public Entity
{
private:
        using Items = std::vector<Item*>;
        Items m_items;

        void AddItem(const Item* item)
        {
                m_items.push_back(const_cast<Item*>(item));
        }

        bool HasWeapon()
        {
                bool hasWeapon = false;

                for (const Item* item : m_items)
                {
                        const Sword* sword = dynamic_cast<const Sword*>(item);
                        if (sword != nullptr)
                        {
                                hasWeapon = true;
                                break;
                        }
                }

                return hasWeapon;
        }
};
```

Listing 19-11 only shows the new code that has been added to Player. We now have an alias for the Item* vector, the vector instance and two new methods, AddItem and HasWeapon.

AddItem is simply used to push new items onto the m_items vector. The HasWeapon method is a little more interesting. It uses a dynamic_cast to determine if the current Item pointer is actually a Sword class. A dynamic_cast will return nullptr if the type conversion is invalid; therefore, only objects that are actually Swords will successfully return a valid Sword pointer. Once we have a valid Sword pointer we know that the player has a weapon, so hasWeapon can be set to true and we can break out of our loop. The loop in question is a range-based for loop that takes advantage of our STL class.

The Player class has a method to determine whether the player is armed or not because we are going to add enemies to some of the Room objects. Listing 19-12 shows the Enemy class.

Listing 19-12. The Enemy Class

```
class Enemy
        : public Entity
{
public:
        enum class EnemyType
        {
                Dragon,
                Orc
        };

private:
        EnemyType m_type;
        bool m_alive{ true };

public:
        Enemy(EnemyType type)
                : m_type{ type }
        {

        }

        bool IsAlive() const
        {
                return m_alive;
        }

        void Kill()
        {
                m_alive = false;
        }
};
```

Text Adventure will support two different kinds of enemies for now, Dragons and Orcs. These types have been represented in the EnemyType enum. The only other member variable is a bool that determines if the Enemy is dead or alive; this goes along with the two helper methods, IsAlive and Kill, which query and set the state of the m_alive variable.

As you might have guessed, there is a new class derived from Option that allows the user to kill the enemies. Listing 19-13 shows the AttackEnemyOption class.

Listing 19-13. The AttackEnemyOption Class

```
class AttackEnemyOption
        : public Option
{
private:
        Enemy* m_enemy;

public:
        AttackEnemyOption(Enemy* enemy, const std::string& outputText);

        virtual void Evaluate(Player& player);
};
```

Listing 19-14 shows the code for the Evaluate method.

Listing 19-14. AttackEnemyOption::Evaluate

```cpp
void AttackEnemyOption::Evaluate(Player& player)
{
        std::cout << std::endl << "You have chosen to " << m_outputText
                << std::endl << std::endl;

        if (player.HasWeapon())
        {
                if (m_enemy->IsAlive())
                {
                        m_enemy->Kill();

                        std::cout << "You killed it!" << std::endl << std::endl;
                }
        }
        else
        {
                std::cout << "You need to find a weapon before attacking monsters!"
                        << std::endl << std::endl;
        }
}
```

The `Player::HasWeapon` method is put to good use here to make sure that the user can only attack enemies when they are armed. The final changes required to tie everything together are in the Game class, which is shown in Listing 19-15.

Listing 19-15. The Updated Game Class

```cpp
class Game
{
private:
        static const unsigned int m_numberOfRooms = 4;
        using Rooms = std::array<Room, m_numberOfRooms>;
        Rooms m_rooms;

        Player m_player;

        AttackEnemyOption m_attackDragonOption;
        AttackEnemyOption m_attackOrcOption;
        MoveOption m_moveNorthOption;
        MoveOption m_moveEastOption;
        MoveOption m_moveSouthOption;
        MoveOption m_moveWestOption;
        OpenChestOption m_openSwordChest;
        QuitOption m_quitOption;

        Sword m_sword;
        Chest m_swordChest;

        Enemy m_dragon;
        Enemy m_orc;
```

```
        void InitializeRooms();
        void WelcomePlayer();
        void GivePlayerOptions() const;
        void GetPlayerInput(std::stringstream& playerInput) const;
        PlayerOptions EvaluateInput(std::stringstream& playerInput);
public:
        Game();

        void RunGame();
};
```

The Game class now has two AttackEnemyOption instances, an OpenChestOption, a Sword, Chest, and two Enemy class instances. These are initialized in the constructor, shown in Listing 19-16.

Listing 19-16. The Game Constructor

```
Game::Game()
        : m_attackDragonOption(&m_dragon, "Attack Dragon")
        , m_attackOrcOption(&m_orc, "Attack Orc")
        , m_moveNorthOption(Room::JoiningDirections::North, PlayerOptions::GoNorth, "Go North")
        , m_moveEastOption(Room::JoiningDirections::East, PlayerOptions::GoEast, "Go East")
        , m_moveSouthOption(Room::JoiningDirections::South, PlayerOptions::GoSouth, "Go South")
        , m_moveWestOption(Room::JoiningDirections::West, PlayerOptions::GoWest, "Go West")
        , m_openSwordChest(&m_swordChest, "Open Chest")
        , m_quitOption("Quit")
        , m_swordChest(&m_sword)
        , m_dragon(Enemy::EnemyType::Dragon)
        , m_orc(Enemy::EnemyType::Orc)
{

}
```

Listing 19-17 shows how these are added to the Room instances using the new AddStaticOption and AddDynamicOption methods. This is done in the Game::InitializeRooms method.

Listing 19-17. Game::InitializeRooms

```
void Game::InitializeRooms()
{
        // Room 0 heads North to Room 1
        m_rooms[0].AddRoom(Room::JoiningDirections::North, &(m_rooms[1]));
        m_rooms[0].AddStaticOption(&m_moveNorthOption);
        m_rooms[0].AddStaticOption(&m_quitOption);
        m_rooms[0].AddDynamicOption(&m_openSwordChest);

        // Room 1 heads East to Room 2, South to Room 0 and West to Room 3
        m_rooms[1].AddRoom(Room::JoiningDirections::East, &(m_rooms[2]));
        m_rooms[1].AddStaticOption(&m_moveEastOption);
        m_rooms[1].AddRoom(Room::JoiningDirections::South, &(m_rooms[0]));
        m_rooms[1].AddStaticOption(&m_moveSouthOption);
        m_rooms[1].AddRoom(Room::JoiningDirections::West, &(m_rooms[3]));
        m_rooms[1].AddStaticOption(&m_moveWestOption);
        m_rooms[1].AddStaticOption(&m_quitOption);
```

```
        // Room 2 heads West to Room 1
        m_rooms[2].AddRoom(Room::JoiningDirections::West, &(m_rooms[1]));
        m_rooms[2].AddStaticOption(&m_moveWestOption);
        m_rooms[2].AddStaticOption(&m_quitOption);
        m_rooms[2].AddDynamicOption(&m_attackDragonOption);

        // Room 3 heads East to Room 1
        m_rooms[3].AddRoom(Room::JoiningDirections::East, &(m_rooms[1]));
        m_rooms[3].AddStaticOption(&m_moveEastOption);
        m_rooms[3].AddStaticOption(&m_quitOption);
        m_rooms[3].AddDynamicOption(&m_attackOrcOption);

        m_player.SetCurrentRoom(&(m_rooms[0]));
}
```

The GivePlayerInput method is now much simpler, as you can see in Listing 19-18.

Listing 19-18. Game::GivePlayerInput

```
void Game::GivePlayerOptions() const
{
        cout << "What would you like to do? (Enter a corresponding number)" << endl << endl;

        // Print the options for the room
        m_player.GetCurrentRoom()->PrintOptions();
}
```

The EvaluateInput method has some slightly more complicated code, shown in Listing 19-19.

Listing 19-19. Game::EvaluateInput

```
PlayerOptions Game::EvaluateInput(stringstream& playerInputStream)
{
        PlayerOptions chosenOption = PlayerOptions::None;
        unsigned int playerInputChoice{ 0 };
        playerInputStream >>playerInputChoice;

        try
        {
                Option* option = m_player.GetCurrentRoom()->EvaluateInput(playerInputChoice);
                option->Evaluate(m_player);
                chosenOption = option->GetChosenOption();
        }
        catch (const std::out_of_range&)
        {
                cout << "I do not recognize that option, try again!" << endl << endl;
        }

        return chosenOption;
}
```

The user's input has been captured into a `stringstream` that is used to get the unsigned `int` option selected. There is then a `try…catch` block. This is exception handling in C++. Exceptions can be generated by any code you call that does not result in a valid operation. In our case we could be passing an invalid option to the `Room::EvaluateInput` method. This invalid option would be used to try to get a pointer from the static options `map` and when the key could not be found, the `map` code would throw an `out_of_range` exception.

> **Note** If we failed to catch this exception, our program execution would stop, but by handling the exception we have been able to show the user an appropriate error message and carry on.

The last method to get an update is the `RunGame` method. Listing 19-20 shows the updates to this method.

Listing 19-20. Game::RunGame

```
void Game::RunGame()
{
        InitializeRooms();

        WelcomePlayer();

        bool playerWon = false;
        bool playerQuit = false;
        while (playerQuit == false && playerWon == false)
        {
                GivePlayerOptions();

                stringstream playerInputStream;
                GetPlayerInput(playerInputStream);

                PlayerOptions selectedOption = EvaluateInput(playerInputStream);
                playerQuit = selectedOption == PlayerOptions::Quit;

                playerWon = m_dragon.IsAlive() == false && m_orc.IsAlive() == false;
        }

        if (playerWon == true)
        {
                cout << "Congratulations, you rid the dungeon of monsters!" << endl;
                cout << "Type goodbye to end" << endl;
                std::string input;
                cin >>input;
        }
}
```

The main change here is that a `win` condition has been added to the game loop. The `while` condition now checks to see whether the user has chosen the quit option or if they have won. The `playerWon` `bool` is set to `true` once both of the enemies in the game world have been killed, which also means the player successfully opened the `Chest`.

Summary

This update to Text Adventure concludes this part of the book. I've given you a whirlwind tour of the most useful STL containers for game developers and you should now be able to use these in your own projects with ease.

This chapter has shown some practical examples of how you can deploy STL containers in game code. You've seen that STL `array` can be used for data that you know will remain constant, such as the `Rooms` in the world or the `JoiningDirections` in each `Room`. You've also seen how a `vector` can be used for more dynamic data structures. Text Adventure uses `vectors` to store dynamic options that are erased after they are used and also to hold the `Player` class's inventory, which would allow the inventory to grow until the memory available on the computer is exhausted. You also saw how a `map` can be used to provide convenient access to objects via a key–data pair relationship.

Hopefully by now you're also comfortable with the C++ syntax for specializing templates. The next part of this book is going to show you how you can create your own template methods and classes to do some really neat and powerful things in the C++ programming language.

Generic Programming

Although the STL provides a ready-made library of templates to cover many requirements, there is no escaping the fact that you will eventually need to use the ability to create your own templates.

The C++ template compiler is a complex, underused, and exceptionally useful piece of software. As well as letting you abstract types out of your classes to create generic and reusable code, the template compiler can also let you calculate constant values at compile time. This type of template programming is known as template metaprogramming.

This part of the book introduces you to the features C++ provides to create your own templates. It also shows you how to use some built-in template metaprograms and even ends with an example of how you can create your own template metaprogram.

Template Programming

Parts 1 and 2 of this book introduced you to concepts and features of the C++ programming language that allow the procedural programming paradigm and the object-oriented programming paradigm. C++ provides functions and control flow statements that allow you to break your programs down into reusable blocks and it provides classes that allow you to encapsulate your data and bundle it with methods that act on that data. C++ also supports a third programming paradigm, generic programming.

Generic programming is conceptually more complicated than the procedural and object-oriented programming paradigms. You can think of generic programming in C++ as programming with types. You've seen examples of this in the previous part of this book when you saw how to specialize STL containers. The STL containers are *generic* in that they do not know which type they are until the code is compiled. When you specialize a template, you are required to pass the types as arguments. This process creates a new type; vector<int> is a completely different type to vector<char>.

Templates were created to provide this type abstraction in programs. After templates were implemented, programmers started to discover that templates could do much, much more than just abstract out types. They discovered that the template compiler could evaluate constant values and compile new constant values. This has given rise to another element to template programming known as *template metaprogramming*.

This chapter gives a brief introduction to template compilation by discussing the difference between compile time and runtime evaluation, the difference between const and constexpr, and the difference between assert and static_assert.

Compile Versus Runtime Time Compilation

Compilers are complex pieces of software that are capable of turning your source code into instructions that can be consumed by a processor. During the compilation process, they are also capable of carrying out other tasks, including preprocessing and optimization. The compiler is also responsible for processing templates. Templates are generic and therefore the source code itself cannot resolve the types in use in the template code. The compiler could try to instantiate a version of the template for every single type and class in your program, but this would likely be very slow and require much more memory than necessary. Instead the compiler creates specializations of templates as and when it encounters them in your code. This process of creating specialized templates from the generic templates is why the compiler considers vector<int> to be a different type to vector<char>.

Note   As you have seen in previous chapters, it can be a great idea to use type aliases to make it clear in your code when a template specialization is declaring a new type.

What the template compiler does then is generate specific source code that is turned into instructions by subsequent steps in the compiler. This has led to the ability of the template compiler to be considered *Turing complete*. Being Turing complete means that the template compiler is considered capable of carrying out all of the computation capabilities of an early computer created by Alan Turing. In effect, the template compiler in C++ is able to do many things outside of just making types generic.

Before we look at how templates can be used in game code in the next chapter, we need to cover some of the basics. Listing 20-1 shows how a simple template can be created.

Listing 20-1. Creating a template Class

```
template <typename T>
class Template
{
private:
        T* m_ptr;

public:
        Template(T* ptr)
                : m_ptr{ptr}
        {

        }
};
```

Listing 20-1 shows how we can tell the compiler that we would like our class to contain a member variable that is of an unspecified type. This is achieved in the very first line with template <typename T>. The <> syntax should be familiar from the STL chapters and is also the form we use to specify the name for our generic type, in this case T.

Note   Where Listing 20-1 uses the typename keyword, it's also possible to use the class keyword. The class keyword was initially used to declare template types, but it was superseded by the typename keyword to reduce the overloading on the class keyword. Some older code might still use the class keyword for compatibility, but typename should be used in any new code.

The class can use the T type in place of a standard type. The compiler will replace the T anywhere it is used with the type supplied when the template is specialized. Listing 20-2 shows how this class template can be specialized.

Listing 20-2. Specializing a Template

```
int value = 1;
Template<int> pointer(&value);
```

When we compile our program the compiler will automatically create a class for the Template<int> type that replaces T with int.

The remainder of this chapter looks at the way we can specify constant values to be used by the template compiler and look at the difference between a runtime and compile time assert.

const Versus constexpr

C++11 introduced the constexpr keyword to coexist with the const keyword. You've already seen const used in this book. In those instances we used const to create variables that were unable to be changed by the program after they were defined. These variables are runtime variables. We can have constants defined inside local variables using values passed from parameters. Parameters themselves can even be constant and in these cases there is no way for the compiler to know whether the values the variables contain are literal constant values or values determined at runtime.

The constexpr keyword has been added to aid in this distinction. If you create a variable using constexpr the compiler will throw a compiler error if it cannot determine the value of the variable at compile time.

> **Note**   Unfortunately, at the time of writing, Microsoft has not yet added support in their latest compiler included with Visual Studio 2013.

Listing 20-3 shows two scenarios where const and constexpr will provide different results.

Listing 20-3. const Versus constexpr

```
const double constValue = sin(0.5);
constexpr double constexprValue = sin(0.5);

void ConstFunction(double value)
{
        const double constValue = value;
        constexpr double constexprValue = value;
}
```

The first two lines of Listing 20-3 will compile without issue. The compiler can work out the value of the result from the sin function at compile time and store the values in the variables. The constexpr variable inside the ConstFunction, however will result in a compile error. GCC gives the following output message: *error: 'value' is not a constant expression*. This happens because the compiler cannot guarantee that the method will not be passed a value that it cannot determine at compile time.

assert Versus static_assert

The assert and static_assert methods have the same runtime versus compile time distinction as const and constexpr. An assert is used to halt your program's execution if you pass in false at runtime. Listing 20-4 shows a use of assert.

Listing 20-4. assert

```
#include <cassert>
int main()
{
        assert(2 == 3);
}
```

The 2 == 3 expression will result in false being passed to the assert. This will cause the code execution to stop in your debugger and allow you to continue. A static_assert on the other hand causes the compiler to throw an error. Listing 20-5 shows a static_assert.

Listing 20-5. static_assert

```
#include <cassert>
int main()
{
        static_assert(2 == 3, "Two does not equal three");
}
```

When you compile this code using GCC you should see the following error: *error: static assertion failed: Two does not equal three*. This is the purpose of the string being passed to the static_assert: It is printed out as part of your compile error. These type of asserts are very useful when trying some template metaprogramming.

Summary

This chapter has shown you the very basics of how to create templates in your own code, including the difference between compile time and runtime evaluation through a look at the difference between const and constexpr, and assert and static_assert. You've seen a basic use of the template and typename keywords and how these are used to create type abstractions in your code.

The remaining chapter in this part of the book covers how you can use templates in the Text Adventure game in the form of template function, template classes, and finally an example of how template metaprogramming can be used to calculate an SDBM hash at compile time.

Chapter 21

Practical Template Programming

This chapter introduces you to some practical template examples so you can see how they can be deployed in your game development projects. You'll see how to implement a `Singleton` class that will allow you to create objects that can be accessed from anywhere in your code base. The `Singleton` pattern also ensures that you can only create a single instance of those classes.

You'll then see how you can create an event broadcasting system. This system itself will not use templates, but we will be creating some friend functions that will be implemented using templates to ensure that the objects being passed as parameters are set up to listen for events. The event manager class will also use a template function that will calculate hash values to uniquely identify the events in our system. Both of these example template functions will be showing you template metaprogramming in action.

This chapter starts with the `Singleton` pattern.

Creating Singleton Classes with Templates

A `Singleton` class is used to create a single instance of an object in your program. This object uses a static member variable and static functions to allow your code to access the object without requiring you to pass it through all of your code. There are multiple methods you can use to implement singletons. One common approach is to add a static member and functions to classes manually. This approach is error prone if you create enough singletons, so it would be better to find a more consistent approach. It turns out that we can use a template and inheritance to create a single implementation that we can add to any class. Listing 21-1 shows the source code required to create a `Singleton`.

Listing 21-1. The Singleton Class

```
template <typename T>
class Singleton
{
private:
        static T* m_instance;
```

```
public:
        Singleton()
        {
                assert(m_instance == nullptr);
                if (m_instance == nullptr)
                {
                        m_instance = static_cast<T*>(this);
                }
        }

        virtual ~Singleton()
        {
                m_instance = nullptr;
        }

        static T& GetSingleton()
        {
                return *m_instance;
        }

        static T* GetSingletonPtr()
        {
                return m_instance;
        }
};

template <typename T>
T* Singleton<T>::m_instance = nullptr;
```

There are three main aspects of this class that you should pay attention to with respect to implementing template classes. The very first line of Listing 21-1 shows that you use the template keyword to tell the compiler that we are creating a template. Using typename T then tells the compiler that the type T will be provided when we specialize this template in our code. The type T is then used to create a static pointer to a T object named m_instance.

The last important piece of template code is the definition of the m_instance variable on the last line. The template <typename T> keywords are needed again as the variable definition exists outside of the template class block.

The Singleton constructor contains an assert to alert you if you try to create more than a single instance of a particular object. There is also a static cast as the pointer in the constructor will be of type Singleton, not type T. It's safe to use a static cast and not a dynamic cast in this instance because we will only ever be casting from a Singleton to the type that derived from Singleton. Listing 21-2 shows how we can use the Singleton template when creating another class, the EventManager.

Listing 21-2. The EventManager Class

```
#include "Singleton.h"

class EventManager
        : public Singleton<EventManager>
{
};
```

You can see here that the Singleton class is derived from by EventManager, but you also pass the type EventManager to the Singleton template. This is a template programming pattern known as the *curiously recurring template pattern* (you can get more information about this topic from http://en.wikipedia.org/wiki/Curiously_recurring_template_pattern). You can now create and delete Singleton derived classes in the manner shown in Listing 21-3.

Listing 21-3. Instantiating the EventManager

```
void Game::RunGame()
{
        new EventManager();

        InitializeRooms();

        WelcomePlayer();

        bool playerWon = false;
        bool playerQuit = false;
        while (playerQuit == false && playerWon == false)
        {
                GivePlayerOptions();

                stringstream playerInputStream;
                GetPlayerInput(playerInputStream);

                PlayerOptions selectedOption = EvaluateInput(playerInputStream);
                playerQuit = selectedOption == PlayerOptions::Quit;

                playerWon = m_dragon.IsAlive() == false && m_orc.IsAlive() == false;
        }

        if (playerWon == true)
        {
                cout << "Congratulations, you rid the dungeon of monsters!" << endl;
                cout << "Type goodbye to end" << endl;
                std::string input;
                cin >>input;
        }

        delete EventManager::GetSingletonPtr();
}
```

The bold lines of code in Listing 21-3 contain the first uses of new and delete that you have seen in this book. You don't need to worry about the details of what these keywords do at the moment, as we'll be covering dynamic memory allocation in detail in Chapter 24. You can however place a breakpoint in the Singleton constructor and destructor to see those in action.

We'll add more code to the EventManager class before it will prove to be useful, so we cover that now.

Implementing the EventManager Class

The EventManager is going to store Event objects in an unordered_map. The keys to this map will be hash values calculated from strings that will be used to register events, attach listeners to events, and eventually send the events. This means that you will need an Event class, an EventHandler class, and a method to convert strings into unique hashes. Once these classes are all in place and operational we'll replace the current method used to detect when the player has chosen to quit the game with the new event system.

The EventHandler Interface

Listing 21-4 shows the code for the EventHandler interface.

Listing 21-4. The EventHandler Interface

```
class Event;

class EventHandler
{
public:
        virtual void HandleEvent(const Event* pEvent) = 0;
};
```

The EventHandler interface is very basic. It simply provides a base class from which other classes can derive to give themselves a common interface that can be used by the rest of the event system. The Event class is one place where this is important, as it stores a vector of EventHandler pointers.

The Event Class

The Event class will be used to represent an individual event within the EventManager. This event class is responsible for forwarding the event to all attached listener objects. To achieve this, the Event class will store EventHandler pointers in a vector. You can see this in Listing 21-5.

Listing 21-5. The Event Class

```
using EventID = int;

class EventHandler;

class Event
{
```

```
private:
        using EventHandlerList = std::vector<EventHandler*>;
        using EventHandlerListIterator = EventHandlerList::iterator;

        EventHandlerList m_listeners;
        EventID m_id;

public:
        explicit Event(EventID eventId);

        void Send();
        void SendToHandler(EventHandler& eventHandler);
        void AttachListener(EventHandler& eventHandler);
        void DetachListener(EventHandler& eventHandler);

        EventID GetID() const { return m_id; }
};
```

The Event class has a vector of EventHandler pointers. These are pointers to objects that have derived from EventHandler and are listening for a specific event. An Event also has an EventID variable that allows the event to be identified.

The explicit keyword before the constructor ensures that instances of the class can only be created when passing in an EventID or integer type. The class also has methods that are used to attach and detach listeners and for sending the event either to all listeners of a specific EventHandler. Listing 21-6 shows the code for the AttachListener and DetachListener methods.

Listing 21-6. The AttachListener and DetachListener Methods

```
void Event::AttachListener(EventHandler& eventHandler)
{
        m_listeners.push_back(&eventHandler);
}

void Event::DetachListener(EventHandler& eventHandler)
{
        for (EventHandlerListIterator iter = m_listeners.begin();
                iter != m_listeners.end();
                ++iter)
        {
                if (&eventHandler == *iter)
                {
                        m_listeners.erase(iter);
                        break;
                }
        }
}
```

The AttachListener and DetachListener methods are responsible for adding and removing a given EventHandler object from the m_listeners vector. This vector becomes useful when you would like to send the Event to all of the pointers it stores, as you can see in Listing 21-7.

Listing 21-7. The Event::Send Method

```
void Event::Send()
{
        for (auto& listener : m_listeners)
        {
                if (listener != nullptr)
                {
                        listener->HandleEvent(this);
                }
        }
}
```

The Send method is straightforward. It simply loops all over the m_listeners vector and calls the HandleEvent method on each valid entry.

The SendToHandler method is given in Listing 21-8. It sends the message to a single EventHandler rather than all of them.

Listing 21-8. The Event::SendToHandler Method

```
void Event::SendToHandler(EventHandler& eventHandler)
{
        auto found = std::find(m_listeners.begin(), m_listeners.end(), &eventHandler);
        if (found != m_listeners.end())
        {
                (*found)->HandleEvent(this);
        }
}
```

This time we use the find STL algorithm to get an iterator to the entry that stores our EventHandler and then call HandleEvent if it is found.

Now that we have an interface for EventHandlers and a class to represent Events, we can look at how the EventManager class is implemented.

The EventManager Implementation

Listing 21-9 shows the member variables and methods contained in the EventManager class.

Listing 21-9. The EventManager Members and Methods

```
class EventManager
        : public Singleton<EventManager>
{
        friend void SendEvent(EventID eventId);

        template <typename T>
        friend void SendEventToHandler(EventID eventId, T* eventHandler);

        friend bool RegisterEvent(EventID eventId);
```

```
        template <typename T>
        friend void AttachEvent(EventID eventId, T* eventHandler);

        template <typename T>
        friend void DetachEvent(EventID eventId, T* eventHandler);

private:
        using EventMap = std::unordered_map<EventID, Event*>;
        using EventMapIterator  = EventMap::iterator;

        EventMap m_eventMap;

        void SendEvent(EventID eventId);

        void SendEventToHandler(EventID eventId, EventHandler& eventHandler);
        bool RegisterEvent(EventID eventId);

        void AttachEvent(EventID eventId, EventHandler& eventHandler);

        void DetachEvent(EventID eventId, EventHandler& eventHandler);

public:
        virtual ~EventManager();
};
```

The EventManager class has an interesting design. The Event objects are stored in an unordered_map using the EventID as a key. There are also private member methods that contain the behavior of the class: SendEvent, SendEventToHandler, RegisterEvent, AttachEvent, and DetachEvent. There are also public friend methods that are used to wrap these function calls and use template code. I'll show you the code for the private methods first then talk you through how and why the public friend functions are used. Listing 21-10 contains the code for the RegisterEvent method.

Listing 21-10. EventManager::RegisterEvent

```
bool EventManager::RegisterEvent(EventID eventId)
{
        bool added = false;

        EventMapIterator result = m_eventMap.find(eventId);
        if (result == m_eventMap.end())
        {
                Event* pNewEvent = new Event(eventId);

                if (pNewEvent)
                {
                        std::pair<EventID, Event*> newEvent(eventId, pNewEvent);
                        auto addedIter = m_eventMap.insert(newEvent);
                        added = addedIter.second;
                }
        }

        assert(added);
        return added;
}
```

The RegisterEvent method first searched the m_eventMap variable using find to see if an Event with the same eventID already exists. If it does not, then a new Event object is created and added to the unordered_map. The AttachEvent and DetachEvent methods find the Event object for the specified eventID and add or detach the supplied EventHandler object, using the code shown in Listing 21-11.

Listing 21-11. The EventManager AttachEvent and DetachEvent Methods

```
void EventManager::AttachEvent(EventID eventId, EventHandler& eventHandler)
{
        EventMapIterator result = m_eventMap.find(eventId);
        assert(result != m_eventMap.end());
        if (result != m_eventMap.end())
        {
                assert(result->second);
                result->second->AttachListener(eventHandler);
        }
}

void EventManager::DetachEvent(EventID eventId, EventHandler& eventHandler)
{
        EventMapIterator result = m_eventMap.find(eventId);
        assert(result != m_eventMap.end());
        if (result != m_eventMap.end())
        {
                assert(result->second);
                result->second->DetachListener(eventHandler);
        }
}
```

These methods are quite simple: They find the Event object for the given eventID and call the Event class's AttachListener or DetachListener, respectively. The SendEvent and SendEventToHandler methods are equally simple and shown in Listing 21-12.

Listing 21-12. The EventManager SendEvent and SendEventToHandler Methods

```
void EventManager::SendEvent(EventID eventId)
{
        EventMapIterator result = m_eventMap.find(eventId);
        if (result != m_eventMap.end())
        {
                assert(result->second);
                if (result->second)
                {
                        result->second->Send();
                }
        }
}
```

```
void EventManager::SendEventToHandler(EventID eventId, EventHandler& eventHandler)
{
        EventMapIterator result = m_eventMap.find(eventId);
        if (result != m_eventMap.end())
        {
                assert(result->second);
                if (result->second)
                {
                        result->second->SendToHandler(eventHandler);
                }
        }
}
```

The destructor for the EventManager class is also interesting. It is responsible for cleaning up the Event objects in the unordered_map. As they were created using the new keyword, they must be destroyed using the delete keyword (I cover this in detail in Chapter 24). The EventManager destructor is given in Listing 21-13.

Listing 21-13. The EventManager Destructor

```
EventManager::~EventManager()
{
        for (EventMapIterator iter = m_eventMap.begin(); iter != m_eventMap.end(); ++iter)
        {
                Event* pEvent = iter->second;
                if (pEvent)
                {
                        delete pEvent;
                        iter->second = nullptr;
                }
        }

        m_eventMap.clear();
}
```

The destructor iterates over the m_eventMap variable, deletes each Event, and sets the second member on the iterator to be nullptr.

Now I can show you the public friend functions that wrap the EventManager private methods. Listing 21-14 shows the code for the SendEvent friend function.

Listing 21-14. The SendEvent friend Function

```
inline void SendEvent(EventID eventId)
{
        EventManager* pEventManager = EventManager::GetSingletonPtr();
        assert(pEventManager);
        if (pEventManager)
        {
                pEventManager->SendEvent(eventId);
        }
}
```

The point of using this friend function is to reduce the amount of code we must write each time we would like to send an Event. If we did not have this friend function, we would need to write the six lines it contains each time. Instead of this we can simply write

```
SendEvent(someEvent);
```

The friend function also safely checks that the Singleton EventManager class has been created. This is useful, as there might be situations in which you might like to test without the EventManager. The SendEvent function itself is relatively simple and calls the SendEvent private member on the EventManager class. This is a benefit of the friend function: It can access the private members and methods of any class it is a friend of. Using this technique you can ensure that only the public friend functions can be used to interact with the EventManager. Listing 21-15 shows the RegisterEvent function, which is equally straightforward.

Listing 21-15. The RegisterEvent Function

```
inline bool RegisterEvent(EventID eventId)
{
        bool added = false;

        EventManager* pEventManager = EventManager::GetSingletonPtr();
        assert(pEventManager);
        if (pEventManager)
        {
                added = pEventManager->RegisterEvent(eventId);
        }

        return added;
}
```

The other three functions interact with the EventManager in a similar way; however, they do have a significant difference. They contain a little template metaprogramming. Listing 21-16 shows all three remaining functions.

Listing 21-16. The SendEventToHandler, AttachEvent, and DetachEvent friend Functions

```
template <typename T>
inline void SendEventToHandler(EventID eventId, T* eventHandler)
{
        static_assert(std::is_base_of<EventHandler, T>::value,
                "Class provided is not derived from EventHandler");

        EventManager* pEventManager = EventManager::GetSingletonPtr();
        assert(pEventManager);
        if (pEventManager)
        {
                pEventManager->SendEventToHandler(
                        eventId, *static_cast<EventHandler*>(eventHandler));
        }
}
```

```
template <typename T>
inline void AttachEvent(EventID eventId, T* eventHandler)
{
        static_assert(std::is_base_of<EventHandler, T>::value,
                "Class provided is not derived from EventHandler");

        EventManager* pEventManager = EventManager::GetSingletonPtr();
        assert(pEventManager);
        if (pEventManager)
        {
                pEventManager->AttachEvent(eventId, *static_cast<EventHandler*>(eventHandler));
        }
}


template <typename T>
inline void DetachEvent(EventID eventId, T* eventHandler)
{
        static_assert(std::is_base_of<EventHandler, T>::value,
                "Class provided is not derived from EventHandler");

        EventManager* pEventManager = EventManager::GetSingletonPtr();
        assert(pEventManager);
        if (pEventManager)
        {
                pEventManager->DetachEvent(eventId, *static_cast<EventHandler*>(eventHandler));
        }
}
```

The important line in these three methods is the static_assert and the code it contains:

```
static_assert(std::is_base_of<EventHandler, T>::value, "Class provided is not derived from EventHandler");
```

The is_base_of keyword is actually a C++11 built-in template metaprogram. It is used to determine at compile time if a type is derived from another. In our case we supply a type to the templates using the typename T syntax as usual and then we pass this type T into the second parameter of is_base_of. The template compiler will calculate if the EventHandler class is a parent of the supplied class and set the value variable to be either true or false. Using this template metaprogram ensures that we can never attach or detach objects that are not derived from EventHandler by combining it with static_assert, which will throw an error when we are building our game.

The EventManager class is complete, but before you can use it I'm going to show you how you can write your own template metaprogram to calculate unique event IDs.

Calculating SDBM Hash Values Using a Template Metaprogram

The SDBM hash algorithm is used to turn a stream of bytes into an integer representation. The algorithm has a very low chance of producing the same value for two different sets of data, which makes it ideal for our purposes. It's also really easy to implement in C++, as you can see in Listing 21-17.

Listing 21-17. The SDBM Hash Function

```
inline unsigned int SDBMHash(const std::string& key)
{
        unsigned int result = 0;

        for (unsigned int i = 0; i < key.length(); ++i)
        {
                int c = key[i];
                result = c + (result << 6) + (result << 16) - result;
        }

        return result;
}
```

The algorithm iterates over the data, in this case a string, and uses the value of each character in an additive algorithm that manipulates the current result using bit shifts and subtractions. The problem with this function as implemented is that it will execute at runtime. This might be desired for some of our data; however, for any constexpr values that we know of at compile time it would be much better to preprocess the hashes. This makes the function a perfect target for template metaprogramming. Listing 21-18 shows the code that achieves this.

Listing 21-18. The SDBMCalculator Template Metaprogram

```
template <int stringLength>
struct SDBMCalculator
{
        static inline int Calculate(const char* const stringToHash, int& value)
        {
                int character =
                        SDBMCalculator<stringLength - 1>::Calculate(stringToHash, value);
                value = character + (value << 6) + (value << 16) - value;
                return stringToHash[stringLength - 1];
        }

        static inline int CalculateValue(const char* const stringToHash)
        {
                int value = 0;
                int character = SDBMCalculator<stringLength>::Calculate(stringToHash, value);
                value = character + (value << 6) + (value << 16) - value;
                return value;
        }
};
```

```
template <>
struct SDBMCalculator<1>
{
        static inline int Calculate(const char* const stringToHash, int& value)
        {
                return stringToHash[0];
        }
};
```

This code is going to be a little tricky for new C++ programmers to get their head around. Listing 21-19 shows how this code would be used in your code.

Listing 21-19. Using the SDBMCalculator Template Metaprogram

```
constexpr int QuitEvent = SDBMCalculator<9>::CalculateValue("QuitEvent");
```

The template metaprogram is passed the length of the string as its template parameter and the string to hash as a function parameter. The static CalculateValue function is the function that is called. This function then calls the static Calculate method in the SDBMCalculator struct. You can see that the Calculate method calls itself. This is the very nature of template metaprogramming: The programs generally consist of recursive function calls. The Calculate method calls Calculate on an SDBMCalculator template, which is passed stringLength - 1 as its parameter.

Our QuitEvent string has a length of 9 so the template metaprogram will recurse down until Calculate can hit the terminating condition. You can see the terminating condition in the specialized version of the struct. This struct doesn't have any template parameters, but its Calculate function has a hard-coded parameter of 1. This specialized version of the function does not call any other version of Calculate so the calls begin to unwind at this point. If we were to print out the character and value after each step, the output would be:

```
Q
81

u
5313636

i
676857093

t
-223462225

E
-175116458

v
1572988576

e
-111689275
```

n
509456361

t
687295179

This works because the stringLength passed to each SDBMCalculator template is used to index into the string with 1 subtracted. Then as we start with the length of the string calling the SDBMCalculate method recursively down until we hit 1, we access the characters in the string in order.

Template metaprogramming can be hard to understand when you're just learning C++. Don't worry about that too much for now. Come back to this code in the future when you're ready to tackle some more template metaprogramming.

We'll update our QuitOption to use messages now that we can create a unique ID for the QuitEvent.

Using an Event to Quit the Game

Using an event to quit the game is relatively straightforward. To begin we'll update the QuitOption::Evaluate method to send the QuitEvent. Listing 21-20 shows how this is done.

Listing 21-20. Updating QuitOption::Evaluate

```
namespace
{
        constexpr int QuitEvent = SDBMCalculator< >::CalculateValue("QuitEvent");
}

void QuitOption::Evaluate(Player& player)
{
        SendEvent(QuitEvent);
}
```

You can finally see the benefit of using the friend functions with the EventManager, as sending the QuitEvent is just a single line of code!

The main change required is to inherit the Game class from EventHandler as shown in Listing 21-21.

Listing 21-21. Updating the Game Class

```
class Game
        : public EventHandler
{
private:
        static const unsigned int m_numberOfRooms = 4;
        using Rooms = std::array<Room, m_numberOfRooms>;
        Rooms m_rooms;

        Player m_player;
```

```
        AttackEnemyOption m_attackDragonOption;
        AttackEnemyOption m_attackOrcOption;
        MoveOption m_moveNorthOption;
        MoveOption m_moveEastOption;
        MoveOption m_moveSouthOption;
        MoveOption m_moveWestOption;
        OpenChestOption m_openSwordChest;
        QuitOption m_quitOption;

        Sword m_sword;
        Chest m_swordChest;

        Enemy m_dragon;
        Enemy m_orc;

        bool m_playerQuit{ false };

        void InitializeRooms();
        void WelcomePlayer();
        void GivePlayerOptions() const;
        void GetPlayerInput(std::stringstream& playerInput) const;
        void EvaluateInput(std::stringstream& playerInput);
public:
        Game();

        void RunGame();

        virtual void HandleEvent(const Event* pEvent);
};
```

The three bold lines are the only changes to the class definition. It is now derived from the EventHandler interface and overrides the HandleEvent method. There is also a bool, m_playerQuit, used to store whether the player has chosen to quit, which is initialized to false.

Listing 21-22 shows the changes that are needed in the Game::RunGame method.

Listing 21-22. Updating Game::RunGame

```
void Game::RunGame()
{
        new EventManager();

        RegisterEvent(QuitEvent);
        AttachEvent(QuitEvent, this);

        InitializeRooms();

        WelcomePlayer();
```

```
        bool playerWon = false;
        while (m_playerQuit == false && playerWon == false)
        {
                GivePlayerOptions();

                stringstream playerInputStream;
                GetPlayerInput(playerInputStream);

                EvaluateInput(playerInputStream);

                playerWon = m_dragon.IsAlive() == false && m_orc.IsAlive() == false;
        }

        if (playerWon == true)
        {
                cout << "Congratulations, you rid the dungeon of monsters!" << endl;
                cout << "Type goodbye to end" << endl;
                std::string input;
                cin >>input;
        }

        DetachEvent(QuitEvent, this);
        delete EventManager::GetSingletonPtr();
}
```

The RunGame method now has code to create an EventManager, to register the QuitEvent, and to attach itself as a listener for that event. The last two lines also detach from the event and delete the EventManager. The other main change is that EvaluateInput is no longer required to return the chosen option. We now catch the event in the HandleEvent method, which you can see in Listing 21-23.

Listing 21-23. The Game::HandleEvent Method

```
void Game::HandleEvent(const Event* pEvent)
{
        if (pEvent->GetID() == QuitEvent)
        {
                m_playerQuit = true;
        }
}
```

Handling events is really easy. You just need to check the ID of the Event and carry out the required action, which in this case is setting the m_playerQuit variable to true. If we had attached to more events we could have used else if statements to check against more EventIDs.

Summary

This chapter has introduced you to some practical examples of template programming. You've seen how to use templates to create classes with variables with types that are determined at compile time. You've also seen how to create functions and methods that use templates.

Using standard templates like this allows you to write generic class implementations that can be specialized with specific types at a later point in time. This is really useful to reduce the need to copy and paste code when you might have been tempted to re-create a class to store a different type of object.

This chapter also introduced the topic of template metaprogramming. This is a complex and useful piece of C++ functionality but isn't used in a lot of code. It can be hard for many programmers to understand and is seen as a relatively advanced topic. You saw in this chapter that C++ has some built-in template metaprograms such as is_base_of and you also saw how you can create your own template metaprograms. These programs are recursive in nature and can provide a good opportunity to optimize your code by shifting calculations from runtime to compile time.

The next part of this book covers more general game programming topics, as this part has drawn the theoretical programming In C++ to a close. The next part covers design patterns, I/O streams, memory management, concurrent programming, and cross-platform game development.

C++ Game Programming

The previous parts of this book have mostly covered the theory of C++ programming with practical examples. This part of the book changes the focus to cover more general game development problems and how you can use the C++ features you've seen in action to solve those problems.

This part of the book introduces concepts from game development such as memory management, design patterns, IO, and concurrent programming. Hopefully these practical game development examples will encourage you to continue your journey and enter the world of professional game development.

Part 5

C++ Game Programming

Chapter 22

Managing Memory for Game Developers

This chapter is the first in the last part of this book, which will cover general game development topics that are important for new programmers to attempt to grasp. The first of these chapters is going to introduce you to the C++ memory model and the implications of using different types of memory.

Memory management is a very important topic in game development. All games go through a period in development where memory is running low and the art team would like some more for extra textures or meshes. The way memory is laid out is also vitally important to the performance of your game. Understanding when to use stack memory, when to use heap memory, and the performance implications of each are important factors in to being able to optimize your programs for cache coherency and data locality. Before you can understand how to approach those problems you will need to understand the different places where C++ programs can store their data.

There are three places in C++ where you can store your memory: There is a static space for storing static variables, the stack for storing local variables and function parameters, and the heap (or free store) from where you can dynamically allocate memory for different purposes.

Static Memory

Static memory is handled by the compiler and there isn't much to say about it. When you build your program using the compiler, it sets aside a chunk of memory large enough to store all of the static and global variables defined in your program. This includes strings that are in your source code, which are included in an area of static memory known as a string table.

There's not much else to say regarding static memory, so we'll move on to discussing the stack.

The C++ Stack Memory Model

The stack is more difficult to understand. Every time you call a function, the compiler generates code behind the scenes to allocate memory for the parameters and local variables for the function being called. Listing 22-1 shows some simple code that we then use to explain how the stack operates.

Listing 22-1. A Simple C++ Program

```
void function2(int variable1)
{
        int variable2{ variable1 };
}

void function1(int variable)
{
        function2(variable);
}

int _tmain(int argc, _TCHAR* argv[])
{
        int variable{ 0 };
        function1(variable);

        return 0;
}
```

The program in Listing 22-1 is very simple: It begins with _tmain, which calls function1 which calls function2. Figure 22-1 illustrates what the stack would look like for the main function.

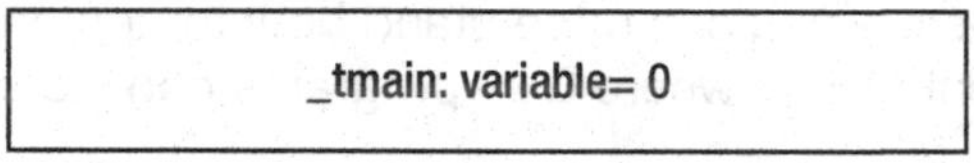

```
_tmain: variable= 0
```

Figure 22-1. The stack for _tmain

The stack space for main is very simple. It has a single storage space for the local variable named variable. These stack spaces for individual functions are known as *stack frames*. When function1 is called, a new stack frame is created on top of the existing frame for _tmain. Figure 22-2 shows this in action.

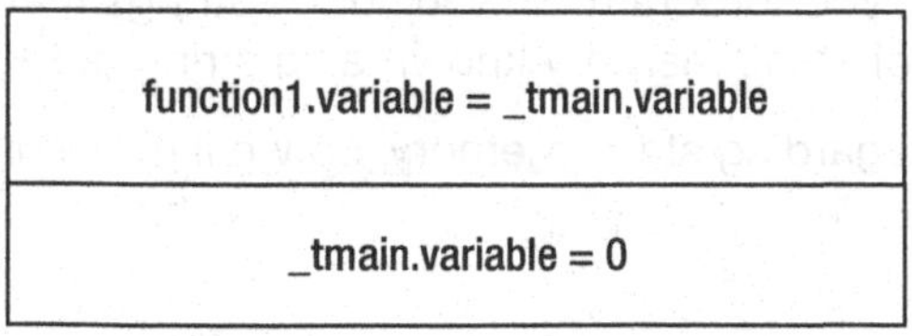

```
function1.variable = _tmain.variable
```
```
_tmain.variable = 0
```

Figure 22-2. The added stack frame for function1

When the compiler creates the code to push the stack frame for function1 onto the stack it also ensures that the parameter variable is initialized with the value stored in variable from _tmain. This is how parameters are passed by value. Finally, Figure 22-3 shows the last stack frame for function2 added to the stack.

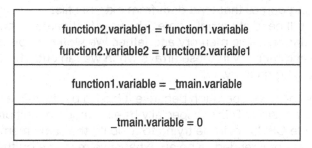

```
function2.variable1 = function1.variable
function2.variable2 = function2.variable1

function1.variable = _tmain.variable

_tmain.variable = 0
```

Figure 22-3. The complete stack frame

The last stack frame is a little more complicated but you should be able to see how the literal value 0 in _tmain has been passed all the way along the stack until it is eventually used to initialize variable2 in function2.

The remaining stack operations are relatively simple. When function2 returns the stack frame generated for that call is *popped* from the stack. This leaves us back at the state presented in Figure 22-2, and when function1 returns we are back at Figure 22-1. That's all you need to know to understand the basic functionality of a stack in C++.

Unfortunately things aren't actually this simple. The stack in C++ is a very complicated thing to fully understand and requires a bit of assembly programming knowledge. That topic is outside the scope of a book aimed at beginners, but it's well worth pursuing once you have a grasp of the basics. The article "Programmers Disassemble" in the September 2012 edition of *Game Developer Magazine* is an excellent introductory article on the operation of the x86 stack and well worth a read, available free from http://www.gdcvault.com/gdmag.

This chapter hasn't covered the ins and outs of how references and pointers are handled on the stack or how return values are implemented. Once you begin to think about this, you might begin to understand how complicated it can be. You might also be wondering why it's useful to understand how the stack works. The answer lies in trying to work out why your game has crashed once it is in a live environment. It's relatively easy to work out why a game crashes while you are developing, as you can simply reproduce the crash in a debugger. On games that have launched, you might receive a file known as a crash dump, which does not have any debugging information and simply has the current state of the stack to go on. At that point you need to look out for the symbol files from the build that let you work out the memory addresses of the functions that have been called, and you can then manually work out which functions have been called from the addresses in the stack and also try to figure out which function passed along an invalid memory address of value on the stack.

This is complicated and time-consuming work, but it does come up every so often in professional game development. Services such as Crashlytics for iOS and Android or BugSentry for Windows PC programs can upload crash dumps and provide a call stack for you on a web service to help alleviate a lot of the pain from trying to manually work out what is going wrong with your game.

The next big topic in memory management in C++ is the heap.

Working with Heap Memory

So far in this book I have avoided using dynamic memory as much as possible because manually managing dynamically allocated memory is sometimes challenging, slower than using stack memory, and also very often unnecessary. Managing dynamic memory will become more important for you once you advance to writing games that load data from external files, as it's often impossible to tell how much memory you'll need at compile time. The very first game I worked on prevented programmers from allocating dynamic memory altogether. We worked around this by allocating arrays of objects and reusing memory in these arrays when we ran out. This is one way to avoid the performance cost of allocating memory.

Allocating memory is an expensive operation because it has to be done in a manner that prevents memory corruption where possible. This is especially true on modern multiprocessor CPU architectures where multiple CPUs could be trying to allocate the same memory at the same time. This chapter, like the last, is not intended to be an exhaustive resource on the topic of memory allocation techniques for game development, but instead introduces the concept of managing heap memory.

You saw the use of the new and delete operators in Chapter 21 when creating the Singleton EventManager object. Listing 22-2 shows a simple program using the new and delete operators.

Listing 22-2. Allocating Memory for a class Dynamically

```
class Simple
{
private:
        int variable{ 0 };

public:
        Simple()
        {
                std::cout << "Constructed" << std::endl;
        }

        ~Simple()
        {
                std::cout << "Destroyed" << std::endl;
        }
};

int _tmain(int argc, _TCHAR* argv[])
{
        Simple* pSimple = new Simple();
        delete pSimple;
        pSimple = nullptr;

        return 0;
}
```

This simple program shows new and delete in action. When you decide to allocate memory in C++ using the new operator, the amount of memory required is calculated automatically. The new operator in Listing 22-2 will reserve enough memory to store the Simple object along with its member variables. If you were to add more members to Simple or inherit it from another class, the program would still operate and enough memory would be reserved for the expanded class definition.

The new operator returns a pointer to the memory that you have requested to allocate. Once you have a pointer to memory that has been dynamically allocated, you are responsible for ensuring that the memory is also freed appropriately. You can see that this is done by passing the pointer to the delete operator. The delete operator is responsible for telling the operating system that the memory we reserved is no longer in use and can be used for other purposes. A last piece of housekeeping is then carried out when the pointer is set to store nullptr. By doing this we help prevent our code from assuming the pointer is still valid and that we can read and write from the memory as though it is still a Simple object. If your programs are crashing in seemingly random and inexplicable ways, accessing freed memory from pointers that have not been cleared is a common suspect.

The standard new and delete operators are used when allocating single objects; however, there are also specific new and delete operators that should be used when allocating and freeing arrays. These are shown in Listing 22-3.

Listing 22-3. Array new and delete

```
int* pIntArray = new int[16];
delete[] pIntArray;
```

This call to new will allocate 64 bytes of memory to store 16 int variables and return a pointer to the address of the first element. Any memory you allocate using the new[] operator should be deleted using the delete[] operator, because using the standard delete can result in not all of the memory you requested being freed.

Note   Not freeing memory and not freeing memory properly is known as a memory leak. Leaking memory in this fashion is bad, as your program will eventually run out of free memory and crash because it eventually won't have any available to fulfill new allocations.

Hopefully you can see from this code why it's beneficial to use the available STL classes to avoid managing memory yourself. If you do find yourself in a position of having to manually allocate memory, the STL also provides the unique_ptr and shared_ptr templates to help delete the memory when appropriate. Listing 22-4 updates the code from Listing 22-2 and Listing 22-3 to use unique_ptr and shared_ptr objects.

Listing 22-4. Using unique_ptr *and* shared_ptr

```
#include <memory>

class Simple
{
private:
        int variable{ 0 };

public:
        Simple()
        {
                std::cout << "Constructed" << std::endl;
        }

        ~Simple()
        {
                std::cout << "Destroyed" << std::endl;
        }
};

int _tmain(int argc, _TCHAR* argv[])
{
        using UniqueSimplePtr = std::unique_ptr<Simple>;
        UniqueSimplePtr pSimple1{ new Simple() };
        std::cout << pSimple1.get() << std::endl;

        UniqueSimplePtr pSimple2;
        pSimple2.swap(pSimple1);
        std::cout << pSimple1.get() << std::endl;
        std::cout << pSimple2.get() << std::endl;

        using IntSharedPtr = std::shared_ptr<int>;
        IntSharedPtr pIntArray1{ new int[16] };
        IntSharedPtr pIntArray2{ pIntArray1 };

        std::cout << std::endl << pIntArray1.get() << std::endl;
        std::cout << pIntArray2.get() << std::endl;

        return 0;
}
```

As the name suggests, unique_ptr is used to ensure that you only have a single reference to allocated memory at a time. Listing 22-3 shows this in action. pSimple1 is assigned a new Simple pointer and pSimple2 is then created as empty. You can try initializing pSimple2 by passing it pSimple1 or using an assignment operator and your code will fail to compile. The only way to pass the pointer from one unique_ptr instance to another is using the swap method. The swap method moves the stored address and sets the pointer in the original unique_ptr instance to be nullptr. The first three lines of output in Figure 22-4 show the addresses stored in the unique_ptr instances.

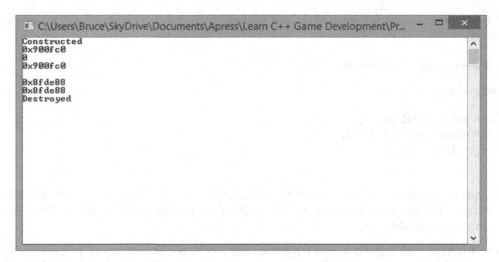

Figure 22-4. The output from Listing 22-4

This output shows that the constructor from the Simple class is called. The pointer stored in pSimple1 is then printed out before the call to swap is made. After the call to swap pSimple1 stores a nullptr that is output as 00000000 and pSimple2 stores the address originally held there. The very final line of the output shows that the destructor for the Simple object has also been called. This is another benefit we receive from using unique_ptr and shared_ptr: Once the objects go out of scope then the memory is freed automatically.

You can see from the two lines of output immediately before the line containing Destroyed that the two shared_ptr instances can store a reference to the same pointer. Only a single unique_ptr can reference a single memory location, but multiple shared_ptr instances can reference an address. The difference manifests itself in the timing of the delete call on the memory store. A unique_ptr will delete the memory it references as soon as it goes out of scope. It can do this because a unique_ptr can be sure that it is the only object referencing that memory. A shared_ptr, on the other hand, does not delete the memory when it goes out of scope; instead the memory is deleted when all of the shared_ptr objects pointing at that address are no longer being used.

This does require a bit of discipline, as if you were to access the pointer using the get method on these objects then you could still be in a situation where you are referencing the memory after it has been deleted. If you are using unique_ptr or shared_ptr make sure that you are only passing the pointer around using the supplied swap and other accessor methods supplied by the templates and not manually using the get method.

Writing a Basic Single Threaded Memory Allocator

This section is going to show you how to overload the new and delete operators to create a very basic memory management system. This system is going to have a lot of drawbacks: It will store a finite amount of memory in a static array, it will suffer from memory fragmentation issues, and it will also leak any freed memory. This section is simply an introduction to some of the processes that occur when allocating memory, and it highlights some of the issues that make writing a fully featured memory manager a difficult task.

Listing 22-5 begins by showing you a structure that will be used as a header for our memory allocations.

Listing 22-5. The `MemoryAllocationHeader` *struct*

```
struct MemoryAllocationHeader
{
        void* pStart{ nullptr };
        void* pNextFree{ nullptr };
        size_t size{ 0 };
};
```

This `struct` stores a pointer to the memory returned to the user in the `pStart` `void*` variable, a pointer to the next free block of memory in the `pNextFree` pointer, and the size of the allocated memory in the `size` variable.

Our memory manager isn't going to use dynamic memory to allocate memory to the user's program. Instead it is going to return an address from inside a static array. This array is created in an unnamed namespace shown in Listing 22-6.

Listing 22-6. The Unnamed namespace *from* `Chapter22-MemoryAllocator.cpp`

```
namespace
{
        const unsigned int ONE_MEGABYTE = 1024 * 1024 * 1024;
        char pMemoryHeap[ONE_MEGABYTE];
        const size_t SIZE_OF_MEMORY_HEADER = sizeof(MemoryAllocationHeader);
}
```

Here you can see that we allocate a static array of 1 MB in size. We know that this is 1 MB as the `char` type is one byte in size on most platforms and we are allocating an array that is 1,024 bytes times 1,024 KB in size for a total of 1,048,576 bytes. The unnamed namespace also has a constant storing the size of our `MemoryAllocationHeader` object, calculated using the `sizeof` function. This size is 12 bytes: 4 bytes for the `pStart` pointer, 4 bytes for the `pNextFree` pointer, and 4 bytes for the `size` variable.

The next important piece for code overloads the new operator. The `new` and `delete` functions that you have seen so far are just functions that can be hidden in the same way you can hide any other function with your own implementation. Listing 22-7 shows our new function.

Listing 22-7. The Overloaded new *Function*

```
void* operator new(size_t size)
{
        MemoryAllocationHeader* pHeader =
                reinterpret_cast<MemoryAllocationHeader*>(pMemoryHeap);
        while (pHeader != nullptr && pHeader->pNextFree != nullptr)
        {
                pHeader = reinterpret_cast<MemoryAllocationHeader*>(pHeader->pNextFree);
        }
```

```
      pHeader->pStart = reinterpret_cast<char*>(pHeader)+SIZE_OF_MEMORY_HEADER;
      pHeader->pNextFree = reinterpret_cast<char*>(pHeader->pStart) + size;
      pHeader->size = size;

      return pHeader->pStart;
}
```

The new operator is passed the size of the allocation we would like to reserve and returns a void* to the beginning of the block of memory to which the user can write. The function begins by looping over the existing memory allocations until it finds the first allocated block with a nullptr in the pNextFree variable.

Once it finds a free block of memory, the pStart pointer is initialized to be the address of the free block plus the size of the memory allocation header. This ensures that every allocation also includes space for the pStart and pNextFree pointer and the size of the allocation. The new function ends by returning the value stored in pHeader->pStart ensuring that the user doesn't know anything about the MemoryAllocationHeader struct. They simply receive a pointer to a block of memory of the size they requested.

Once we have allocated memory, we can also free that memory. The overloaded delete operator clears the allocations from our heap in Listing 22-8.

Listing 22-8. The Overloaded delete Function

```
void operator delete(void* pMemory)
{
      MemoryAllocationHeader* pLast = nullptr;
      MemoryAllocationHeader* pCurrent =
            reinterpret_cast<MemoryAllocationHeader*>(pMemoryHeap);
      while (pCurrent != nullptr && pCurrent->pStart != pMemory)
      {
            pLast = pCurrent;
            pCurrent = reinterpret_cast<MemoryAllocationHeader*>(pCurrent->pNextFree);
      }

      if (pLast != nullptr)
      {
            pLast->pNextFree = reinterpret_cast<char*>(pCurrent->pNextFree);
      }

      pCurrent->pStart = nullptr;
      pCurrent->pNextFree = nullptr;
      pCurrent->size = 0;
}
```

This operator traverses the heap using two pointers, pLast and pCurrent. The heap is traversed until the pointer passed in pMemory is matched against an allocated memory block stored in the pStart pointer in a MemoryAllocationHeader struct. Once we find the matching allocation we set the pNextFree pointer to the address stored in pCurrent->pNextFree. This is the point at which we create two problems. We have fragmented our memory by freeing memory potentially between two other blocks of allocated memory, meaning that only an allocation of the same size or smaller can be filled from this block. In this example, the fragmentation is redundant because we have not implemented any way of tracking our free blocks of memory. One option would be to use a list to store all of the free blocks rather than storing them in the memory allocation headers themselves. Writing a full-featured memory allocator is a complicated task that could fill an entire book.

> **Note**   You can see that we have a valid case for using `reinterpret_cast` in our new and delete operators. There aren't many valid cases for this type of cast. In this case we want to represent the same memory address using a different type and therefore the `reinterpret_cast` is the correct option.

Listing 22-9 contains the last memory function for this section and it is used to print out the contents of all active `MemoryAllocationHeader` objects in our heap.

Listing 22-9. The `PrintAllocations` Function

```
void PrintAllocations()
{
        MemoryAllocationHeader* pHeader =
                reinterpret_cast<MemoryAllocationHeader*>(pMemoryHeap);

        while (pHeader != nullptr)
        {
                std::cout << pHeader << std::endl;
                std::cout << pHeader->pStart << std::endl;
                std::cout << pHeader->pNextFree << std::endl;
                std::cout << pHeader->size << std::endl;

                pHeader = reinterpret_cast<MemoryAllocationHeader*>(pHeader->pNextFree);

                std::cout << std::endl << std::endl;
        }
}
```

This function loops over all of the valid `MemoryAllocationHeader` pointers in our head and prints their pStart, pNextFree, and size variables. Listing 22-10 shows an example main function that uses these functions.

Listing 22-10. Using the Memory Heap

```
int _tmain(int argc, _TCHAR* argv[])
{
        memset(pMemoryHeap, 0, SIZE_OF_MEMORY_HEADER);

        PrintAllocations();

        Simple* pSimple1 = new Simple();
```

```
        PrintAllocations();

        Simple* pSimple2 = new Simple();

        PrintAllocations();

        Simple* pSimple3 = new Simple();

        PrintAllocations();

        delete pSimple2;
        pSimple2 = nullptr;

        PrintAllocations();

        pSimple2 = new Simple();

        PrintAllocations();

        delete pSimple2;
        pSimple2 = nullptr;

        PrintAllocations();

        delete pSimple3;
        pSimple3 = nullptr;

        PrintAllocations();

        delete pSimple1;
        pSimple1 = nullptr;

        PrintAllocations();

        return 0;
}
```

This is a very simple function. It begins by using the memset function to initialize the first 12 bytes of the memory heap. memset works by taking an address, then a value to use, then the number of bytes to set. Each byte is then set to the value of the byte passed as the second parameter. In our case we are setting the first 12 bytes of pMemoryHeap to 0.

We then have our first call to PrintAllocations and the output from my run is the following.

```
0x00870320
0x00000000
0x00000000
0
```

The first line is the address of the MemoryAllocationHeader struct, which for our first call is also the address stored in pMemoryHeap. The next line is the value stored in pStart, then pNextFree, then size. These are all 0 as we have not yet made any allocations. The memory addresses are being printed as 32-bit hexadecimal values.

Our first Simple object is then allocated. It turns out that because the Simple class only contains a single int variable, we only need to allocate 4 bytes to store it. The output from the second PrintAllocations call confirms this.

```
Constructed
0x00870320
0x0087032C
0x00870330
4

0x00870330
0x00000000
0x00000000
0
```

We can see the Constructed text, which was printed in the constructor for the Simple class and then that our first MemoryAllocationHeader struct has been filled in. The address of the first allocation remains the same, as it is the beginning of the heap. The pStart variable stores the address from 12 bytes after the beginning as we have left enough space to store the header. The pNextFree variable stores the address after adding the 4 bytes required to store the pSimple variable, and the size variable stores the 4 from the size passed to new. We then have the printout of the first free block, starting at 00870330, which is conveniently 16 bytes after the first.

The program then allocates another two Simple objects to produce the following output.

```
Constructed
0x00870320
0x0087032C
0x00870330
4

0x00870330
0x0087033C
0x00870340
4

0x00870340
0x0087034C
0x00870350
4

0x00870350
0x00000000
0x00000000
0
```

In this output you can see the three allocated 4-byte objects and each of the start and next addresses in each allocation header. The output is updated again after deleting the second object.

```
Destroyed
0x00870320
0x0087032C
0x00870340
4

0x00870340
0x0087034C
0x00870350
4

0x00870350
0x00000000
0x00000000
0
```

The first allocated object now points to the third and the second allocated object has been removed from the heap. A fourth object is allocated just to see what would happen.

```
Constructed
0x00870320
0x0087032C
0x00870340
4

0x00870340
0x0087034C
0x00870350
4

0x00870350
0x0087035C
0x00870360
4

0x00870360
0x00000000
0x00000000
0
```

At this point pSimple1 is stored at address 0x0087032C, pSimple2 is at 0x0087035C, and pSimple3 is at 0x0087034C. The program then ends by deleting each allocated object one by one.

Despite the problems that would prevent you from using this memory manager in production code, it does serve as a useful example of how a heap operates. Some method of tracking allocations is used so that the memory management system can tell which memory is in use and which memory is free to be allocated.

Summary

This chapter has given you a very simple introduction to the C++ memory management model. You've seen that your programs will use static memory, stack memory, and heap memory to store the objects and data to be used by your games.

Static memory and stack memory are handled automatically by the compiler, and you've already been using these types of memory throughout this book without having to do anything in particular. Heap memory has higher management overhead, as it requires that you also free the memory once you have finished using it. You've seen that the STL provides the unique_ptr and shared_ptr templates to help automatically manage dynamic memory allocations. Finally, you were introduced to a simple memory manager. This memory manager would be unsuitable for production code, but it does provide you with an overview of how memory is allocated from a heap and how you can overload the global new and delete methods to hook in your own memory manager.

Extending this memory manager to be fully featured would involve adding support for reallocating freed blocks, defragmenting contiguous free blocks in the heap, and eventually ensuring the allocation system is thread safe. Modern games also tend to create multiple heaps to serve different purposes. It's not uncommon for games to create memory allocators to handle mesh data, textures, audio, and online systems. There could also be thread-safe allocators and allocators that are not thread safe that can be used in situations where memory accesses will not be made by more than one thread. Complex memory management systems also have small block allocators to handle memory requests below a certain size to help alleviate memory fragmentation, which could be caused by frequent small allocations made by the STL for string storage, and so on. As you can see, the topic of memory management in modern games is a far more complex problem than can be covered in this chapter alone.

Chapter 23

Useful Design Patterns for Game Development

Design patters are like blueprints for your code. They are systems you can use to complete tasks that are very similar in nature that arise while you are developing games. Just as STL data structures are reusable collections that can be used when needed to solve specific problems, design patterns can be utilized to solve logical problems in your code.

There are benefits to using design patterns in your game projects. First, they allow you to use a common language that many other developers will understand. This helps reduce the length of time it takes new programmers to get up to speed when helping on your projects because they might already be familiar with the concepts you have used when building your game's infrastructure.

Design patterns can also be implemented using common code. This means that you can reuse this code for a given pattern. Code reuse reduces the number of lines of code in use in your game, which leads to a more stable and more easily maintainable code base, both of which mean you can write better games more quickly.

You've already seen at least one design patter used in this book already. Chapter 21 showed how you could use a template class to create a `Singleton` object. You can think of a `Singleton` as a reusable logical object that provides you with the ability to ensure that only a single instance of a given class is created and accessed throughout your game code. This chapter introduces you to three more patterns: the Factory, the Observer and the Visitor.

Using the Factory Pattern in Games

The factory pattern is a useful way to abstract out the creation of dynamic objects at runtime. A factory for our purposes is simply a function that takes a type of object as a parameter and returns a pointer to a new object instance. The returned object is created on the heap and therefore it is the caller's responsibility to ensure that the object is deleted appropriately. Listing 23-1 shows a factory method that I have created to instantiate the different types of `Option` objects used in Text Adventure.

Listing 23-1. A Factory for Creating Option Instances

```
Option* CreateOption(PlayerOptions optionType)
{
        Option* pOption = nullptr;

        switch (optionType)
        {
        case PlayerOptions::GoNorth:
                pOption = new MoveOption(
                        Room::JoiningDirections::North,
                        PlayerOptions::GoNorth, "Go North");
                break;
        case PlayerOptions::GoEast:
                pOption = new MoveOption(
                        Room::JoiningDirections::East,
                        PlayerOptions::GoEast, "Go East");
                break;
        case PlayerOptions::GoSouth:
                pOption = new MoveOption(
                        Room::JoiningDirections::South,
                        PlayerOptions::GoSouth,
                        "Go South");
                break;
        case PlayerOptions::GoWest:
                pOption = new MoveOption(
                        Room::JoiningDirections::West,
                        PlayerOptions::GoWest,
                        "Go West");
                break;
        case PlayerOptions::OpenChest:
                pOption = new OpenChestOption("Open Chest");
                break;
        case PlayerOptions::AttackEnemy:
                pOption = new AttackEnemyOption();
                break;
        case PlayerOptions::Quit:
                pOption = new QuitOption("Quit");
                break;
        case PlayerOptions::None:
                break;
        default:
                break;
        }

        return pOption;
}
```

As you can see, the CreateOption factory function takes a PlayerOption enum as a parameter and then returns an appropriately constructed Option. This relies on polymorphism to return a base pointer for the object. The knock-on effect of this use of polymorphism is that any factory function can only create objects that derive from its return type. Many game engines manage this by having all creatable objects derive from a common base class. For our purposes, in the context of learning, it's better to cover a couple of examples. Listing 23-2 shows a factory for the Enemy derived classes.

Listing 23-2. The Enemy Factory

```
Enemy* CreateEnemy(EnemyType enemyType)
{
        Enemy* pEnemy = nullptr;
        switch (enemyType)
        {
        case EnemyType::Dragon:
                pEnemy = new Enemy(EnemyType::Dragon);
                break;
        case EnemyType::Orc:
                pEnemy = new Enemy(EnemyType::Orc);
                break;
        default:
                assert(false); // Unknown enemy type
                break;
        }
        return pEnemy;
}
```

If you were to create new inherited classes for these enemy types at some point in the future, you would only be required to update the factory function to add these new classes to your game. This is a handy feature of using factory methods to take advantage of polymorphic base classes.

So far all of the Option and Enemy objects in Text Adventure have been member variables within the Game class. This doesn't work too well with factory objects because the factory will create the objects on the heap, not using stack memory; therefore the Game class must be updated to store pointers to the Option and Enemy instances. You can see how this is done in Listing 23-3.

Listing 23-3. Updating Game to Store Pointers to Option and Enemy Instances

```
class Game
        : public EventHandler
{
private:
        static const unsigned int m_numberOfRooms = 4;
        using Rooms = std::array<Room::Pointer, m_numberOfRooms>;
        Rooms m_rooms;

        Player m_player;

        Option::Pointer m_attackDragonOption;
        Option::Pointer m_attackOrcOption;
        Option::Pointer m_moveNorthOption;
        Option::Pointer m_moveEastOption;
        Option::Pointer m_moveSouthOption;
        Option::Pointer m_moveWestOption;
        Option::Pointer m_openSwordChest;
        Option::Pointer m_quitOption;
```

```
        Sword m_sword;
        Chest m_swordChest;

        using Enemies = std::vector<Enemy::Pointer>;
        Enemies m_enemies;

        bool m_playerQuit{ false };

        void InitializeRooms();
        void WelcomePlayer();
        void GivePlayerOptions() const;
        void GetPlayerInput(std::stringstream& playerInput) const;
        void EvaluateInput(std::stringstream& playerInput);
public:
        Game();

        void RunGame();

        virtual void HandleEvent(const Event* pEvent);
};
```

Game now references the Option and Enemy instances via a type alias that is defined in the respective
Option and Enemy class definitions. These aliases are shown in Listing 23-4.

Listing 23-4. The Option::Pointer and Enemy::Pointer Type Aliases

```
class Option
{
public:
        using Pointer = std::shared_ptr<Option>;

protected:
        PlayerOptions m_chosenOption;
        std::string m_outputText;

public:
        Option(PlayerOptions chosenOption, const std::string& outputText)
                : m_chosenOption(chosenOption)
                , m_outputText(outputText)
        {

        }

        const std::string& GetOutputText() const
        {
                return m_outputText;
        }

        virtual void Evaluate(Player& player) = 0;
};
```

```
class Enemy
        : public Entity
{
public:
        using Pointer = std::shared_ptr<Enemy>;
private:
        EnemyType m_type;
        bool m_alive{ true };

public:
        Enemy(EnemyType type)
                : m_type{ type }
        {

        }

        EnemyType GetType() const
        {
                return m_type;
        }

        bool IsAlive() const
        {
                return m_alive;
        }

        void Kill()
        {
                m_alive = false;
        }
};
```

The Pointer aliases in both classes have been defined using the shared_ptr template. This means that once the instances have been created by the factories you will not need to worry about where the objects should be deleted. The shared_ptr will automatically delete the instance as soon as you no longer hold a shared_ptr reference.

Updating the Game class constructor is the next important change when using the two factory functions. This constructor is shown in Listing 23-5.

Listing 23-5. The Updated Game Constructor

```
Game::Game()
        : m_attackDragonOption{ CreateOption(PlayerOptions::AttackEnemy) }
        , m_attackOrcOption{ CreateOption(PlayerOptions::AttackEnemy) }
        , m_moveNorthOption{ CreateOption(PlayerOptions::GoNorth) }
        , m_moveEastOption{ CreateOption(PlayerOptions::GoEast) }
        , m_moveSouthOption{ CreateOption(PlayerOptions::GoSouth) }
        , m_moveWestOption{ CreateOption(PlayerOptions::GoWest) }
        , m_openSwordChest{ CreateOption(PlayerOptions::OpenChest) }
        , m_quitOption{ CreateOption(PlayerOptions::Quit) }
        , m_swordChest{ &m_sword }
```

```
{
        static_cast<OpenChestOption*>(m_openSwordChest.get())->SetChest(&m_swordChest);

        m_enemies.emplace_back(CreateEnemy(EnemyType::Dragon));
        static_cast<AttackEnemyOption*>(m_attackDragonOption.get())->SetEnemy(m_enemies[0]);

        m_enemies.emplace_back(CreateEnemy(EnemyType::Orc));
        static_cast<AttackEnemyOption*>(m_attackOrcOption.get())->SetEnemy(m_enemies[1]);
}
```

The constructor now calls the factory methods to create the proper instances needed to initialize the
shared_ptr for each Option and Enemy. Each Option has its own pointer, but the Enemy instances are
now placed into a vector using the emplace_back method. I've done this to show you how you can
use the shared_ptr::get method along with static_cast to convert the polymorphic base class to
the derived class needed to add the Enemy. The same type of cast is needed to add the address of
m_swordChest to the m_openSwordChest option.

That's all there is to creating basic factory functions in C++. These functions come into their own
when writing level loading code. Your data can store the type of object you'd like to create at any
given time and just pass it into a factory that knows how to instantiate the correct object. This
reduces the amount of code in your loading logic, which can help reduce bugs! This is definitely a
worthwhile goal.

Decoupling with the Observer Pattern

The observer pattern is very useful in decoupling your code. Coupled code is code that shares too
much information about itself with other classes. This could be specific methods in its interface or
variables that are exposed between classes. Coupling has a couple of major drawbacks. The first
is that it increases the number of places where your code must be updated when making changes
to exposed methods or functions and the second is that your code becomes much less reusable.
Coupled code is less reusable because you have to take over any coupled and dependent classes
when deciding to reuse just a single class.

Observers help with decoupling by providing an interface for classes to derive which provide
event methods that will be called on objects when certain changes happen on another class. The
Event system introduced earlier had an informal version of the observer pattern. The Event class
maintained a list of listeners that had their HandleEvent method called whenever an event they were
listening for was triggered. The observer pattern formalizes this concept into a Notifier template
class and interfaces that can be used to create observer classes. Listing 23-6 shows the code for
the Notifier class.

Listing 23-6. The Notifier Template Class

```
template <typename Observer>
class Notifier
{
private:
        using Observers = std::vector<Observer*>;
        Observers m_observers;
```

```
public:
        void AddObserver(Observer* observer);
        void RemoveObserver(Observer* observer);

        template <void (Observer::*Method)()>
        void Notify();
};
```

The `Notifier` class defines a vector of pointers to `Observer` objects. There are complementary methods to add and remove observers to the `Notifier` and finally a template method named `Notify`, which will be used to notify `Observer` objects of an event. Listing 23-7 shows the `AddObserver` and `RemoveObserver` method definitions.

Listing 23-7. The AddObserver and RemoveObserver method definitions

```
template <typename Observer>
void Notifier<Observer>::AddObserver(Observer* observer)
{
        assert(find(m_observers.begin(), m_observers.end(), observer) == m_observers.end());
        m_observers.emplace_back(observer);
}

template <typename Observer>
void Notifier<Observer>::RemoveObserver(Observer* observer)
{
        auto object = find(m_observers.begin(), m_observers.end(), observer);
        if (object != m_observers.end())
        {
                m_observers.erase(object);
        }
}
```

Adding an `Observer` is as simple as calling `emplace_back` on the `m_observers` vector. The assert is used to inform us if we are adding more than one copy of each `Observer` to the vector. The `remove` is achieved by using `find` to get an `iterator` to the object to be removed and calling `erase` if the iterator is valid.

The `Notify` method uses a C++ feature that you have not seen so far, ***method pointers***. A method pointer allows us to pass the address of a method from a class definition that should be called on a specific object. Listing 23-8 contains the code for the `Notify` method.

Listing 23-8. The Notifier<Observer>::Notify Method

```
template <typename Observer>
template <void(Observer::*Method)()>
void Notifier<Observer>::Notify()
{
        for (auto& observer : m_observers)
        {
                (observer->*Method)();
        }
}
```

The Notify template method specifies a method pointer parameter. The method pointer must have a void return type and take no arguments. The type of a method pointer takes the following format.

*void (Class::*VariableName)()*

Class here represents the name of the class the method belongs to and VariableName is the name we use to reference the method pointer in our code. You can see this in action in the Notify method when we call the method using the Method identifier. The object we are calling the method on here is an Observer* and the address of the method is dereferenced using the pointer operator.

Once our Notifier class is complete, we can use it to create Notifier objects. Listing 23-9 inherits a Notifier into the QuitOption class.

Listing 23-9. Updating QuitOption

```
class QuitOption
        : public Option
        , public Notifier<QuitObserver>
{
public:
        QuitOption(const std::string& outputText)
                : Option(PlayerOptions::Quit, outputText)
        {

        }

        virtual void Evaluate(Player& player);
};
```

QuitOption now inherits from the Notifier class, which is passed a new class as its template parameter. Listing 23-10 shows the QuitObserver class.

Listing 23-10. The QuitObserver Class

```
class QuitObserver
{
public:
        virtual void OnQuit() = 0;
};
```

QuitObserver is simply an interface that provides a method, OnQuit, to deriving classes. Listing 23-11 shows how you should update the QuitOption::Evaluate method to take advantage of the Notifier functionality.

Listing 23-11. Updating QuitOption::Notifier

```
void QuitOption::Evaluate(Player& player)
{
        Notify<&QuitObserver::OnQuit>();
}
```

Now you can see the very clean template method call. This simple call will call the OnQuit method on every object that has been added as an observer on the QuitOption. That's our next step: The Game class is updated to inherit from QuitObserver in Listing 23-12.

Listing 23-12. The Game Class QuitObserver

```
class Game
        : public EventHandler
        , public QuitObserver
{
private:
        static const unsigned int m_numberOfRooms = 4;
        using Rooms = std::array<Room::Pointer, m_numberOfRooms>;
        Rooms m_rooms;

        Player m_player;

        Option::Pointer m_attackDragonOption;
        Option::Pointer m_attackOrcOption;
        Option::Pointer m_moveNorthOption;
        Option::Pointer m_moveEastOption;
        Option::Pointer m_moveSouthOption;
        Option::Pointer m_moveWestOption;
        Option::Pointer m_openSwordChest;
        Option::Pointer m_quitOption;

        Sword m_sword;
        Chest m_swordChest;

        using Enemies = std::vector<Enemy::Pointer>;
        Enemies m_enemies;

        bool m_playerQuit{ false };

        void InitializeRooms();
        void WelcomePlayer();
        void GivePlayerOptions() const;
        void GetPlayerInput(std::stringstream& playerInput) const;
        void EvaluateInput(std::stringstream& playerInput);
public:
        Game();
        ~Game();

        void RunGame();

        virtual void HandleEvent(const Event* pEvent);

        // From QuitObserver
        virtual void OnQuit();
};
```

The bolded lines show that the Game class inherits from QuitObserver, now has a destructor, and overloads the OnQuit method. Listing 23-13 shows how the constructor and destructor are responsible for adding and removing the class as a listener to QuitOption.

Listing 23-13.NThe Game Class Constructor and Destructor

```
Game::Game()
: m_attackDragonOption{ CreateOption(PlayerOptions::AttackEnemy) }
, m_attackOrcOption{ CreateOption(PlayerOptions::AttackEnemy) }
, m_moveNorthOption{ CreateOption(PlayerOptions::GoNorth) }
, m_moveEastOption{ CreateOption(PlayerOptions::GoEast) }
, m_moveSouthOption{ CreateOption(PlayerOptions::GoSouth) }
, m_moveWestOption{ CreateOption(PlayerOptions::GoWest) }
, m_openSwordChest{ CreateOption(PlayerOptions::OpenChest) }
, m_quitOption{ CreateOption(PlayerOptions::Quit) }
, m_swordChest{ &m_sword }
{
        static_cast<OpenChestOption*>(m_openSwordChest.get())->SetChest(&m_swordChest);

        m_enemies.emplace_back(CreateEnemy(EnemyType::Dragon));
        static_cast<AttackEnemyOption*>(m_attackDragonOption.get())->SetEnemy(m_enemies[0]);

        m_enemies.emplace_back(CreateEnemy(EnemyType::Orc));
        static_cast<AttackEnemyOption*>(m_attackOrcOption.get())->SetEnemy(m_enemies[1]);

        static_cast<QuitOption*>(m_quitOption.get())->AddObserver(this);
}

Game::~Game()
{
        static_cast<QuitOption*>(m_quitOption.get())->RemoveObserver(this);
}
```

The bolded lines again show the relevant updates to the code. The last update in Listing 23-14 implements the OnQuit method.

Listing 23-14. The Game::OnQuit Method

```
void Game::OnQuit()
{
        m_playerQuit = true;
}
```

This is all there is to implementing the observer pattern. This has achieved another decoupling between the QuitOption class and any other classes in the game that need to know about quit events. The observer class is especially useful when creating game framework code for systems such as online features. You can imagine a situation where you implement a class to download leaderboards from a web server. This class could be used in multiple game projects and each individual game could simply implement its own class to observe the downloader and act appropriately when the leaderboard data has been received.

Easily Adding New Functionality with the Visitor Pattern

One of the main goals of writing reusable game engine code is to try to avoid including game-specific functionality in your classes. This can be hard to achieve with a pure object-oriented approach, as the aim of encapsulation is to hide the data in your classes behind interfaces. This could mean that you are required to add methods to classes to work on data that are very specific to a certain class.

We can get around this problem by loosening our encapsulation on classes that must interact with game code, but we do so in a very structured manner. You can achieve this by using the visitor pattern. A visitor is an object that knows how to carry out a specific task on a type of object. These are incredibly useful when you need to carry out similar tasks on many objects that might inherit from the same base class but have different parameters or types. Listing 23-15 shows an interface class you can use to implement Visitor objects.

Listing 23-15. The Visitor Class

```
class Visitor
{
private:
        friend class Visitable;
        virtual void OnVisit(Visitable& visitable) = 0;
};
```

The Visitor class provides a pure virtual method OnVisit, which is passed an object that inherits from a class named Visitable. Listing 23-16 lists the Visitable class.

Listing 23-16. The Visitable Class

```
class Visitable
{
public:
        virtual ~Visitable() {}

        void Visit(Visitor& visitor)
        {
                visitor.OnVisit(*this);
        }
};
```

The Visitable class provides a Visit method that is passed the Visitor object. The Visit method calls the OnVisit method on the Visitor. This allows us to make the OnVisit method private, which ensures that only Visitable objects can be visited and that we are always passing a valid reference to the OnVisit method.

The visitor pattern is very simple to set up. You can see a concrete example of how to use the pattern in Listing 23-17, where the Option class from Text Adventure has been inherited from Visitable.

Listing 23-17. The Updated Option Class

```cpp
class Option
        : public Visitable
{
public:
        using Pointer = std::shared_ptr<Option>;

protected:
        PlayerOptions m_chosenOption;
        std::string m_outputText;

public:
        Option(PlayerOptions chosenOption, const std::string& outputText)
                : m_chosenOption(chosenOption)
                , m_outputText(outputText)
        {

        }

        const std::string& GetOutputText() const
        {
                return m_outputText;
        }

        virtual void Evaluate(Player& player) = 0;
};
```

The only change required is to inherit the Option class from Visitable. To take advantage of this, a Visitor named EvaluateVisitor is created in Listing 23-18.

Listing 23-18. The EvaluateVisitor Class

```cpp
class EvaluateVisitor
        : public Visitor
{
private:
        Player& m_player;

public:
        EvaluateVisitor(Player& player)
        : m_player{ player }
        {

        }

        virtual void OnVisit(Visitable& visitable)
        {
                Option* pOption = dynamic_cast<Option*>(&visitable);
```

```
            if (pOption != nullptr)
            {
                    pOption->Evaluate(m_player);
            }
        }
};
```

The EvaluateListener::OnVisit method uses a dynamic_cast to determine if the supplied visitable variable is an object derived from the Option class. If it is, the Option::Evaluate method is called. The only remaining update is to use the EvaluateVisitor class to interface with the chosen option in Game::EvaluateInput. This update is shown in Listing 23-19.

Listing 23-19. The Game::EvaluateInput Method

```
void Game::EvaluateInput(stringstream& playerInputStream)
{
        PlayerOptions chosenOption = PlayerOptions::None;
        unsigned int playerInputChoice{ 0 };
        playerInputStream >>playerInputChoice;

        try
        {
                Option::Pointer option =
                        m_player.GetCurrentRoom()->EvaluateInput(playerInputChoice);
                EvaluateVisitor evaluator{ m_player };
                option->Visit(evaluator);
        }
        catch (const std::out_of_range&)
        {
                cout << "I do not recognize that option, try again!" << endl << endl;
        }
}
```

As you can see, the code has been updated to call the Visit method on the Option rather than calling the Evaluate method directly. That's all we needed to do to add the Visitor pattern to the Text Adventure game.

This example isn't the best use of the Visitor pattern, as it is relatively simple. Visitors can come into their own in places such as a render queue in 3-D games. You can implement different types of rendering operations in Visitor objects and use that to determine how individual games render their 3-D objects. Once you get the hang of abstracting out logic in this way, you might find many places where being able to provide different implementations independently of the data is very useful.

Summary

This chapter has given you a brief introduction to the concept of design patterns. Design patterns are exceptionally useful as they provide a ready-made toolbox of techniques that can be used to solve many diverse problems. You've seen the Singleton, Factory, Observer, and Visitor patterns used in this book, but there are many, many more.

The de facto standard textbook on software engineering design patterns is *Design Patterns: Elements of Reusable Object Oriented Software* by Gamma, Helm, Johnson, and Vlissides (also known as the "Gang of Four"). If you find this concept interesting, you should read their book. It covers the examples shown here as well as other useful patterns. Bob Nystrom, a former software engineer at EA, has provided a free online collection of design patterns relevant to game development. You can find his web site here: http://gameprogrammingpatterns.com/.

You'll find many patterns relevant and helpful when trying to solve game development problems. They also make your code easier to work with for other developers who are also versed in the common techniques that design patterns provide. Our next chapter is going to look at C++ IO streams and how we can use them to load and save game data.

24

Using File IO to Save and Load Games

Saving and loading game progress is a standard feature of all but the most basic games today. This means that you will need to know how to handle the loading and saving of game objects. This chapter covers one possible strategy for writing out the data you will need to be able to reinstate a player's game.

First we look at the SerializationManager class, which uses the STL classes ifstream and ofstream to read and write from files. Then we cover how to update the Text Adventure game to be able to save which room the player is in, which items have been picked up, which enemies are dead, and which dynamic options have been removed.

What Is Serialization?

It would be good to cover what serialization is before we serialize the game's different classes. Serialization in computer programming covers the process of converting data into a format that can be written out by the program and read in at a later point in time. There are three major systems in modern games that take advantage of serialization.

The first is the save game system that will also be the basis for this chapter. Classes are serialized into a binary data file that can be read by the game at a later point in time. This type of serialization is essential for players to be able to retain their game data between different runs of the game and even on different computers. Transferring saved games between different machines is now a key feature of Xbox Live, PlayStation Network, Steam, and Origin.

The second main use of serialization is in multiplayer gaming. Multiplayer games need to be able to convert game object state into a small a number of bytes as possible for transmission over the Internet. The program on the receiving end then needs to be able to reinterpret the stream of incoming data to update the position, rotation, and state of opponent players' and projectiles. Multiplayer games are also required to serialize the win conditions of the round players are participating in so that winners and losers can be worked out.

The remaining systems are more useful during game development. Modern game toolsets and engines provide the ability to update game data at runtime. Player properties such as health or the amount of damage dealt by weapons can be updated by game designers while the game is running. This is made possible using serialization to convert data from the tool into a data stream that the game can then use to update its current state. This form of serialization can speed up the iteration process of game design. I've even worked with a tool that allows designers to update all of the current connected players in a multiplayer session midround.

These aren't the only forms of serialization you will encounter during game development, but they are likely to be the most common. This chapter focuses on serializing game data out and in using the C++ classes `ofstream` and `ifstream`. These classes provide the ability to serialize C++'s built-in types to and from files stored in your device's file system. This chapter shows you how to create classes that are aware of how to write out and read in their data using `ifstream` and `ofstream`. It will also show you a method for managing which objects need to be serialized and how to refer to relationships between objects using unique object IDs.

The Serialization Manager

The `SerializationManager` class is a `Singleton` that is responsible for keeping track of every object in the game that can have its state streamed out or is referenced by another savable object. Listing 24-1 covers the class definition for the `SerializationManager`.

Listing 24-1. The SerializationManager Class

```cpp
class SerializationManager
        : public Singleton<SerializationManager>
{
private:
        using Serializables = std::unordered_map<unsigned int, Serializable*>;
        Serializables m_serializables;

        const char* const m_filename{"Save.txt"};

public:
        void RegisterSerializable(Serializable* pSerializable);

        void RemoveSerializable(Serializable* pSerializable);

        Serializable* GetSerializable(unsigned int serializableId) const;

        void ClearSave();

        void Save();

        bool Load();
};
```

The SerializationManager class stores pointers to Serializable objects in an unordered_map. Each of the Serializable objects will be given a unique ID that is used as the key in this collection. The file name we would like to use for the save file is stored in the m_filename variable.

There are three methods used to manage the objects that are handled by the SerializationManager class. The RegisterSerializable, RemoveSerializable, and GetSerializable methods are shown in Listing 24-2.

Listing 24-2. The RegisterSerializable, RemoveSerializable, and GetSerializable Methods

```
void SerializationManager::RegisterSerializable(Serializable* pSerializable)
{
        assert(m_serializables.find(pSerializable->GetId()) == m_serializables.end());
        m_serializables.emplace{ pSerializable->GetId(), pSerializable };
}

void SerializationManager::RemoveSerializable(Serializable* pSerializable)
{
        auto iter = m_serializables.find(pSerializable->GetId());
        if (iter != m_serializables.end())
        {
                m_serializables.erase(iter);
        }
}

Serializable* SerializationManager::GetSerializable(unsigned int serializableId) const
{
        Serializable* pSerializable{ nullptr };
        auto iter = m_serializables.find(serializableId);
        if (iter != m_serializables.end())
        {
                pSerializable = iter->second;
        }
        return pSerializable;
}
```

These methods are all fairly straightforward and manage adding, removing, and retrieving Serializable addresses from the m_serializables unordered_map.

The Save method is responsible for looping over all of the Serializable objects and asking them to write their data to an ofstream object. Listing 24-3 shows the Save method and how the ofstream object is initialized and moved.

Listing 24-3. The SerializableManager::Save

```
void SerializationManager::Save()
{
        std::ofstream file{ m_filename };
        file << true;
        file << std::endl;
```

```
        for (auto& serializable : m_serializables)
        {
                Serializable* pSerializable = serializable.second;
                file << pSerializable->GetId();
                file << std::endl;
                pSerializable->OnSave(file);

                file << std::endl;
                file << std::endl;
        }
}
```

An ofstream object is initialized by passing it the file name you wish to write to. You can then use the standard << operator to write data to the file. The o in ofstream stands for output, the f for file, and stream for its ability to stream data, meaning we are working with an *output file stream*.

The Save method begins by writing out a true. This bool is used to determine if the save game has a reinstatable save game inside. We write out false later when the player has completed the game. Save then loops over all of the stored Serializable objects, writes out their unique ID, and calls the OnSave method. The std::endl is being written out just to make the text file a little more readable and easier to debug.

The opposite action to Save is Load, shown in Listing 24-4.

Listing 24-4. The SerializationManager::Load Method

```
bool SerializationManager::Load()
{
        std::ifstream file{ m_filename };
        bool found = file.is_open();
        if (found)
        {
                bool isValid;
                file >> isValid;
                if (isValid)
                {
                        std::cout <<
                                "Save game found, would you like to load? (Type yes to load)"
                                << std::endl << std::endl;
                        std::string shouldLoad;
                        std::cin >> shouldLoad;
                        if (shouldLoad == "yes")
                        {
                                while (!file.eof())
                                {
                                        unsigned int serializableId{ 0 };
                                        file >> serializableId;
                                        auto iter = m_serializables.find(serializableId);
```

```
                                  if (iter != m_serializables.end())
                                  {
                                          iter->second->OnLoad(file);
                                  }
                          }
                  }
          }
          else
          {
                  found = false;
          }
      }
      return found;
}
```

The Load method is a little more involved than Save. You can see that it is using an ifstream, *input file stream*, rather than an ofstream. The ifstream is initialized using the file name to load. The is_open method in ifstream is used to determine if a file with the given name was found. If the player has never played the game, then no save file will exist; this check ensures that we do not try to load a game when no save game exists.

The next check is used to determine if the save file that does exist has a valid save state inside. This is done using the >> operator, just as is done when using cin. This is what happens next when cin is used to ask the player if he or she would like to load the save game. If the player types anything but *yes,* then game will start without loading.

There is then a while loop that is checking if the eof method is returning true. The eof method is determining whether the method has hit the *end of file*. The inner section of this loop reads the unique ID from the file, retrieves the Serializable from the map, and then calls the OnLoad method on that object.

The last SerializationManager method is ClearSave, which is used to write out a file with false as its only value. Listing 24-5 shows this method.

Listing 24-5. The SerializationManager::ClearSave Method

```
void SerializationManager::ClearSave()
{
        std::ofstream file{ m_filename };
        file << false;
}
```

The SerializationManager class is fairly simple. The Serializable class is also straightforward and is listed in Listing 24-6.

Listing 24-6. The Serializable Class

```
class Serializable
{
        unsigned int m_id{ 0 };
```

```
public:
        explicit Serializable(unsigned int id)
                : m_id{ id }
        {
                SerializationManager::GetSingleton().RegisterSerializable(this);
        }

        Serializable::~Serializable()
        {
                SerializationManager* pSerializationManager =
                        SerializationManager::GetSingletonPtr();
                if (pSerializationManager)
                {
                        pSerializationManager->RemoveSerializable(this);
                }
        }

        virtual void OnSave(std::ofstream& file) = 0;
        virtual void OnLoad(std::ifstream& file) = 0;

        unsigned int GetId() const { return m_id; }
};
```

The Serializable class is intended to be inherited by the classes you would like to be able to save between game sessions and is therefore implemented as an interface. This is achieved by making the OnSave and OnLoad method purely virtual.

Each Serializable also stores an ID in the m_id variable. The constructor and destructor automatically adds and removes the object from the SerializationManager object that it accesses via the Singleton pattern.

Saving and Loading Text Adventure

The first step toward being able to save and load the game is to create the SerializationManager. Listing 24-7 shows the updated main function.

Listing 24-7. The Updated main Function

```
int _tmain(int argc, _TCHAR* argv[])
{
        new SerializationManager();

        Game game;
        game.RunGame();

        delete SerializationManager::GetSingletonPtr();

        return 0;
}
```

Creating and deleting the SerializationManager in main ensures that it exists for the entirety of the Game::RunGame method. The game is saved when the player chooses to quit, and Listing 24-8 shows how this is achieved.

Listing 24-8. Saving the Game

```
void Game::OnQuit()
{
        SerializationManager::GetSingleton().Save();
        m_playerQuit = true;
}
```

A call to SerializationManager::Save is added to the Game::OnQuit method. The Load and ClearSave methods are added to Game::RunGame in Listing 24-9.

Listing 24-9. The Game::RunGame Method

```
void Game::RunGame()
{
        InitializeRooms();

        const bool loaded = SerializationManager::GetSingleton().Load();
        WelcomePlayer(loaded);

        bool playerWon = false;
        while (m_playerQuit == false && playerWon == false)
        {
                GivePlayerOptions();

                stringstream playerInputStream;
                GetPlayerInput(playerInputStream);

                EvaluateInput(playerInputStream);

                for (auto& enemy : m_enemies)
                {
                        playerWon = enemy->IsAlive() == false;
                }
        }

        if (playerWon == true)
        {
                SerializationManager::GetSingleton().ClearSave();
                cout << "Congratulations, you rid the dungeon of monsters!" << endl;
                cout << "Type goodbye to end" << endl;
                std::string input;
                cin >> input;
        }
}
```

The WelcomePlayer method is now updated to ask the players if they would like to load their save game in Listing 24-10.

Listing 24-10. Updating Game::WelcomePlayer

```
void Game::WelcomePlayer(const bool loaded)
{
        if (!loaded)
        {
                cout << "Welcome to Text Adventure!" << endl << endl;
                cout << "What is your name?" << endl << endl;

                string name;
                cin >> name;
                m_player.SetName(name);

                cout << endl << "Hello " << m_player.GetName() << endl;
        }
        else
        {
                cout << endl << "Welcome Back " << m_player.GetName() << endl << endl;
        }
}
```

WelcomePlayer now greets players with a Welcome Back message once the game has loaded and reinstated the name they entered when they first played the game.

The next change to the Game class code is to pass a unique ID into the constructor of each object we would like to be a Serializable. The Game constructor is one place where this happens, as shown in Listing 24-11.

Listing 24-11. The Game Class Constructor

```
Game::Game()
: m_attackDragonOption{
        CreateOption(
                PlayerOptions::AttackEnemy,
                SDBMCalculator<18>::CalculateValue("AttackDragonOption")) }
, m_attackOrcOption{
        CreateOption(
                PlayerOptions::AttackEnemy,
                SDBMCalculator<15>::CalculateValue("AttackOrcOption")) }
, m_moveNorthOption{
        CreateOption(
                PlayerOptions::GoNorth,
                SDBMCalculator<15>::CalculateValue("MoveNorthOption")) }
, m_moveEastOption{
        CreateOption(
                PlayerOptions::GoEast,
                SDBMCalculator<14>::CalculateValue("MoveEastOption")) }
```

```
, m_moveSouthOption{
        CreateOption(
                PlayerOptions::GoSouth,
                SDBMCalculator<15>::CalculateValue("MoveSouthOption")) }
, m_moveWestOption{
        CreateOption(
                PlayerOptions::GoWest,
                SDBMCalculator<14>::CalculateValue("MoveWestOption")) }
, m_openSwordChest{
        CreateOption(
                PlayerOptions::OpenChest,
                SDBMCalculator<20>::CalculateValue("OpenSwordChestOption")) }
, m_quitOption{
        CreateOption(
                PlayerOptions::Quit,
                SDBMCalculator<10>::CalculateValue("QuitOption")) }
, m_swordChest{ &m_sword, SDBMCalculator<5>::CalculateValue("Chest") }
{
        static_cast<OpenChestOption*>(m_openSwordChest.get())->SetChest(&m_swordChest);

        m_enemies.emplace_back(
                CreateEnemy(
                        EnemyType::Dragon,
                        SDBMCalculator<6>::CalculateValue("Dragon")));
        static_cast<AttackEnemyOption*>(m_attackDragonOption.get())->SetEnemy(m_enemies[0]);

        m_enemies.emplace_back(
                CreateEnemy(
                        EnemyType::Orc,
                        SDBMCalculator<3>::CalculateValue("Orc")));
        static_cast<AttackEnemyOption*>(m_attackOrcOption.get())->SetEnemy(m_enemies[1]);

        static_cast<QuitOption*>(m_quitOption.get())->AddObserver(this);
}
```

As you can see, each factory function now takes a hashed string that is used to construct the object and supply a unique ID for the SerializationManager's unordered_map. This unique key is also useful for game objects to be able to save out their references to other objects. You can see this in Listing 24-12, in which the source code for Player::OnSave is shown.

Listing 24-12. The Player::OnSave Method

```
void Player::OnSave(std::ofstream& file)
{
        file << m_name;
        file << std::endl;
        file << m_items.size();
        file << std::endl;
```

```
        for (auto& item : m_items)
        {
                file << item->GetId();
                file << std::endl;
        }
        file << m_pCurrentRoom->GetId();
        file << std::endl;
}
```

The Player::OnSave method writes out the name the user supplied when beginning his or her game. It then writes out the number of items in the m_items collection. Each item's ID is written out and finally the m_pCurrentRoom ID is written out. The block of text in the save file for a player looks like the following:

```
1923481025
Bruce
1
3714624381
625001751
```

The first line is the unique ID of the Player object, followed by the m_name, the number of Items, the ID of the one item, and finally the ID of the Room the player was in at the time he or she quit.

The Player::OnSave method is mirrored by the Player::OnLoad method in Listing 24-13.

Listing 24-13. The Player::OnLoad Method

```
void Player::OnLoad(std::ifstream& file)
{
        file >> m_name;
        unsigned int numItems;
        file >> numItems;
        for (unsigned int i = 0; i < numItems; ++i)
        {
                unsigned int itemId;
                file >> itemId;
                Item* pItem =
                dynamic_cast<Item*>(
                        SerializationManager::GetSingleton().GetSerializable(itemId));
                m_items.emplace_back{ pItem };
        }

        unsigned int roomId;
        file >> roomId;
        Room* pRoom =
                dynamic_cast<Room*>(
                        SerializationManager::GetSingleton().GetSerializable(roomId));
        m_pCurrentRoom = pRoom->GetPointer();
}
```

The OnLoad method reads the m_name variable out of the file, then the number of items. There is then a for loop that reads out the IDs of each item and retrieves a pointer to the Item from the SerializationManager. Each Serializable pointer is converted into an Item pointer using a dynamic_cast.

The Room pointer is a little more challenging. The Player class does not store a raw pointer to the Room object; instead, a shared_ptr was used. Listing 24-14 shows how the Room class has been updated to store a shared_ptr to itself, which can be used to retrieve a valid shared_ptr when retrieving the object from the SerializationManager.

Listing 24-14. The Room Class

```cpp
class Room
        : public Entity
        , public Serializable
{
public:
        using Pointer = std::shared_ptr<Room>;

        enum class JoiningDirections
        {
                North = 0,
                East,
                South,
                West,
                Max
        };

private:
        using JoiningRooms = std::array<Pointer, static_cast<size_t>(JoiningDirections::Max)>;
        JoiningRooms m_pJoiningRooms;

        using StaticOptions = std::map<unsigned int, Option::Pointer>;
        StaticOptions m_staticOptions;
        unsigned int m_staticOptionStartKey{ 1 };

        using DynamicOptions = std::vector<Option::Pointer>;
        DynamicOptions m_dynamicOptions;

        Pointer m_pointer{ this };

public:
        explicit Room(unsigned int serializableId);

        void AddRoom(JoiningDirections direction, Pointer room);
        Pointer GetRoom(JoiningDirections direction) const;

        Option::Pointer EvaluateInput(unsigned int playerInput);
        void AddStaticOption(Option::Pointer option);
        void AddDynamicOption(Option::Pointer option);
        void PrintOptions() const;
```

```
        virtual void OnSave(std::ofstream& file);
        virtual void OnLoad(std::ifstream& file);

        Pointer GetPointer() const { return m_pointer; }
};
```

Now any time any part of our code wishes to store a shared_ptr to a Serializable object, it should be retrieving the pointer from a shared place. The easiest place for this to be is on the object itself, which is registered with the SerializationManager via its unique ID.

The Room class has to save and load the state of its dynamic options. Listing 24-15 shows the save and load methods.

Listing 24-15. Room::OnSave and Room::OnLoad

```cpp
void Room::OnSave(std::ofstream& file)
{
        file << m_dynamicOptions.size();
        file << std::endl;
        for (auto& dynamicOption : m_dynamicOptions)
        {
                file << dynamicOption->GetId();
                file << std::endl;
        }
}


void Room::OnLoad(std::ifstream& file)
{
        m_dynamicOptions.clear();

        unsigned int numDynamicOptions;
        file >> numDynamicOptions;
        if (numDynamicOptions > 0)
        {
                for (unsigned int i = 0; i < numDynamicOptions; ++i)
                {
                        unsigned int optionId;
                        file >> optionId;
                        Option* pOption =
                                dynamic_cast<Option*>(
                SerializationManager::GetSingleton().GetSerializable(optionId));
                        if (pOption)
                        {
                                Option::Pointer sharedPointer = pOption->GetPointer();
                                m_dynamicOptions.emplace_back{ sharedPointer };
                        }
                }
        }
}
```

The OnSave method loops over all of the dynamic options and saves their unique IDs after saving the number of dynamic options the state has. The OnLoad method begins by clearing the existing dynamic options and then reinstates each option from the SerializationManager. Once again this is done using a dynamic_cast and retrieving a shared_ptr from the Option class instances.

The Chest class and the Enemy classes are the only other classes with added OnSave and OnLoad methods. These are used to save the m_isOpen and m_alive variables from these classes and are shown in Listing 24-16.

Listing 24-16. The Chest::OnSave, Chest::OnLoad, Enemy::OnSave, *and* Enemy::OnLoad *Methods*

```
virtual void Chest::OnSave(std::ofstream& file)
{
        file << m_isOpen;
}

virtual void Chest::OnLoad(std::ifstream& file)
{
        file >> m_isOpen;
}

virtual void Enemy::OnSave(std::ofstream& file)
{
        file << m_alive;
}

virtual void Enemy::OnLoad(std::ifstream& file)
{
        file >> m_alive;
}
```

These simple methods round out the last of the class changes to support the saving and loading of the Text Adventure game. At this point I'd encourage you to get the sample code from the accompanying web site and take a look at the execution of the program in your debugger to get a feeling for how the ability to be able to reference objects via a centralized system using unique IDs can be very useful.

Summary

This chapter has given you an overview of a simple mechanism for implementing the ability to save and load your games. The ifstream and ofstream classes provide a simple mechanism for writing and reading file data for your programs. These classes follow the usual conventions for stream types in C++ and should be easily recognizable from the cin, cout, and stringstream examples you have already seen throughout this book.

One of the most important lessons to take away from this chapter is the fact that pointers are not transferrable from one game session to the next. This is true for trying to implement a loading and saving system and is also true for implementing a multiplayer game. Pointer addresses cannot be sent from one computer to another to refer to any given object. Instead objects need to be created with a consistent and persistent unique ID and registered with a centralized system, which ensures there are no key clashes and can provide access to objects wherever it might be needed in your code.

Chapter 25

Speeding Up Games with Concurrent Programming

Processor manufacturers have hit a ceiling on the number of cycles their CPUs can execute per second. This can be seen with modern CPUs in desktop computers, tablets, and mobile phones where CPU speeds are rarely seen over the 2.5 Ghz mark.

CPU manufacturers have taken to adding more and more cores to their CPUs to provide more and more performance. The Xbox One, PlayStation 4, Samsung Galaxy phones, and desktop CPUs all have access to eight CPU cores to execute programs. This means that programmers of modern software need to embrace multithreaded, concurrent programming if they wish their programs to get the most out of modern computing devices and feel fluid and responsive for their users. Game programmers have to think about concurrency even across different processors. The Xbox One and PlayStation 4 actually have dual quad-core CPUs, audio CPUs, and GPUs all executing code at the same time.

This chapter will introduce multicore CPU programming so that you can have a basic understanding of how C++ allows you to execute code on multiple threads, how to ensure that those threads share resources responsibly, and how to make sure that all of the threads are destroyed before your program ends.

Running Text Adventure in Its Own Thread

I'm going to show you how to create a thread in this section that will execute the Game::RunGame method. This will mean that the main game loop is running in its own execution thread and our main function is left to carry out other tasks. Listing 25-1 shows how to create a game thread.

Listing 25-1. Creating a Thread

```
#include "GameLoop.h"
#include <thread>

void RunGameThread(Game& game)
{
        game.RunGame();
}

int _tmain(int argc, _TCHAR* argv[])
{
        new SerializationManager();

        Game game;
        std::thread gameThread{ RunGameThread, std::ref{ game } };
        assert(gameThread.joinable());
        gameThread.join();

        delete SerializationManager::GetSingletonPtr();

        return 0;
}
```

C++ provides the thread class that will automatically create a native operating system thread and execute a function that you pass into its constructor. In this example, we are creating a thread named gameThread that will run the RunGameThread function.

RunGameThread takes a reference to a Game object as a parameter. You can see that we are using std::ref to pass the game object to gameThread. You need to do this because the thread class constructor makes a copy of the object being passed in. Once it has this copy and starts the thread, the destructor is called on the copy. Calling ~Game will call ~Player, which will unregister our m_player object from the SerializationManager. If this happens, our game will crash, as the m_player object will not exist whenever the game tries to load the user's save game. The std::ref object avoids this by storing a reference to the game object internally and making copies of itself. When the destructors are being called, they are called on the ref object and not on the object passed. This prevents the crash you would otherwise experience.

Execution continues on your original thread once the new thread has been created and is running the function you supplied. At this point you can carry out some other tasks. Text Adventure doesn't have any other jobs to complete at the moment, and therefore execution would carry on, delete the SerializationManager, and return. This would cause another crash because your gameThread would go out of scope and try to destroy your running thread. What you really want to happen is for _tmain to stop executing until the task being carried out in gameThread has completed. Threads complete when their function returns and in our case we will be waiting for the player to either quit or win the game.

You make a running thread wait for another by calling join on the other thread's object. The joinable method is supplied to make sure that the thread you would like to wait on is one that is valid and running. You can test this by placing a breakpoint on the delete SerializationManager line. Your breakpoint will not be hit until you complete your game.

That's all there is to creating, running, and waiting for threads in C++. The next task is to work out how to make sure that threads can share data between each other without causing issues.

Sharing Data Between Threads Using Mutexes

Multithreaded programming introduces problems. What happens if two threads try to access the same variables at exactly the same time? Data can be inconsistent, data can be wrong, and changes can be lost. In the very worst examples your programs will crash. The updated main function in Listing 25-2 shows an example of a program that would crash when both threads access the same functions at the same time.

Listing 25-2. A Version of _tmain That Would Crash

```
int _tmain(int argc, _TCHAR* argv[])
{
        new SerializationManager();

        Game game;
        std::thread gameThread{ RunGameThread, std::ref{ game } };
        assert(gameThread.joinable());
        while (!game.HasFinished())
        {
                // Stick a breakpoint below to see that this code
                // is running at the same time as RunGame!
                int x = 0;
        }
        gameThread.join();

        delete SerializationManager::GetSingletonPtr();

        return 0;
}
```

This code would crash because the Game::HasFinished method is being called repeatedly. It is guaranteed that both the main thread and the game thread would try to access the variables inside HasFinished at the same time. Listing 25-3 contains the Game::HasFinished method.

Listing 25-3. Game::HasFinished

```
bool HasFinished() const
{
        return (m_playerQuit || m_playerWon);
}
```

The Game class tries to write to the m_playerWon variable once every loop. Eventually the main thread will try to read the m_playerWon variable at the same time as the game thread is writing to it and the program will close. You solve this problem by using mutual exclusion. C++ provides a mutex class that blocks execution on multiple threads around accesses to shared variables. By adding the code from Listing 25-4 you can create a mutex in the Game class.

Listing 25-4. Creating a mutex

```
std::mutex m_mutex;
std::unique_lock<std::mutex> m_finishedQueryLock{ m_mutex, std::defer_lock };
```

We have two parts to our mutex, the mutex itself and a wrapper template named unique_lock, which provides convenient access to the behavior of the mutex. The unique_lock constructor takes a mutex object as its main parameter. This is the mutex that it acts on. The second parameter is optional; if it is not supplied, the unique_lock obtains a lock on the mutex immediately but by passing std::defer_lock we can prevent this from happening.

At this point you might be wondering exactly how a mutex works. A mutex can be locked and unlocked. We class the process of locking a mutex as obtaining a lock. The unique_lock template provides three methods to work with the mutex: lock, unlock, and try_lock.

The lock method is a *blocking* call. This means that your thread's execution will stall until the mutex has been successfully locked by the thread you called lock from. If the mutex is already locked by another thread, your thread will wait until the mutex becomes unlocked before proceeding.

The unlock method unlocks a locked mutex. Best practice is to hold your lock for as few lines of code as possible. Generally this means that you should do any calculations you need before obtaining a lock, obtain the lock, write the result to the shared variable, and then unlock immediately to allow other threads to lock the mutex.

The try_lock method is a nonblocking version of lock. This method returns true if the lock was obtained or false if the lock was not obtained. This allows you to do other work, usually in a loop within the thread until such time that the try_lock method returns true.

Now that you have seen the code to create a lock, I can show you how to use the unique_lock template to prevent your Text Adventure game from crashing. Listing 25-5 uses the lock to protect access to the m_playerQuit and m_playerWon variables in the HasFinished method.

Listing 25-5. Updating Game::HasFinished with the unique_lock

```
bool HasFinished() const
{
        m_finishedQueryLock.lock();
        bool hasFinished = m_playerQuit || m_playerWon;
        m_finishedQueryLock.unlock();
        return hasFinished;
}
```

The HasFinished method now calls the lock method on m_finishedQueryLock before it calculates the value to be stored in the hasFinished variable. The lock is released before the return statement in the method to allow any waiting threads to be able to lock the mutex.

This is only the first step in being able to protect our program from crashes. The HasFinished method is called on the main thread but the m_playerWon and m_playerQuit variables are written to from the game thread. I have added three new methods to protect these variables in the game thread in Listing 25-6.

Listing 25-6. The Game::SetPlayerQuit and Game::SetPlayerWon Methods

```
void SetPlayerQuit()
{
        m_finishedQueryLock.lock();
        m_playerQuit = true;
        m_finishedQueryLock.unlock();
}

void SetPlayerWon()
{
        m_finishedQueryLock.lock();
        m_playerWon = true;
        m_finishedQueryLock.unlock();
}

bool GetPlayerWon()
{
        m_finishedQueryLock.lock();
        bool playerWon = m_playerWon;
        m_finishedQueryLock.unlock();
        return playerWon;
}
```

This means that we are required to update the Game::OnQuit method as shown in Listing 25-7.

Listing 25-7. The Game::OnQuit Method

```
void Game::OnQuit()
{
        SerializationManager::GetSingleton().Save();
        SetPlayerQuit();
}
```

The Game::OnQuit method now calls the SetPlayerQuit method, which uses the m_finishedQueryLock to protect the variable access. The RunGame method needs to be updated to use the SetPlayerWon and GetPlayerWon methods and is shown in Listing 25-8.

Listing 25-8. Updating Game::RunGame

```
void Game::RunGame()
{
        InitializeRooms();

        const bool loaded = SerializationManager::GetSingleton().Load();
        WelcomePlayer(loaded);

        while (!HasFinished())
        {
                GivePlayerOptions();
```

```
                stringstream playerInputStream;
                GetPlayerInput(playerInputStream);

                EvaluateInput(playerInputStream);

                bool playerWon = true;
                for (auto& enemy : m_enemies)
                {
                        playerWon &= enemy->IsAlive() == false;
                }

                if (playerWon)
                {
                        SetPlayerWon();
                }
        }

        if (GetPlayerWon())
        {
                SerializationManager::GetSingleton().ClearSave();
                cout << "Congratulations, you rid the dungeon of monsters!" << endl;
                cout << "Type goodbye to end" << endl;
                std::string input;
                cin >>input;
        }
}
```

The bold lines show the updates to this method to support the mutex protection around our shared variables. There's an attempt to follow best practice by using a local variable to work out if the player has won the game before calling the SetPlayerWon method. You could wrap the entire loop in a mutex lock mechanism, but this would slow your program, as both threads would be spending longer in a state where they were simply waiting for locks to be unlocked and not executing code.

This extra work is one reason why splitting a program into two separate threads does not give a 100% increase in performance as there is some overhead to waiting for lock to synchronize access to shared memory between the threads. Reducing these synchronization points is key to extracting as much performance as possible from multithreaded code.

Threads and mutexes make up a low-level view of multithreaded programming. They represent abstract versions of operating system threads and locks. C++ also provides higher level threading abstractions that you should use more often than threads. These are provided in the promise and future classes.

Using Futures and Promises

The future and promise classes are used in a pair. The promise executes a task and places its result in a future. A future blocks execution on a thread until the promise result is available. Fortunately C++ provides a third template to create a promise and future for us so that we don't have to manually do this over and over.

Listing 25-9 updates the `Game::RunGame` to use a `packaged_task` to load the user's save game data.

Listing 25-9. Using a packaged_task

```
bool LoadSaveGame()
{
        return SerializationManager::GetSingleton().Load();
}

void Game::RunGame()
{
        InitializeRooms();

        std::packaged_task< bool() > loaderTask{ LoadSaveGame };
        std::thread loaderThread{ std::ref{ loaderTask } };
        auto loaderFuture = loaderTask.get_future();
        while (loaderFuture.wait_for(std::chrono::seconds{ 0 }) != std::future_status::ready)
        {
                // Wait until the future is ready.
                // In a full game you could update a spinning progress icon!
                int x = 0;
        }
        bool userSaveLoaded = loaderFuture.get();
        WelcomePlayer(userSaveLoaded);

        while (!HasFinished())
        {
                GivePlayerOptions();

                stringstream playerInputStream;
                GetPlayerInput(playerInputStream);

                EvaluateInput(playerInputStream);

                bool playerWon = true;
                for (auto& enemy : m_enemies)
                {
                        playerWon &= enemy->IsAlive() == false;
                }

                if (playerWon)
                {
                        SetPlayerWon();
                }
        }
}
```

```
        if (GetPlayerWon())
        {
                SerializationManager::GetSingleton().ClearSave();
                cout << "Congratulations, you rid the dungeon of monsters!" << endl;
                cout << "Type goodbye to end" << endl;
                std::string input;
                cin >>input;
        }
}
```

The first step was to create a function, LoadSaveGame, to be executed in another thread. LoadSaveGame calls the SerializationManager::Load method. The LoadSaveGame function pointer is passed into the packaged_task constructor. The packaged_task template has been specialized with the type bool(). This is the type of the function; it returns a bool and does not take any parameters.

Then std::ref is used to pass the packaged_task into a thread. When a packaged_task is passed to a thread it can be executed, as a thread object knows how to handle packaged_task objects. This is true because a packaged_task object overloads an operator, which allows it to be called just like a function. This overloaded function call operator calls the actual function used to construct the packaged_task.

The main thread can now call the get_future method on the packaged_task. A future is used in threaded programs to allow you to set up tasks that will provide returned values at some point in the *future*. You could call get immediately on the future, but as get is a blocking call, your thread would stall until the future result is available. Listing 25-9 shows an alternate implementation where wait_for is used to check if the future result is available.

The future::wait_for method takes a value from the std::chrono set of duration classes. In this case, we are passing in std::chrono::seconds{ 0 }, which means the method will return instantly with a result. The possible return values in our case come from the std::future_status enum class and are ready or timeout. The timeout value will be returned until the player's game is loaded or he or she chooses to start a new game. At that point we can call the future::get method, which stores the value returned from SerializationManager::Load, via the LoadSaveGame function passed to loaderTask.

That wraps up your brief introduction to multithreaded C++ programming.

Summary

In this chapter you have been introduced to some of the classes C++ provides to allow you to add multiple execution threads to your programs. You first saw how threads can be created to execute functions. Calling functions in this manner allows the operating system to run your threads on more than one CPU thread and speed up the execution of your program.

When you use threads you need to make sure that your threads do not conflict when accessing variables and sharing data. You saw that the mutex can be used to manually provide mutually exclusive access to variables. After showing a mutex in action, I then introduced you to the packaged_task template, which automatically creates a promise and a future to better manage your concurrent tasks at a higher level than the base thread and mutex.

Using threads like this can allow you to provide better responsiveness to players. They aren't particularly effective in this task in a text-based game, but they can be used to provide more CPU execution time per frame in a 3D graphics-based game or for situations such as having a constantly updating loading or progress bar when long-running tasks are executing on other CPUs. Better responsiveness or faster frame rates improve usability and players' perception of your games.

The next and last chapter in this book will show you techniques that you can use to write code that will compile on multiple platforms. This will be useful if you find yourself in a situation where you want to write games that can run on iOS, Android and Windows Phones, or Windows and Linux, or even consoles such as the Xbox One and PlayStation 4. You might even write a game that can run on all of these in the same way an engine such as Unity can.

Chapter 26

Supporting Multiple Platforms in C++

There will come a time in your game development career when you have to write code that will only work on a single platform. That code will have to be compiled out of other platforms. You will more than likely also have to find alternative implementations for each of the platforms you will be working on. Classic examples of such code can usually be found in interactions between your game and online login and microtransaction solutions such as Game Center, Google+, Xbox Live, PlayStation Network, and Steam.

There can be more complicated problems between different platforms. iOS devices run on Arm processors; Android supports Arm, x86, and MIPS; and most other operating systems can be run on more than a single instruction set. The problem that can arise is that compilers for each of these CPU instruction sets can use different sizes for their built-in types. This is especially true when moving from 32-bit CPUs to 64-bit CPUs. In these situations pointers are no longer 32 bits in size; they are, in fact, 64 bits. This can cause all sorts of portability problems if you assume that types and pointers are of a fixed size. These issues can be very difficult to track down and will usually cause either graphical corruption or you will see your programs simply crash at random times.

Ensuring Types Are the Same Size on Multiple Platforms

Ensuring that your program uses the same size of types in your programs on multiple platforms will be easier than you might initially think. The C++ STL provides a header called `cstdint` that contains types that are of a consistent size. These types are:

```
int8_t and uint8_t
int16_t and uint16_t
int32_t and uint32_t
int64_t and uint64_t
```

The int8_t and uint8_t provide integers that are 8 bits or one byte in length. The *u* version is unsigned and the non-u version is signed. The other types are similar but of their equivalent fixed length. There are 16-bit versions, 32-bit versions, and 64-bit versions of integers.

> **Note** You should avoid using the 64-bit integers for the time being unless you explicitly need numbers that cannot be stored within 32 bits. Most processors still operator on 32-bit integers when doing arithmetic. Even 64-bit processors that have 64-bit memory addresses for pointers still do normal arithmetic using 32-bit ints. In addition, 64-bit values use twice as much memory as 32-bit values, which increases the RAM required to execute your program.

The next problem that might arise is that the char type might not be the same on all platforms. C++ does not supply a fixed-size char type, so we need to improvise a little. Every platform I have developed games on has used 8-bit char types, so we're only going to account for that. We will, however, define our own char type alias so that if you ever do port code to a platform with chars larger than 8 bits then you will only have to solve the problem in a single place. Listing 26-1 shows the code for a new header, FixedTypes.h.

Listing 26-1. FixedTypes.h

```
#pragma once
#include <cassert>
#include <cstdint>
#include <climits>

static_assert(CHAR_BIT == 8, "Compiling on a platform with large char type!");
using char8_t = char;
using uchar8_t = unsigned char;
```

The FixedTypes.h file includes cstdint, which gives us access to the 8- to 64-bit fixed-width integers. We then have a static_assert that ensures that the CHAR_BIT constant is equal to 8. The CHAR_BIT constant is supplied by the climits header and contains the number of bits that are used by the char type on your target platform. This static_assert will ensure that our code, which includes the FixedTypes header, will not compile on platforms that use a char with more than 8 bits. The header then defines two type aliases, char8_t and uchar8_t, which you should use when you know you specifically need 8-bit chars. This isn't necessarily everywhere. Generally you will need 8-bit char types when loading data that was written out using tools on another computer that did use 8-bit character values because the length of the strings in the data will have one byte per character rather than more. If you're not sure if you do or don't need 8 bits specifically, you're better sticking to always using 8-bit chars.

The last problem solved in the cstdint header is for using pointers on platforms with different-sized pointers to integers. Consider the code in Listing 26-2.

Listing 26-2. An Example Bad Pointer Cast

```
bool CompareAddresses(void* pAddress1, void* pAddress2)
{
        uint32_t address1 = reinterpret_cast<uint32_t>(pAddress1);
        uint32_t address2 = reinterpret_cast<uint32_t>(pAddress2);
        return address1 == address2;
}
```

There are a handful of cases where you might be required to compare the values of two addresses and you could case the pointers to 32-bit unsigned ints to achieve this comparison. This code, however, is not portable. The following two hexadecimal values represent different memory locations on 64-bit computers:

```
0xFFFFFFFF00000000
0x0000000000000000
```

If you cast these two values to uint32_t the two hex values stored in the unsigned integers will be:

```
0x00000000
0x00000000
```

The CompareAddresses function would return true for two different addresses because the upper 32 bits of the 64-bit addresses have been narrowed without warning by reinterpret_cast. This function would always work on systems with 32-bit pointers or less and only break on 64-bit systems. Listing 26-3 contains the solution to this problem.

Listing 26-3. An Example of a Good Pointer Comparison

```
bool CompareAddresses(void* pAddress1, void* pAddress2)
{
        uintptr_t address1 = reinterpret_cast<uintptr_t>(pAddress1);
        uintptr_t address2 = reinterpret_cast<uintptr_t>(pAddress2);
        return address1 == address2;
}
```

The cstdint header provides intptr_t and uintptr_t, which are signed and unsigned integers with enough bytes to completely store an address on your target platform. You should always use these types when casting pointers into integer values if you would like to write portable code!

Now that we've covered the different issues we can encounter with different-sized integers and pointers on different platforms, we'll look at how we can provide different implementations of classes on different platforms.

Using the Preprocessor to Determine Target Platform

Straight off the bat in this section, I'll show you a header file that defines preprocessor macros to determine which platform you are currently targeting. Listing 26-4 contains the code for the Platforms.h header file.

Listing 26-4. `Platforms.h`

```
#pragma once

#if defined(_WIN32) || defined(_WIN64)

#define PLATFORM_WINDOWS 1
#define PLATFORM_ANDROID 0
#define PLATFORM_IOS 0

#elif defined(__ANDROID__)

#define PLATFORM_WINDOWS 0
#define PLATFORM_ANDROID 1
#define PLATFORM_IOS 0

#elif defined(TARGET_OS_IPHONE)

#define PLATFORM_WINDOWS 0
#define PLATFORM_ANDROID 0
#define PLATFORM_IOS 1

#endif
```

This header achieves the task of converting preprocessor symbols provided by the Windows, Android, and iOS build tools into single definitions that we can now use in our own code. The _WIN32 and _WIN64 macros are added to your build on Windows machines, whereas __ANDROID__ and TARGET_OS_IPHONE exist when building Android and iOS applications. These definitions can change over time, and an obvious example is the _WIN64 macro, which did not exist before the 64-bit versions of the Windows operating system and this is the reason for wanting to create our own platform macros. We can add or remove from Platforms.h as we see fit without affecting the rest of our program.

I've updated the Enemy classes to have platform-specific implementations to show you how you can put these platform-specific classes into action. Listing 26-5 shows that the Enemy class has been renamed EnemyBase.

Listing 26-5. Renaming Enemy to EnemyBase

```
#pragma once

#include "Entity.h"
#include "EnemyFactory.h"
#include "Serializable.h"
#include <memory>

class EnemyBase
        : public Entity
        , public Serializable
```

```
{
public:
        using Pointer = std::shared_ptr<EnemyBase>;

private:
        EnemyType m_type;
        bool m_alive{ true };

public:
        EnemyBase(EnemyType type, const uint32_t serializableId)
                : m_type{ type }
                , Serializable(serializableId)
        {

        }

        EnemyType GetType() const
        {
                return m_type;
        }

        bool IsAlive() const
        {
                return m_alive;
        }

        void Kill()
        {
                m_alive = false;
        }

        virtual void OnSave(std::ofstream& file)
        {
                file << m_alive;
        }

        virtual void OnLoad(std::ifstream& file)
        {
                file >>m_alive;
        }
};
```

The class isn't pure virtual as we don't actually have any platform-specific code to add as this is an exercise for illustrative purposes. You can imagine that a proper base class for platform abstraction would have pure virtual methods that would have platform-specific code added.

The next step is to create three classes for our different platforms. These are shown in Listing 26-6.

Listing 26-6. WindowsEnemy, AndroidEnemy, and iOSEnemy

```cpp
class WindowsEnemy
        : public EnemyBase
{
public:
        WindowsEnemy(EnemyType type, const uint32_t serializableId)
                : EnemyBase(type, serializableId)
        {
                std::cout << "Created Windows Enemy!" << std::endl;
        }
};

class AndroidEnemy
        : public EnemyBase
{
public:
        AndroidEnemy(EnemyType type, const uint32_t serializableId)
                : EnemyBase( type , serializableId )
        {
                std::cout << "Created Android Enemy!" << std::endl;
        }
};

class iOSEnemy
        : public EnemyBase
{
public:
        iOSEnemy(EnemyType type, const uint32_t serializableId)
                : EnemyBase(type, serializableId)
        {
                std::cout << "Created iOS Enemy!" << std::endl;
        }
};
```

These three classes rely on polymorphism to allow the rest of the program to work with the
EnemyBase class rather than the platform-specific implementations. The last problem to solve is how
to create these classes. Fortunately the Factory pattern gives us a ready-made solution. Listing 26-7
updates EnemyFactory to create the correct type of EnemyBase for our implementation.

Listing 26-7. Updating EnemyFactory with Platform-Specific Types

```cpp
namespace
{
#if PLATFORM_WINDOWS
#include "WindowsEnemy.h"
        using Enemy = WindowsEnemy;
#elif PLATFORM_ANDROID
#include "AndroidEnemy.h"
        using Enemy = AndroidEnemy;
```

```
#elif PLATFORM_IOS
#include "iOSEnemy.h"
        using Enemy = iOSEnemy;
#endif
}

EnemyBase* CreateEnemy(EnemyType enemyType, const uint32_t serializableId)
{
        Enemy* pEnemy = nullptr;
        switch (enemyType)
        {
        case EnemyType::Dragon:
                pEnemy = new Enemy(EnemyType::Dragon, serializableId);
                break;
        case EnemyType::Orc:
                pEnemy = new Enemy(EnemyType::Orc, serializableId);
                break;
        default:
                assert(false); // Unknown enemy type
                break;
        }
        return pEnemy;
}
```

The CreateEnemy function itself has only changed in one way. Its return type is now EnemyBase rather than Enemy. This is the case because I've used a type alias to have the Enemy keyword map to the correct platform-specific Enemy version. You can see this in action in the unnamed namespace before the function. I check each platform definition, include the appropriate header, and finally add using Enemy = to set the type alias to the correct type.

The Factory pattern is the perfect method to use when you need to implement platform-specific versions of classes. The Factory allows you to hide the implementation details of the creation of objects from the rest of your program. This leads to code that is easier to maintain and reduces the number of places in your codebase where you have to change things around to add new platforms. Reducing the time to port to a new platform could be a lucrative business opportunity and open up new potential revenue streams for your company.

Summary

This brings us to the end of your introduction to game programming in C++. This book has walked you through the main programming paradigms in C++ from procedural programming to object-oriented programming through to generic programming. You've also seen how the STL can provide you with ready-made data structures as well as algorithms to work on and with those structures.

The last part of this book has introduced you to some topics that will be important for you to learn as you go through your game development career. Mastering managing memory, concurrent programming, and higher level topics such as design patterns will ensure that you and your programs can adapt to whatever the future brings.

Chapter 27

Wrapping Up

The C++ programming language is a tool that will serve you well while trying to build video games. It provides low-level access to processors, which allows you to write efficient code for a wide variety of computer processors.

This book has shown you various techniques, features, and paradigms that you can apply to your own programming efforts. You've seen that C++ can be used to write procedural programs or object-oriented programs. Procedural programs can be created consisting only of functions, variables, and structs, whereas object-oriented programs are built from classes.

C++ extends these two paradigms by also allowing for generic programming. This type of programming is supported through the ability to create templates. Templates are used to create blueprints for classes with abstract types. The template compiler is responsible for creating specialized instances of template classes at compile time. C++ uses templates to provide the Standard Template Library. The STL supplies many data structures and algorithms so that you do not have to write every program from scratch.

An Overview of Text Adventure

This book ended with a very simple text adventure game that you can now expand into a full game if you wish. Listing 27-1 shows the Game class definition. This class encapsulates all of the types of programming C++ provides.

Listing 27-1. The Game Class Definition

```
class Game
        : public EventHandler
        , public QuitObserver
{
private:
        static const uint32_t m_numberOfRooms = 4;
        using Rooms = std::array<Room::Pointer, m_numberOfRooms>;
        Rooms m_rooms;
```

```cpp
        Player m_player;

        Option::Pointer m_attackDragonOption;
        Option::Pointer m_attackOrcOption;
        Option::Pointer m_moveNorthOption;
        Option::Pointer m_moveEastOption;
        Option::Pointer m_moveSouthOption;
        Option::Pointer m_moveWestOption;
        Option::Pointer m_openSwordChest;
        Option::Pointer m_quitOption;

        Sword m_sword;
        Chest m_swordChest;

        using Enemies = std::vector<EnemyBase::Pointer>;
        Enemies m_enemies;

        std::mutex m_mutex;
        mutable std::unique_lock<std::mutex> m_finishedQueryLock{ m_mutex, std::defer_lock };
        bool m_playerQuit{ false };
        void SetPlayerQuit()
        {
                m_finishedQueryLock.lock();
                m_playerQuit = true;
                m_finishedQueryLock.unlock();
        }

        bool m_playerWon{ false };
        void SetPlayerWon()
        {
                m_finishedQueryLock.lock();
                m_playerWon = true;
                m_finishedQueryLock.unlock();
        }

        bool GetPlayerWon()
        {
                m_finishedQueryLock.lock();
                bool playerWon = m_playerWon;
                m_finishedQueryLock.unlock();
                return playerWon;
        }

        void InitializeRooms();
        void WelcomePlayer(const bool loaded);
        void GivePlayerOptions() const;
        void GetPlayerInput(std::stringstream& playerInput) const;
        void EvaluateInput(std::stringstream& playerInput);
public:
        Game();
        virtual ~Game();
```

```
        void RunGame();

        virtual void HandleEvent(const Event* pEvent);

        // From QuitObserver
        virtual void OnQuit();

        bool HasFinished() const
        {
                m_finishedQueryLock.lock();
                bool hasFinished = m_playerQuit || m_playerWon;
                m_finishedQueryLock.unlock();
                return hasFinished;
        }
};
```

The Game class shows how you can construct classes in C++. There is a parent class from which Game derives. This class provides an interface that includes virtual methods. The Game class overrides these virtual methods with specific instances of its own. A perfect example of this is the HandleEvent method.

Game also shows how you can customize STL templates for your own uses. There is an array of Room::Pointer instances as well as a vector of EnemyBase::Pointer instances. These types of pointers are created using type aliases. Type aliases in C++ allow you to create your own named types and are generally a good idea. If you ever need to change the type of an object at a later date you can get away with just changing the type alias. If you hadn't used an alias you would be required to manually change every location where the type had been used.

There is also a mutex present in the Game class. This mutex is a clue to the fact that C++ allows you to write programs that can execute on multiple CPU cores at once. A mutex is a mutual exclusion object that allows you to ensure that only a single thread is accessing a single variable at one time.

Listing 27-2 contains the final source code for the Game::RunGame method. This method consists of code that shows how you can iterate over collections and use futures.

Listing 27-2. The Game::RunGame Method

```
void Game::RunGame()
{
        InitializeRooms();

        std::packaged_task< bool() > loaderTask{ LoadSaveGame };
        std::thread loaderThread{ std::ref{ loaderTask } };
        auto loaderFuture = loaderTask.get_future();
        while (loaderFuture.wait_for(std::chrono::seconds{ 0 }) != std::future_status::ready)
        {
                // Wait until the future is ready.
                // In a full game you could update a spinning progress icon!
                int32_t x = 0;
        }
        bool userSaveLoaded = loaderFuture.get();
        WelcomePlayer(userSaveLoaded);
```

```
    while (!HasFinished())
    {
            GivePlayerOptions();

            stringstream playerInputStream;
            GetPlayerInput(playerInputStream);

            EvaluateInput(playerInputStream);

            bool playerWon = true;
            for (auto& enemy : m_enemies)
            {
                    playerWon &= enemy->IsAlive() == false;
            }

            if (playerWon)
            {
                    SetPlayerWon();
            }
    }

    if (GetPlayerWon())
    {
            SerializationManager::GetSingleton().ClearSave();
            cout << "Congratulations, you rid the dungeon of monsters!" << endl;
            cout << "Type goodbye to end" << endl;
            std::string input;
            cin >>input;
    }
}
```

The range-based for loop can be used in conjunction with the auto keyword to provide easy, portable iteration over many STL collections. You can see it in action in RunGame where there is a loop over the m_enemies vector.

A paired_task is used to execute save game loading on a separate thread of execution. The std::thread::get_future method is used to acquire a future object that lets you know when the task you were executing has been completed. This approach to loading can be used to allow you to load games while updating a dynamic loading screen.

There is also an example of how to use cin and cout to read player input and write out messages to the console. Input and output are fundamental concepts for game developers as they are essential to providing the interactivity that players expect from games.

Summary

Game development is a fun but demanding field to enter. There are many areas to explore, learn, and attempt to master. Very few people become proficient in all areas of game development, but their programming skills are usually transferable. Programmers can specialize in graphics programming, network programming, gameplay programming, or other fields such as audio and animation. There will never be a shortage of tasks for programmers to undertake as most large games are written in C++ with code bases that have been around for 10 to 20 years. Engines such as Cryengine, Unreal, and Unity are written in C++ and provide support for scripting languages to create game logic. C++ is a perfect choice for someone looking to begin a career in game development that will take them into an AAA game development studio at some point.

I hope you've found this book an enjoyable entry into your journey down the path of your chosen career.

Index

D

Get the eBook for only $10!

> Now you can take the weightless companion with you anywhere, anytime. Your purchase of this book entitles you to 3 electronic versions for only $10.

This Apress title will prove so indispensible that you'll want to carry it with you everywhere, which is why we are offering the eBook in **3 formats** for only $10 if you have already purchased the print book.

Convenient and fully searchable, the PDF version enables you to easily find and copy code—or perform examples by quickly toggling between instructions and applications. The MOBI format is ideal for your Kindle, while the ePUB can be utilized on a variety of mobile devices.

Go to www.apress.com/promo/tendollars to purchase your companion eBook.

Apress®
THE EXPERT'S VOICE™